Using Artificial Intelligence (AI) to Minimize Errors in Business Enterprise Management

Helmut Becker

Using Artificial Intelligence (AI) to Minimize Errors in Business Enterprise Management

Springer Gabler

Helmut Becker
University of Library Studies
and Information Technologies (ULSIT)
Sofia, Bulgaria

This book is based on the author's doctoral dissertation, completed at the Faculty of Information Sciences, Department of Information Systems and Technologies, at the University of Library Studies and Information Technologies (ULSIT), Sofia. The research was conducted in the field of 'Social Communications and Information Sciences' (Professional Field 3.5) as part of the doctoral program 'Organization and Management of Information Processes.' The work was supervised by Prof. Dr. Georgi Petrov Dimitrov, Ph.D.

ISBN 978-3-658-47242-9 ISBN 978-3-658-47243-6 (eBook)
https://doi.org/10.1007/978-3-658-47243-6

This Springer Gabler imprint is published by the registered company Springer Fachmedien Wiesbaden GmbH, part of Springer Nature.
The registered company address is: Abraham-Lincoln-Str. 46, 65189 Wiesbaden, Germany

Supervisor's Foreword

Every day we make numerous decisions. How to get dressed, which route to choose on our way to work, which tasks to prioritize at the office, what to do in our free time, what to buy with our money. When we move into the field of enterprise management, such decisions could be who to hire, promote or fire, what products to develop, which markets to enter, what technologies to use, where to allocate the company's resources, what prices, cost cuts and investments to make. The examples could be numerous. Sometimes these decisions result in errors which cost a lot of money, sometimes the price is entire careers or the company's existence. And if these errors could be foreseen with a large degree of certainty and avoided, the business would function in a more secure environment.

What is a decision? According to the Oxford Learner's Dictionary, the word "decision" has two meanings—*"a choice or judgement that you make after thinking and talking about what is the best thing to do"* and the *"the process of deciding something"*[1]. To do the necessary preparatory activities in this process, namely thinking and talking, you actually need to *collect* relevant information about the surrounding environment and *assess* this information—alone or with the help of others. The more relevant information you collect, the better foundation you have for assessing it and thus—to make the correct decisions and to avoid making an error.

In a world where we are constantly flooded with all sorts of data from all sorts of sources, some credible, some not, it comes as a no surprise that humanity is

[1] Oxford Learner's Dictionary, URL: <https://www.oxfordlearnersdictionaries.com/definition/english/decision?q=decision> (last visited at 07.12.2024).

seeking to implement new and advanced technologies to help them with assessing this information and ultimately—to make better decisions. This is in line with the global tendency of rapid development of information and communication technologies (ICT) and their implementation in all spheres of human activity which is summarized under the notion of digital transformation. One of the technologies that can collect and assess a very large amount of data and help us with decision-making is artificial intelligence (AI). AI holds enormous potential and is perhaps the technology that can radically transform social relations. Therefore, only a thorough analysis of the possible benefits and risks of its use can lead to its sustainable implementation in human activity, including in risk management processes in business.

In the above context, the present monograph of Dr. Helmut Becker is devoted exactly to these topical problems. The author aims to explore the existing systems for risk management such as ISO 31000:2018 and COSO ERM Integrated Framework in the context of High Reliability Organizations (HROs) and their possible applications to other business organizations. Dr. Becker successfully defends the thesis that the integration of AI into error culture and risk management practices has the potential to improve the resilience of the existing companies and to limit the chances of committing management errors.

Among the most substantial contributions from the present research paper the following should be recognized:

- It is proven that systems for risk management in the enterprises ISO 31000:2018 and COSO ERM Integrated Framework show weaknesses when capturing errors that could be either eliminated, or at least significantly limited through the usage of AI;
- A new conceptual model has been elaborated that includes 56 criteria, including the (Mindful Organizing Scale—MOS) criteria. The latter are tailored for use in an AI solution system and can be integrated into existing information processes;
- New knowledge has been synthesized regarding the matter of how the error management concepts for recording and increasing error culture have a very high potential to be transformed into an AI-based solution;
- A visual representation of how AI can be used for measuring the error culture in organizations. The book shows how this makes possible the creation of an early warning system to identify weaknesses in the existing error management system;

- A visual representation of how via integration of the MOS criteria the existing weaknesses related to the human factor within the existing risk management system frameworks ISO 31000:2018 and COSO ERM can be addressed.

What are the approaches for risk management in HROs and to what extent are they effective in different business conditions? What criteria can be used to evaluate the error culture in organizations? How do ISO 31000:2018 and COSO ERM capture human error? How can the MOS criteria and AI be integrated? The answers to these and to other important questions about correlation between AI and the sphere of enterprise management can be found in the present paper.

The monograph is an important step towards a better understanding of the capabilities of AI and its possible application in the business context. It is a valuable source of new knowledge that may be used by managers, IT specialists, lawyers, researchers in the areas of AI and ICT, organizational management and decision-making, and everybody with an interest in new technologies and business management. Such research is especially valuable amid growing fears that AI will replace humans. Almost no technology is by default good or bad—it depends how humanity uses it. And with the help of papers like the one of Dr. Becker, our hopes that AI will be used constructively and creatively in favor of humanity can only grow. Enjoy reading the next lines!

09 December 2024

Assoc. Prof. Martin Zahariev
PhD—Department "National Security" at
the University of Library Studies
and Information Technologies
Sofia, Bulgaria

Partner at Dimitrov, Petrov & Co. Law Firm
Sofia, Bulgaria

Senior Legal Expert at the Law and Internet
Foundation
Sofia, Bulgaria

Author's Foreword

The focus of this work was to develop a novel approach for integrating artificial intelligence (AI) into error management to enhance organizational resilience and achieve a sustainable improvement in error culture.

The inspiration for this research stems from my extensive professional experience, during which I observed the profound impact of errors in organizations—not only on operational outcomes but also on the people behind the processes. The challenges organizations face in creating a constructive error culture motivated me to explore innovative solutions that combine technological advancements with a human-centered approach.

My academic journey has been significantly shaped by my diverse professional and academic background. From 2014 to 2016, I pursued an Executive MBA at the Technical University of Munich (TUM), where my Master's thesis focused on error culture and error management in healthcare. This research deepened my understanding of how error culture can drive organizational performance and safety and laid the foundation for further exploration of these concepts in broader business contexts.

With over 25 years of experience as a licensed attorney and extensive expertise in human resources management, I have had the privilege of working at the intersection of law, business strategy, and organizational leadership. These experiences have shaped my perspective on how legal, managerial, and technological frameworks can converge to address complex challenges in modern enterprises.

At the heart of this research is the application of principles from High Reliability Organizations (HRO) and their combination with innovative AI technologies.

The insights aim to provide both practitioners and academics with strategies to better manage human errors and reduce risks.

Looking to the future, I could very well imagine the results of this research being translated into a practical AI application that helps organizations proactively identify and address error sources.

Writing this dissertation was not only an academic endeavor but also a deeply personal learning experience. My wife, Lenka, and our three daughters, Leni, Emma, and Lotte, often had to forgo my time and attention during this project. Their patience, understanding, and support gave me the strength to navigate this intensive phase. For that, I am profoundly grateful. I would also like to extend my deepest gratitude to my doctoral advisor, Prof. Dr. Georgi Petrov Dimitrov, Ph.D., whose expertise and guidance shaped the direction of this research.

I hope that the content of this book provides valuable insights for both theoretical discussions and practical applications in the field of business management and inspires further innovations in error management and organizational resilience.

Dr. Helmut Becker, LL.M., MBA

Abstract

Becker, H.: Using Artificial Intelligence (AI) to Minimize Errors in Business Enterprise Management. Scientific Advisor: Prof. Dr. Georgi Petrov Dimitrov, Ph.D. Information Systems and Technologies Department to the Faculty of Information Sciences, Doctoral Program: "Organization and Management of Information Processes". ULSIT, Sofia, 2024. 221 pages; 191 information sources; 22 figures; 63 tables.

This dissertation examines the integration of Artificial Intelligence (AI) in business enterprise management, focusing on minimizing errors through enhanced error management and error culture. The research hinges on the adaptability of High Reliability Organizations' (HRO) error management practices to a wider range of business contexts and the integration of AI with the Mindful Organizing Scale (MOS) criteria.

The Sub-Hypotheses include the transferability of HRO error management practices to diverse organizations, the transformation of MOS into an AI-based solution to enhance error culture, and the identification of gaps in existing risk management systems ISO 31000, COSO ERM Framework in addressing human factors. Through a comprehensive literature review and case studies, the dissertation explores AI's potential in real-time data analysis, predictive insights, and task automation, while also considering its limitations and ethical implications.

The research contributes to understanding how AI and HRO principles can synergize to improve organizational resilience and safety culture. It provides insights for academics, practitioners, and policymakers on leveraging AI in error minimization within business operations.

Keywords: Artificial Intelligence · Error Culture · Error Management · High Reliability Organizations · Mindful Organizing Scale · Risk Management · Business Enterprise Management · ISO 31000 · COSO ERM Framework

Introduction

State of the art

Reports about crises of formerly highly esteemed companies fill the business newspapers. Former stock market stars such as Enron and WorldCom share the sin bank of value destroyers with traditional corporations such as Swissair, DaimlerChrysler or ABB. Despite these numerous practical examples, management theorists have so far been much less interested in the crashes of once successful companies than in the search for success factors. They usually see decline as part of a natural process: Companies go through various life cycles, at the end of which is precisely death.

Unfortunately, this theoretical approach does not explain the spectacular corporate crises of recent years. ABB, Enron, Swissair or WorldCom were among the most successful representatives of their industries until their demise. The problems did not come at the end of the natural life cycle, but rather in the prime of life. Why is it that companies that for years were among the most successful and respected so often run into difficulties?

This paper therefore seeks to address the issue of how management failures in companies can be reduced. The use of Artificial Intelligence (AI), as a branch of computer science that deals with replicating aspects of human thought and action with computers, can help here.

Numerous efforts are being made to ensure operational risk management for the safety of companies as well as the workforce. Numerous measures, some of which are obligatory, are available to companies in order to operate successfully on the global market from a risk perspective.

Nevertheless, scandals of enormous proportions occur. Prominent examples include the Volkswagen Group's diesel emissions scandal (Goerzen et al., 2023) and, most recently, the Wirecard scandal.

The question arises whether knowledge-based systems based on formalized expertise allow logical conclusions to be drawn about possible weaknesses in corporate risk management. For it seems to be the human being who is the weak point, in whose place an AI system promises more success and seems to be less prone to error.

The central importance of a safety culture for corporate safety and security is already widely accepted in High Reliability Organizations (HROs). Reliability is the probability that a system functions as normal (i.e. does not fail) (Aven, 2008). HROs are thus to be understood as highly reliable systems. With an argumentative first-right conclusion, the positive, open handling of individual errors and system errors for error prevention should also play a central role for companies that are not usually counted as HROs, such as banks, automotive companies or plant and machinery manufacturers.

Thus, it is not surprising that the literature attempts to outline the key features that could improve organizations and their performance to emulate HROs, both the formal structures and the informal practices that complement these structures (Carroll and Rudolph, 2006). In their meta-analysis, Tolk, Cantu and Beruvides (Tolk et al., 2015) show that many researchers combine HRO theory with common theories of organizational behaviour and organizational psychology.

A positive "error culture" is often called for in connection with the demand for a safety culture. For the development of error prevention strategies in companies, it seems indispensable that all actors involved in the complex company processes based on the division of labour help to identify sources of error and work together to avoid errors. However, this can only succeed if a culture of learning together from mistakes is anchored in the company. But unfortunately, everyday corporate life still looks unsatisfactory. This is because mistakes are unfortunately not infrequently understood as exclusively personal failures or addressed as such in everyday professional life.

This corresponds to the traditional view of mistakes in the workplace, which promotes a blame culture. Nevertheless, a culture of trust seems to be indispensable for a culture of error. Since trust cannot be introduced by company order and is dependent on many factors, it is advisable to complement error management measures with an AI system that can be used as an early warning system for an effective error management system in the company.

At HRO, recording the safety culture is an important part of error management. This requires a reliable and valid measurement method. However, measuring safety culture requires measurement at all three levels of organizational culture from different perspectives using complex and imaginative methods of assessment and analysis; questionnaires or similar measurement methods are not suitable for this purpose (Glendon and Stanton, 2000).

In comparison, it is easier and less costly to measure the safety climate with questionnaires and especially with appropriate employee surveys. With various questionnaires developed in the USA, the "safety climate" can be recorded and measured. These include, for example, the "Hospital Survey on Patient Safety Culture" (Blegen et al., 2009); (Sorra and Dyer, 2010) and "Safety Attitudes Questionnaire" (Sexton et al., 2006). Another safety climate questionnaire used in this work is the Mindful Organising Scale (MOS) (formerly Safety Organising Scale—"SOS") developed by Vogus & Sutcliffe (Vogus and Sutcliffe, 2007). MOS is based on the systemic failure approach and is based on detailed case studies of HRO's (Vogus and Sutcliffe, 2007). MOS provides a scale for measuring mindful organizing. Through observational research and numerous case studies on the functioning of high-reliability organizations (HROs), researchers found that a form of collective mindfulness (or mindful organizing) is at the heart of this high-reliability performance. MOS was further strengthened in its reliability and validity (Ausserhofer et al., 2013). This also applies to the German version of the MOS data collection questionnaire (Ausserhofer et al., 2012, Becker, 2016).

Based on MOS, conclusions can be drawn about the collective mindfulness and thus the error culture of the organization.

Research object and research subject

The dissertation aims to investigate the integration of Artificial Intelligence (AI) into error culture and risk management practices to improve organizational resilience and reduce the likelihood of management errors. The focus is on how organizations and information management can be optimized through the use of AI to promote a proactive and sustainable error culture.

Furthermore, the research will examine the integration of AI technology into existing risk management frameworks, specifically ISO 31000:2018 and the COSO ERM Integrated Framework, to address human factors, which are significant sources of error in corporate environments.

Research aim

The goal of this research is to investigate the potential of AI solutions, particularly utilizing the Mindful Organising Scale (MOS), to improve error culture and error management within organizations, thereby enhancing overall risk management effectiveness.

Research tasks
The research tasks are as follows:

- Evaluating the current situation regarding management failures and risk management practices in companies.
- Selecting appropriate research methods and tools, including the integration of AI and the utilization of MOS.
- Conducting research to assess the effectiveness of AI-based solutions in enhancing error culture and risk management.
- Evaluating the results obtained and formulating conclusions and recommendations for implementing AI-driven improvements in corporate risk management systems.

This dissertation compares two prominent management systems in the field of corporate risk management, namely ISO 31000:2018 and the COSO ERM Integrated Framework and examines, whether and to what extend both consider human factors, which are still the biggest potential sources of error.

At first time a combination of MOS and further well-chosen further items, namely by recognized human factors in the relevant literature on safety culture, serves as holistic examination criteria. It will be investigated whether and to what extent MOS can be made usable for an AI solution for business enterprises, to improve ISO 31000:2018 and the COSO ERM Integrated framework after identifying potential improvements to them.

Dissertation structure
This dissertation is structured as follows:

In Chapter I the categories of analysis and relevant theories are presented. This includes the presentation of the theories of error and deals with the analysis, change and development of organizational cultures. In this context, great attention is paid to the theories of safety culture and safety climate, in particular error culture and HRO. Furthermore, is looked on error and risk management with special consideration of MOS and active shaping of the error culture. In the following it is discussed whether and to what extent error and risk management systems can be made more efficient and effective through artificial intelligence (AI) and whether AI can be used to sustainably promote error culture and error management.

After the explanation of the methodological approach of the dissertation in **Chapter II**, the risk management systems ISO 31000:2018 and COSO ERM Integrated Framework are then compared with each other in **Chapter III**. The results obtained through the matrix comparison in Chapter III are interpreted in **Chapter IV.**

The dissertation is concluded with the final summary of the key points and findings of the research study Conclusion and Recommendations **in Chapter V**.

Working hypothesis

Using Artificial Intelligence (AI) has the potential to Minimize Errors in Business Enterprise Management.

Supporting sub-hypotheses:

1) Error management approaches developed for High Reliability Organizations (HRO) can be largely transferred to all other business enterprises and organizations subject to risk management systems.
2) MOS has the potential to be transferred into an AI solution in order to sustainably promote error culture and error management in the organization.
3) The error culture can be measured and operationalized by an AI system.
4) The risk management systems ISO 31000:2018 and COSO ERM Integrated Framework show significant weaknesses on the field of human factors that can be mitigated by MOS criteria, operationalized by an AI system.

For the first time, the possibility of using AI will be investigated, taking into account error management systems developed for HROs and established measures to promote an error culture in the corporate context.

The dissertation will show that, based on defined study items, the error culture can be measured and operationalized by an AI system.

Thus, based on formalized and recognized expertise on error culture and error management, a knowledge-based system can be developed as an AI that allows logical conclusions to be drawn on the characteristics of error culture and thus identifies weaknesses in corporate risk management.

The use of artificial intelligence to measure the error culture benefits all companies and organizations; even those who already use well known risk management systems—namely ISO 31000:2018 and the COSO ERM Integrated framework -in place.

An AI solution for measuring error culture can be used to establish an early warning system for weaknesses in the existing error management system due to an insufficient error culture. At the same time, potential for improvement can be identified to increase error culture and improve existing error management systems.

Some of the results have already been published:

1. Becker, H. (2022a) 'Error Culture for Strengthening Entrepreneurial Resilience' In: National Security, Identity and Media in the Conditions of Global Political and Economic Crisis. Sofia: Za Bukvite—O Pismeneh, pp. 106-116. ISBN 978-619-185-567-4
2. Becker, H. (2022b): 'Using Artificial Intelligence for Strengthening Entrepreneurial Resilience' Contemporary Strategies and Innovations in the Knowledge Management, Sofia: Za Bukvite—O Pismeneh, pp. 316-327. ISSN 2535-0250
3. Becker, H. (2023) 'Error Culture for Strengthening Resilience of Critical Infrastructure' In: Proceedings of National Scientific Conference with International Participation "Security and Defence", held on 21 April 2023. Sofia: Za Bukvite—O Pismeneh, pp. 706-717. ISBN: 978-619-185-593-3

The findings from the dissertation on the use of artificial intelligence (AI) for the sustainable strengthening of error culture and error management in business enterprises can be used by the enterprises themselves, business consultants and business lawyers in their day-to-day business practice.

Contents

1 Error Theories; Analysis, Change and Development of Organizational Culture, Artificial Intelligence 1
1.1 Error 1
1.2 Safety and Security 2
1.3 Errors and Critical Incidents 5
1.4 Human Error 8
1.5 Error Types and Generic Error Modelling System 10
1.6 Knowingly Violating the Rules or Gross Negligence 14
1.7 Four Levels of Culpability (Mens Rea) 15
1.8 Person-Related Error Approach 17
1.9 System-Related Error Approach 17
1.10 Active and Latent Errors 18
1.11 The Swiss-Cheese Model 19
1.12 Human Factors 20
1.13 Dirty Dozen 20
1.14 SHELL-Model 21
1.15 Schein's 3-Level Model 29
1.16 Competing Values Framework (CVF) 30
1.16.1 The hierarchical organizational culture 32
1.16.2 The Market Culture 33
1.16.3 The Clan Culture 33
1.16.4 Adhocracy Culture 33

1.17 Nine Dimensions of Organizational Culture and Concept of Reconciling Corporate Culture 34
1.18 Safety Culture 37
1.19 Safety Climate 41
1.20 High Reliability Organizations (HROs). 42
1.21 Error Management 44
1.22 Error Culture and Error Management Culture 47
1.23 The Mindful Organizing Scale (MOS) 49
1.24 Active Shaping of Error Culture 52
1.25 Prosocial Motivation and Emotional Ambivalence 53
1.26 Risk Management Systems 54
1.26.1 ISO Standard 31000:2018 55
1.26.2 COSO ERM Integrated Framework 59
1.26.3 Key Weaknesses of Risk Management Systems 61
1.27 AI in Promoting Error Culture and Error Management 62
1.28 Organization and Management of the Information Process in Business Management 66
1.28.1 Integration of Technology Assessment Frameworks in Corporate Strategies 66
1.28.2 Feedback Mechanisms and Stakeholder Engagement 68
1.28.3 AI in Strategic Decision-Making 68
1.28.4 Implementing AI for Error Minimization 70
1.28.5 AI Technology and Corporate Social Responsibility 71
1.28.6 Anticipatory Governance 71
1.28.7 Global Information Governance 71
1.29 Conclusion 72

2 Development and Application of an Integrated Audit Approach to Identify the Weaknesses of the Risk Management Systems ISO 31000 and COSO ERM Framework in Capturing the Error Culture, Which has the Potential for Operationalization through AI 75
2.1 Methodology for Literature Research on Error Management in HROs and AI Transformation of MOS 75
2.2 Methodology for Comparing ISO 31000 and COSO ERM Frameworks 76

2.2.1 Criteria ... 76
2.2.1.1 Competing value framework ... 77
2.2.1.2 MOS Items ... 77
2.2.1.3 GEMS Criteria ... 78
2.2.1.4 SHELL criteria ... 79
2.2.1.5 Dirty Dozen ... 81
2.2.2 Matrix and Scale ... 82

3 Comparison of the Risk Management Systems ISO 31000:2018 and COSO ERM Framework with regard to their Ability to Capture the Error Culture ... 85
3.1 Competing Value Framework (CVF) ... 85
3.2 MOS Criteria ... 88
3.2.1 MOS: Deal with Failure ... 88
3.2.2 MOS: Questioning Simplistic Interpretations ... 94
3.2.3 MOS: Sensitivity to Operational Processes ... 99
3.2.4 MOS: Striving for Resilience ... 106
3.2.5 MOS: Pay Attention to Subject Matter Expertise ... 112
3.3 The GEMS Model Criteria ... 119
3.3.1 Skill-based Errors (Slips and Oversights) ... 119
3.3.2 Rule-based Errors (Errors of Confusion and Recognition) ... 125
3.3.3 Knowledge-based Errors (Errors of Reasoning and Judgment) ... 131
3.4 SHELL-criteria ... 137
3.4.1 Software ... 137
3.4.2 Hardware ... 142
3.4.3 Environment ... 146
3.4.4 Liveware ... 155
3.4.5 Liveware-Liveware Interface ... 160

4 Interpretation of Results: Evaluating ISO 31000:2018 and COSO ERM Frameworks in Capturing Error Culture and Potential Improvement through AI Solutions using a Holistic Approach with MOS ... 171
4.1 Adaptability and Response to Failures ... 171
4.2 Handling of Operational Sensitivities ... 171
4.3 Management of Human Error ... 172

4.4 Technological Aspects of Risk Management 172
4.5 Leadership and Communication in Risk Management 172

5 Conclusion and Recommendations 173

Bibliography 177

Abbreviations

ACSNI	Advisory Committee on the Safety of Nuclear Installations
ADR	Adverse Drug Reactions
AI	Artificial Intelligence
APS	Aktionsbündnis Patientensicherheit e.V.
b/w	Black and White
BMJ	British Medical Journal
BT-Drs.	Bundestagsdrucksache
BZB	Bavarian Dental Journal
Calif Management Rev	California Management Review
CIP	Critical Infrastructure Protection
CIRS	Critical Incident Reporting System
CMAJ	Canadian Medical Association Journal
COSO	Committee of Sponsoring Organizations of the Treadway Commission
Crit Care Med	Critical Care Medicine
CRM	Crew Resource Management
CVF	Competing Values Framework
e.V.	Eingetragener Verein (Registered Association)
ed.	Edition
Eds.	Editors
ERM	Enterprise Risk Management

ESARR	Eurocontrol Safety Regulatory Requirement
FMEA	Failure Mode and Effects Analysis
G-BA	Joint Federal Committee
GEMS	Generic Error Modeling System
HFACS	Human Factors Analysis and Classification System
HMD	Health and Medicine Division
HRO	High Reliability Organizations
HRT	High Reliability Theory
HSC	British Health and Safety Commission
HSE	Health and Safety Executive
IfP	Institute for Patient Safety
Inc.	Incorporated
INSAG	International Nuclear Safety Advisory Group
INT J QUAL HEALTH CARE	International Journal for Quality in Health Care
IOM	Institute of Medicine
IQTIG	Institute for Quality Assurance and Transparency in Health Care
J Occup Health Psychol	Journal of Occupational Health Psychology
JAMA	Journal of the American Medical Association
JCAHO	Joint Commission on Accreditation of Healthcare Organizations
KHSG	Hospital Structure Act
KQM-RL	Quality Management Guideline Hospitals
kRM	Clinical Risk Management
Med Clin	Medical Clinic
MOS	Mindfulness Organizing Scale
No.	Number
NZS	New Zealand Standards
p.	Page
pp.	Pages
QM	Quality Management
Qual Saf Health Care	Quality & Safety in Health Care
RN4Cast	Registered Nurse Forecasting
S.	Section
SGB	Sozialgesetzbuch (Social Code)

SHI	Statutory Health Insurance
SOAM	Systemic Occurrence Analysis Methodology
SOS	Safety Organizing Scale
Vol.	Volume
WHO	World Health Organization

List of Figures

Fig. 1.1	Heinrich's law (Heinrich, 1941), p. 27	5
Fig. 1.2	SOAM version of the Reason Model (Eurocontrol, 2005), p. 22	20
Fig. 1.3	Shel(l) Model Molloy & O'Boyle, 2005, p. 153	23
Fig. 1.4	Schein's onion layers of organizational culture, adapted from Schein (Schein, 1985)	30
Fig. 1.5	Competing Values Framework (Cameron, 2009), page 3	32
Fig. 1.6	Six Elements of the safety culture	40
Fig. 1.7	Error Management Troika	46
Fig. 1.8	4 levels of risk in AI (European Commission, 2024)	64
Fig. 3.1	Bar chart comparing the ISO 31000:2018 and COSO ERM Framework for Competing Value Framework Criteria	88
Fig. 3.2	Bar chart comparing the ISO 31000:2018 and COSO ERM Framework for Deal with Failure criteria	93
Fig. 3.3	Bar chart comparing the ISO 31000:2018 and COSO ERM Framework for Questioning Simplistic Interpretations Criteria	99
Fig. 3.4	Bar chart comparing the ISO 31000:2018 and COSO ERM Framework for Sensitivity to Operational Processes Criteria	105
Fig. 3.5	Bar chart comparing the ISO 31000:2018 and COSO ERM Framework for Striving for Resilience Criteria	111

Fig. 3.6 Bar chart comparing the ISO 31000:2018 and COSO ERM Framework for Pay Attention to Subject Matter Expertise Criteria 118
Fig. 3.7 Bar chart comparing the ISO 31000:2018 and COSO ERM Framework for Errors Criteria 124
Fig. 3.8 Bar chart comparing the ISO 31000:2018 and COSO ERM Framework for Rule-based Errors Criteria 130
Fig. 3.9 Bar chart comparing the ISO 31000:2018 and COSO ERM Framework for Knowledge-based Error Criteria 136
Fig. 3.10 Bar chart comparing the ISO 31000:2018 and COSO ERM Framework for various Software criteria 141
Fig. 3.11 Bar chart comparing the ISO 31000:2018 and COSO ERM Framework for various Hardware criteria 145
Fig. 3.12 Bar chart comparing the ISO 31000:2018 and COSO ERM Framework for various Environment criteria 155
Fig. 3.13 Bar chart comparing the ISO 31000:2018 and COSO ERM Framework for various Liveware criteria 160
Fig. 3.14 Bar chart comparing the ISO 31000:2018 and COSO ERM Framework for various Liveware-Liveware criteria 164

List of Tables

Table 1.1	Safety and Security	5
Table 1.2	Three levels of cognitive control of actions and corresponding error types	12
Table 1.3	Operationalizing GEMS Criteria for AI Solutions	14
Table 1.4	Operationalization of the SHELL model criteria for AI solutions: Criteria and data source overview	28
Table 1.5	based on Five dimensions of collective mindfulness and corresponding MOS items (Sutcliffe and Vogus, 2007), p. 48, extended by objective test criteria	51
Table 2.1	Test criteria	83
Table 3.1	Competition versus partnership orientation dilemma: ISO 31000:2018 and COSO ERM Framework	85
Table 3.2	Stable continuity versus dynamic change: ISO 31000:2018 and COSO ERM Framework	86
Table 3.3	Number of reported failures within a given time period: ISO 31000:2018 and COSO ERM Framework	88
Table 3.4	Percentage of reported failures that were analyzed and addressed: ISO 31000:2018 and COSO ERM Framework	89
Table 3.5	Time taken to analyze and address failures: ISO 31000:2018 and COSO ERM Framework	91
Table 3.6	Effectiveness of the solutions implemented to address failures: ISO 31000:2018 and COSO ERM Framework	92

Table 3.7 Frequency of questioning by team members during meetings or discussions: ISO 31000:2018 and COSO ERM Framework ... 94
Table 3.8 Number of different perspectives considered when making decisions: ISO 31000:2018 and COSO ERM Framework ... 95
Table 3.9 Percentage of decisions made after considering multiple perspectives: ISO 31000:2018 and COSO ERM Framework ... 96
Table 3.10 Effectiveness of decisions made after considering multiple perspectives: ISO 31000:2018 and COSO ERM Framework ... 97
Table 3.11 Number of reported process deviations within a given period: ISO 31000:2018 and COSO ERM Framework ... 99
Table 3.12 Percentage of process deviations that were analyzed and addressed: ISO 31000:2018 and COSO ERM Framework ... 100
Table 3.13 Time taken to analyze and address process deviations: ISO 31000:2018 and COSO ERM Framework ... 102
Table 3.14 Effectiveness of the solutions implemented to address process deviations: ISO 31000:2018 and COSO ERM Framework ... 103
Table 3.15 Frequency of proactive measures taken to prevent failures or process deviations: ISO 31000:2018 and COSO ERM Framework ... 106
Table 3.16 Number of backup or redundancy systems in place: ISO 31000:2018 and COSO ERM Framework ... 107
Table 3.17 Time taken to recover from failures or process deviations: ISO 31000:2018 and COSO ERM Framework ... 108
Table 3.18 Effectiveness of the solutions implemented to recover from failures or process deviations: ISO 31000:2018 and COSO ERM Framework ... 109
Table 3.19 Number of reported incidents related to lack of expertise within a given time period: ISO 31000:2018 and COSO ERM Framework ... 112
Table 3.20 Percentage of team members with relevant expertise or qualifications: ISO 31000:2018 and COSO ERM Framewor ... 113

Table 3.21 Frequency of seeking advice or guidance from team members with relevant expertise: ISO 31000:2018 and COSO ERM Framework 115
Table 3.22 Effectiveness of the solutions implemented based on advice or guidance from team members with relevant expertise: ISO 31000:2018 and COSO ERM Framework 116
Table 3.23 Frequency of certain errors compared to the expected number of errors given the task complexity and individual skill level: ISO 31000:2018 and COSO ERM Framework 119
Table 3.24 Time taken to complete a task compared to the expected time given the task complexity and individual skill level: ISO 31000:2018 and COSO ERM Framework 120
Table 3.25 Consistency in performing the task correctly over multiple attempts: ISO 31000:2018 and COSO ERM Framework 121
Table 3.26 Reaction time to unexpected events or changes in the task: ISO 31000:2018 and COSO ERM Framework 123
Table 3.27 Number of times a rule was misinterpreted or not followed correctly: ISO 31000:2018 and COSO ERM Framework 125
Table 3.28 Frequency of incorrect responses to specific stimuli or cues: ISO 31000:2018 and COSO ERM Framework 126
Table 3.29 Percentage of correct responses to similar but distinct stimuli or cues: ISO 31000:2018 and COSO ERM Framework 127
Table 3.30 Time taken to recognize and correct an error: ISO 31000:2018 and COSO ERM Framework 128
Table 3.31 Number of logical fallacies committed during decision-making or problem-solving:: ISO 31000:2018 and COSO ERM Framework 131
Table 3.32 Consistency of decision-making with established principles or guidelines: ISO 31000:2018 and COSO ERM Framework 132

Table 3.33 Time taken to reach a decision compared to the expected time given the complexity of the problem and available information: ISO 31000:2018 and COSO ERM Framework 133
Table 3.34 The degree of deviation from optimal outcomes or solutions: ISO 31000:2018 and COSO ERM Framework 134
Table 3.35 Robust incident response plan in place: ISO 31000:2018 and COSO ERM Framework 137
Table 3.36 Regularly updating software and ensuring it is secure and up-to-date: ISO 31000:2018 and COSO ERM Framework 138
Table 3.37 Conducting software testing to identify any potential vulnerabilities or weaknesses: ISO 31000:2018 and COSO ERM Framework 139
Table 3.38 Training to employees on how to use software and technology tools properly: ISO 31000:2018 and COSO Framework 140
Table 3.39 Conducting regular inspections and maintenance of hardware to ensure it is in good working condition: ISO 31000:2018 and COSO ERM Framework 142
Table 3.40 Using high-quality hardware that meets safety standards: ISO 31000:2018 and COSO ERM Framework 143
Table 3.41 Providing training to employees on how to use hardware safely and effectively: ISO 31000:2018 and COSO ERM Framework 144
Table 3.42 Conducting regular safety inspections to identify potential hazards in the workplace: ISO 31000:2018 and COSO ERM Framework 146
Table 3.43 Providing adequate lighting, ventilation, and other environmental controls to ensure a safe working environment: ISO 31000:2018 and COSO ERM Framework 147
Table 3.44 Providing training to employees on how to recognize and avoid environmental hazards: ISO 31000:2018 and COSO ERM Framework 148

Table 3.45 Encouraging a safety culture within the organization through regular communication, training, and feedback: ISO 31000:2018 and COSO ERM Framework 149
Table 3.46 Holding employees accountable for following security policies and procedures. ISO 31000:2018 and COSO ERM Framework 150
Table 3.47 Encouraging employees to report safety concerns or incidents: ISO 31000:2018 and COSO ERM Framework 151
Table 3.48 Monitoring the level of cognitive, physical, and emotional demands placed on individuals or teams, as well as the distribution of workload among team members: ISO 31000:2018 and COSO ERM Framework 152
Table 3.49 Stress and Fatigue: ISO 31000:2018 and COSO ERM Framework 153
Table 3.50 Recruiting and Retention of qualified and experience staff: ISO 31000:2018 and COSO ERM Framework 155
Table 3.51 Conducting background checks on all employees who have access to sensitive information: ISO 31000:2018 and COSO ERM Framework 156
Table 3.52 Training and Experience: ISO 31000:2018 and COSO ERM Framework 157
Table 3.53 Providing training to employees on how to work safely and effectively: ISO 31000:2018 and COSO ERM Framework 158
Table 3.54 Communication: ISO 31000:2018 and COSO ERM Framework 160
Table 3.55 Teamwork: ISO 31000:2018 and COSO ERM Framework 162
Table 3.56 Leadership style and conflict resolution: ISO 31000:2018 and COSO ERM Framework 163
Table 3.57 Overall findings 165

Error Theories; Analysis, Change and Development of Organizational Culture, Artificial Intelligence

1

For better understanding the mechanisms of action of an error culture, but also of an error management, types of errors and error theories are examined in more detail.

1.1 Error

An error can be defined abstractly as a situation or process that deviates from a target state (Bauer et al., 2004). Aktionsbündnis Patientensicherheit[1] (APS) has a more differentiated definition and sees an error as an action or omission in which there is a deviation from the plan, an incorrect plan or no plan at all; it is irrelevant for the definition of an error whether damage occurs (Aktionsbündnis Patientensicherheit (APS), 2016)

Whether and to what extent an error is present depends essentially on which normative criterion is used as a standard of evaluation. In research and development departments, for example, "trial and error" is a fundamental principle of innovation. "Errors" are desirable to that extent. In hospitals, on the other hand, the focus is on patient safety and thus also on the safety aspect. Errors should therefore remain the exception rather than the rule in the hospital sector. This normative change of course is fundamental, because it also decides decisively on the relevance of target/actual deviations. But even in business activities, mistakes should be avoided as far as possible, as they can jeopardize the existence of the company or even lead to its insolvency. The insolvency of a business entity can metaphorically be regarded as a life-threatening crisis, leading to its dissolution.

[1] Patient Safety Action Alliance.

H. Becker, *Using Artificial Intelligence (AI) to Minimize Errors in Business Enterprise Management*, https://doi.org/10.1007/978-3-658-47243-6_1

1.2 Safety and Security

The detection and correction of "errors" is a key issue in both domains of safety and security. This requires careful analysis of potential errors and vulnerabilities in order to develop effective counter-strategies. In many sectors, especially in critical infrastructures, an integrated view of safety and security is necessary to control and minimize both accidental and intentional risks. In practice, this often means that security systems must be designed to be robust against a wide range of failure modes and threat scenarios.

Safety and security, though often used interchangeably in common language, represent two distinct yet closely related concepts (International Organization for Standardization (ISO), 2018a, The European Union information agency for occupational safety and health (EU-OSA), 2022). Broadly, safety pertains to safeguarding against harm, injury, or accidental danger, while security involves protection from intentional threats or attacks (American Society for Industrial Security (ASIS), 2015); (The International Telecommunication Union (ITU), 2024)

These concepts hold immense significance across diverse industries, such as healthcare, high-reliability organizations (HROs), financial institutions, and other businesses (International Organization for Standardization (ISO), 2018a, The European Union information agency for occupational safety and health (EU-OSA), 2022). However, discussions about safety and security are particularly prevalent in healthcare and HROs due to the potentially severe, even life-threatening consequences of errors or failures.

In healthcare, safety and security are of paramount concern, given that patients' lives frequently hang in the balance (International Organization for Standardization (ISO), 2018b). Errors in medication, treatment, or diagnosis can have grave consequences, including patient harm or loss of life (International Organization for Standardization (ISO), 2018b).Consequently, healthcare providers and organizations place great emphasis on safety protocols, risk management strategies, and continuous quality improvement initiatives to mitigate risks and enhance patient safety (International Organization for Standardization (ISO), 2018b).

Similarly, industries like aviation and nuclear power, classified as HROs, prioritize safety and security due to the potential catastrophic outcomes associated with errors (ISO, 2018b). These sectors adhere to rigorous safety protocols, often mandated by strict regulations, to ensure the well-being of workers and the public (International Organization for Standardization (ISO), 2018b).

However, the strategies developed for effective error management, particularly in healthcare and HROs, can be adapted for broader economic sectors (International Organization for Standardization (ISO), 2018b). The key distinction lies in the fact that industries like banking and other businesses are more prone to security-related risks, such as theft, fraud, or cyberattacks (International Organization for Standardization (ISO), 2018b).The consequences of such events are typically financial rather than life-threatening.

Errors can have far-reaching implications, affecting not only safety and security but also business sustainability, potentially resulting in financial losses and legal liabilities (International Organization for Standardization (ISO), 2018b). Critical infrastructures, which encompass sectors essential to a nation's security, economic stability, and public health, are particularly vulnerable to a spectrum of risks, both internal and external (The White House, 2013).

In today's geopolitical landscape, operators of critical infrastructures, whether private or state-run, are exposed to real threat scenarios, necessitating a robust protection framework (The White House, 2013). The safeguarding of critical infrastructures, comprising vital sectors such as energy, transportation, and information technology, is a fundamental responsibility of governments and corporate entities (The White House, 2013).

Given the global nature of modern economies and international cooperation in various domains, the protection of critical infrastructure has transcended national boundaries (Lazari and Mikac, 2022). The European Commission, in its pursuit of a common approach to critical infrastructure protection (CIP), promotes collaboration beyond the borders of the European Union, fostering cooperation with neighboring countries, including prospective EU members (Lazari and Mikac, 2022).

Critical infrastructures face an array of hazards, ranging from extreme weather events to technical failures, human errors, and criminal activities (The White House, 2013). The increasing interconnectivity of critical infrastructure, facilitated by IT networks and the internet, exposes them to global vulnerabilities (The White House, 2013).

Protecting cyber assets, including information systems and associated data, has assumed paramount importance, with a particular focus on countering cyberattacks (The White House, 2013). Nonetheless, it's essential to recognize that even as efforts to safeguard the physical and operational aspects of critical infrastructure advance, room for improvement remains (The White House, 2013).

Critical infrastructures share a commonality with other organizations, namely their vulnerability to human risks, both internal and external (The White House,

2013). The distinguishing factor lies in the profound societal and national consequences of their failure, setting them apart from non-critical enterprises (The White House, 2013).

In the realm of safety and security, multiple definitions exist, often contingent on the specific context, such as workplace safety, public policy, or information technology (International Organization for Standardization (ISO), 2018a, The European Union information agency for occupational safety and health (EU-OSA), 2022). However, standardized definitions endorsed by experts and authoritative bodies in respective fields are prevalent (International Organization for Standardization (ISO), 2018a, The European Union information agency for occupational safety and health (EU-OSA), 2022). For instance, the International Organization for Standardization (ISO) defines safety as the condition of being shielded from, or unlikely to cause, danger, risk, or injury (International Organization for Standardization (ISO), 2018b). In a workplace context, the European Union information agency for occupational safety and health (EU-OSA) characterizes safety as the state of being free from the occurrence or risk of injury, danger, or loss (The European Union information agency for occupational safety and health (EU-OSA), 2022).

These definitions of "Safety" underscore the central theme of protection against accidental harm, risk, or injury. Conversely, the International Association for "Security" Professionals (American Society for Industrial Security (ASIS), 2015) defines Security as the safeguarding of human beings, physical assets, and information, coupled with the prevention and investigation of crimes against these assets (American Society for Industrial Security (ASIS), 2015). In the realm of information technology, security primarily pertains to shielding data and systems from unauthorized access and cyber threats (American Society for Industrial Security (ASIS), 2015). The International Telecommunication Union (ITU) defines cyber security as the set of security concepts, tools, policies, protective measures, guidelines, risk management approaches, measures, training, best practices, safeguards and technologies that are used together to protect the digital environment and the assets of an organization and its users (The International Telecommunication Union (ITU), 2024).

These definitions illuminate the core tenets of each concept: Safety's focus on averting unintentional harm and mitigating risk, and security's mission to counter intentional threats and attacks. Notably, these definitions may exhibit variations based on industry, regulatory frameworks (Table 1.1).

Table 1.1 Safety and Security

Scope	Goal	Risks	Countermeasures
Safety	To avoid harm or reduce its impact	Natural disasters, accidents, or unintentional human error	Focus on prevention, such as implementing safety protocols, providing training, or making physical changes to reduce risk
Security	Prevent unauthorized access, protect assets, and deter criminal activity	intentional threats or attacks, intentional misbehaviour	Proactive response, such as installing security systems, increasing surveillance, or hiring security personnel.

1.3 Errors and Critical Incidents

Damage events are not per se unpredictable, random or fated. Small failures may well be early indicators that something is not "running smoothly" (Edmondson, 2004). The connection between early warning indicators and damage events is shown by Heinrich's Law (Heinrich, 1941) (Fig. 1.1).

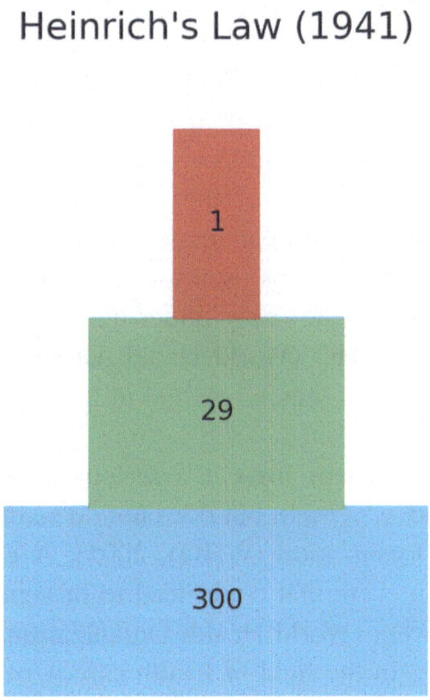

Fig. 1.1 Heinrich's law (Heinrich, 1941), p. 27

The ratios shown in the figure above -1-29-300—show that in a group of 330 similar accidents the majority of 300 critical incidents occur without much publicity, but they form the basis for 29 incidents with minor injuries to those affected and for one case with catastrophic consequences (Heinrich, 1941). The serious injury can be caused either by the first accident or by another accident in the group (Heinrich, 1941).

Heinrich's law suggests that critical incidents should be recorded and systematically analysed, and that the process containing the error should be corrected in a second step. Error reporting systems offer a possibility to learn from errors. Reason (Reason, 2000a) sees their use as an indispensable prerequisite for identifying recurring error traps or identifying limits without exceeding them. There is no one error reporting system, but different forms with different objectives (Aktionsbündnis Patientensicherheit (APS), 2016); (Kahla-Witzsch, 2005). The importance of error reporting systems or critical incident systems to improve the safety situation is particularly evident in the healthcare industry, because errors in medication, treatment, or diagnosis can have serious consequences and even lead to patient harm or death. Therefore, there is an increased interest in identifying and eliminating sources of error at an early stage. In principle, this interest should be shared by all companies, regardless of whether life, health or company assets or economic existence are endangered by mistakes.

Reporting systems collecting data on adverse events and incidents at the point of care are now widespread around the world (World Health Organization (WHO), 2021, World Health Organization (WHO), 2020). In reporting systems errors are classified according to whether harm has already occurred or according to the degree of probability of harm. Incident reports can capture events in one or more of the following three basic categories: adverse events, no harm events and near misses (World Health Organization (WHO), 2009). The definitions of terms used are those developed as part of an international classification for patient safety under the auspices of the World Alliance for Patient Safety of the WHO (World Health Organization (WHO), 2009). An **adverse event** is an incident which resulted in harm to a patient (World Health Organization (WHO), 2009).

A **near miss** is a serious error or mishap that has the potential to cause an adverse event but does not do so due to chance or timely avoidance (World Health Organization (WHO), 2005). A **critical event**, on the other hand, is defined as an event that could lead to or significantly increases the likelihood of an adverse event (World Health Organization (WHO), 2005).

In the field of health care, Critical Incident Reporting System (CIRS) plays a significant role. In Germany, this is even prescribed by law. In contrast to "error reporting" systems, which aim to record clear errors that regularly lead to an adverse event, a CIRS starts earlier. They already record near misses or critical incidents or latent conditions (Kahla-Witzsch, 2005).

The advantage of CIRS compared to an error reporting system is that a larger amount of data can be collected in the same amount of time. This is because, with reference to Heinrich's Law, critical incidents occur more frequently than moderate or serious errors. On the other hand, nothing has happened yet in the case of a critical incident, so there is no liability problem (Mildenberger and Ulsenheimer, 2003). In this respect, the psychological hurdles for employees to report are also lower. However, according to Reason (Reason, 1995), an indispensable prerequisite for an error reporting system is that the reports are preferably anonymous. The anonymity of the reporter is also an advantage for a CIRS. This is because it lowers the inhibition threshold for reporting, as the reporter does not have to fear any sanctions due to anonymity.

Hospitals in Germany were required for the first time to introduce CIRS in addition to risk management systems under the Gesetz zur Verbesserung der Rechte von Patientinnen und Patienten[2].

The Gemeinsame Bundesausschuss[3] (G-BA)—the highest decision-making body of the joint self-administration of physicians, dentists, psychotherapists, hospitals and health insurance funds in Germany—has defined minimum standards for error reporting systems in the medical care of SHI-insured patients in accordance with the legal mandate. These can be found in § 5 of the guideline of the Joint Federal Committee on the basic requirements for quality management within a health care facility for hospitals accredited according to § 108 SGB V (Gemeinsamer Bundesausschuss (G-BA), 2016). Accordingly, a CIRS accessible and easy to manage for all employees across departments and occupational groups accessible and easy to manage. I.e. the CIRS addresses all staff members, from the cleaning staff to the reception staff to the nursing staff, doctors and managers of a hospital. At the same time reports must be made voluntarily, anonymously and without sanctions by the employees.

The legislator does not stipulate the concrete specification of a CIRS. According to Reason (Reason, 1995), however, it is indispensable that in the error reporting system individual, task-related, situation-related and organizational factors and to relate them to critical incidents and near misses. Therefore, the

---

[2] Act on the Improvement of Patients' Rights of 20 February 2013; § 135a Absatz 2 Nummer 2 des SGB V.

[3] Joint Federal Committee.

German legislator demands that CIRS be embedded in a clinical risk management system.

Moreover, although CIRS or error reporting systems are an indispensable part of error management, they are insufficient in themselves to ensure safety and quality in hospitals. In addition, regular monitoring of the vital signs of the entire organization from the point of view of safety must be added to support proactive error prevention (Reason, 1995).The indicators used for measurement differ according to the respective analysis tools.

1.4 Human Error

In various industries, human errors pose a significant threat to both individuals and organizations, echoing the insights of English industrial and organizational psychologist James Reason (Reason, 1990). These errors manifest as deviations from expected behaviors or desired goals of action, actions that the agent could have realistically performed or achieved. The consequences of human errors reverberate across diverse sectors, with high-technology systems particularly susceptible to their adverse effects.

The gravity of human error is strikingly evident in healthcare, as highlighted by Reason in 1995 (Reason, 1995). Hospitals, as vital components of the medical system, are not exempt from this formidable challenge. Medical systems, while pioneering remarkable advancements in patient care, remain vulnerable to the multifaceted nature of human error. To effectively address and mitigate these errors, a profound comprehension of the underlying mechanisms and contributing factors is essential. Well known examples of human errors include high-profile incidents such as:

Challenger Space Shuttle Disaster (1986): A critical failure in the O-rings due to mismanagement and miscommunication led to the tragic explosion of the Challenger space shuttle, resulting in the loss of seven astronauts' lives (Committee on science and technology—House of representatives, 1986).

Three Mile Island Nuclear Accident (1979): A combination of operator errors, design flaws, and equipment malfunctions resulted in a partial meltdown at the Three Mile Island nuclear power plant, raising concerns about nuclear safety (Rogovin and Frampton George T., 1979).

Deepwater Horizon Oil Spill (2010): A series of human errors, including inadequate safety measures and misjudgments, contributed to the largest marine oil spill in history, with devastating environmental and economic consequences (Commission on the BP Deepwater Horizon Oil Spill, 2011).

Fukushima Daiichi Nuclear Disaster in 2011 was natural disaster, combined with inadequate preparedness and operator errors, resulted in a nuclear meltdown at the Fukushima Daiichi nuclear power plant, leading to radiation leaks and long-term environmental impacts (International Atomic Energy Agency (IAEA), 2015).

Therac-25 Radiation Therapy Machine Accidents: Software and user interface design flaws in the Therac-25 radiation therapy machine caused patients to receive lethal doses of radiation due to programming errors and inadequate safety checks (Leveson and Turner, 1993).

SpaceX Falcon 1 Launch Failure (2006): A design flaw in a fuel tank caused the failure of the first launch of the SpaceX Falcon 1 rocket (McCartney, 2006), highlighting the challenges and risks in the aerospace industry.

In 2009 and 2010, Toyota recalled nearly eight million vehicles as part of the sticky pedal and pedal entrapment recalls (Toyota Unintended Acceleration Recall). In addition, Toyota paid $48.8 million in civil penalties as the result of The National Highway Traffic Safety Administration (NHTSA) investigations into the timeliness of several safety recalls. Software and design issues in certain Toyota vehicles led to unintended acceleration incidents, resulting in accidents and recalls, underscoring the importance of quality control in the automotive sector (U.S. Department Of Transportation (DOT), 2019);(U.S. Department of Transportation (DOT), 2012).

These prominent examples underscore the critical importance of understanding and addressing human errors across diverse fields, emphasizing the need for proactive measures, improved safety protocols, and ongoing research to minimize their impact on high-technology systems and society as a whole.

For the last six years there can be listed further prominent examples of human errors:

Boeing 737 MAX Crashes (2018–2019): Two fatal crashes involving the Boeing 737 MAX aircraft occurred in 2018 and 2019, resulting in the grounding of the entire MAX fleet. Investigations revealed design flaws and insufficient pilot training, emphasizing the critical role of human factors in aviation safety (National Transportation Safety Board (NTSB), 2019).

Facebook Cambridge Analytica Scandal (2018): The improper handling of user data by Facebook and the exploitation of this data by Cambridge Analytica for political purposes highlighted the potential consequences of data breaches and the need for stricter data protection measures (Committee on Energy and Commerce, 2018).

Boeing Starliner CST-100 test flight anomaly in 2019: Boeing's CST-100 Starliner spacecraft suffered a critical software failure during an unmanned test flight to the International Space Station, highlighting the importance of thorough testing and quality control in spaceflight (NASA areospace safety advisory panel, 2021).

COVID-19 Vaccine Distribution Challenges (2020-ongoing): The global distribution of COVID-19 vaccines has faced various logistical and communication challenges, highlighting the importance of efficient planning, coordination, and addressing potential errors in the distribution process (Forman et al., 2021).

These recent cases serve as reminders of the wide-ranging impact of human error and the critical need for proactive measures, improved safety protocols, and ongoing research to minimize its effects across different industries and sectors.

1.5 Error Types and Generic Error Modelling System

GEMS is an error classification scheme developed by Reason (Reason, 1990) that focuses on cognitive factors in human error as opposed to environmental or other context-related factors. GEMS is based heavily on Rasmussen's three major categories of errors: skill-based slips and lapses, rule-based mistakes, and knowledge-based mistakes.

The Generic Error Modelling System (GEMS) framework is used to analyze and avoid human errors in complex systems. It consists of a set of tools and techniques for identifying, analysing, and mitigating errors in complex systems.

GEMS considers human errors as the result of the interaction between various factors, including individual performance, system design and organizational factors. It takes a systems approach. It thus considers both technical and social aspects of the systems in which human errors may occur.

GEMS identifies four levels of system complexity and belonging factor that can contribute to the occurrence of errors:

Organizational influences: This level includes the factors that influence the organization and its environment, including organizational culture, leadership, resource availability, regulatory requirements, and economic conditions.

Conditions for unsafe acts: This level includes the factors that can lead to unsafe acts, including lack of experience, stress, overload, distraction and ineffectiveness of rules and procedures.

Unsafe acts themselves: This level involves the actual actions or behaviors undertaken by individuals that directly lead to errors or safety breaches.

Consequences: This level includes the direct and indirect consequences of errors, including damage to the health and safety of people, economic costs, loss of image and legal consequences.

GEMS takes a holistic approach, recognizing that human errors are a result of the interaction of many factors, and it thus looks at the system, rather than just one part of it. The practical use of the GEMS framework is to provide practical and actionable recommendations for error prevention and reduction in complex systems. GEMS can be applied flexibly to different types of systems, including technical systems, social systems and organizations.

The "conditions for unsafe acts" level in the GEMS framework provides an appropriate context for understanding the interactions between the three levels of cognitive control—skill-based, rule-based and knowledge-based—and other systemic factors that can lead to errors and unsafe acts.

The three levels of cognitive control of actions refer to the stages of learning and performing a task, from the initial skill-based level to the more advanced knowledge-based level. The basic assumption is that human actions are primarily controlled at the skill-based and rule-based levels (Reason, 1990). The rationale for this is seen in the fact that information processing at these levels is particularly efficient and without much effort due to the parallel processing mode. According to Reason (Reason, 1990), when problems occur during action, the first attempt is usually to solve them at the rule-based level by using known and successful or proven action patterns in similar situations. Only if this is unsuccessful is the action problem dealt with at the knowledge-based level, whereby here, too, rather simple solution strategies (e.g. the trial-and-error strategy) are preferred in the first step. Extensive situation analyses and considerations for problem solving are therefore avoided as long as possible (Reason, 1990).

Based on the three levels of cognitive control of actions, there are three types of errors, each corresponding to a different level of cognitive control: skill-based errors (slips and lapses), rule-based errors (mistakes involving confusion or misrecognition), and knowledge-based errors (errors in reasoning and judgment) (Nerdinger et al., 2011).

Skill-based errors, such as slips and oversights, occur at the lowest level of cognitive control, where a task is automated and requires little conscious attention. Rule-based errors, such as errors of confusion and recognition, occur when a task requires conscious attention to follow established rules or procedures. Knowledge-based errors, such as errors of reasoning and judgment, occur when a task requires higher-level cognitive processing and decision-making (Table 1.2).

Table 1.2 Three levels of cognitive control of actions and corresponding error types

Level of cognitive control of action	Error type
Skill based	slips and oversights
Rule based	error of confusion and recognition
Knowledge based	error of reasoning and judgement

This level of cognitive control describes the factors that can lead to unsafe acts, including lack of experience, stress, overload, distraction and ineffectiveness of rules and procedures. The GEMS framework recognizes that unsafe acts can often be due to a failure in cognitive control and therefore proposes solutions to improve rules, procedures, and training to reduce the risk of errors.

The GEMS model can potentially be used for analyzing by AI as it provides a framework for understanding how cognitive control is exercised over actions. Each level of cognitive control (i.e., skill-based, rule-based, and knowledge-based) can be operationalized into objective assessment criteria that can be analyzed by AI. For example, skill-based errors can be assessed by measuring the frequency and type of slips and oversights made by an individual or a team. Rule-based errors can be assessed by evaluating the degree of confusion or misapplication of rules in decision-making processes. Knowledge-based errors can be assessed by analyzing the reasoning and judgment processes used by individuals or teams in complex situations. By breaking down cognitive control into objective assessment criteria, AI can potentially analyze and evaluate an organization's cognitive processes and identify areas for improvement. GEMS-assessment criteria are as follows:

Skill-based errors (slips and oversights):

- Frequency of certain errors compared to the expected number of errors given the task complexity and individual skill level.
- Time taken to complete a task compared to the expected time given the task complexity and individual skill level.
- Consistency in performing the task correctly over multiple attempts.
- Reaction time to unexpected events or changes in the task.

Rule-based errors (errors of confusion and recognition):

- Number of times a rule was misinterpreted or not followed correctly.
- Frequency of incorrect responses to specific stimuli or cues.
- Percentage of correct responses to similar but distinct stimuli or cues.
- Time taken to recognize and correct an error.

Knowledge-based errors (errors of reasoning and judgment).

- Number of logical fallacies committed during decision-making or problem-solving.
- Consistency of decision-making with established principles or guidelines.
- Time taken to reach a decision compared to the expected time given the complexity of the problem and available information.
- The degree of deviation from optimal outcomes or solutions.

To illustrate how the criteria from the Generic Error Modelling System (GEMS) can be operationalized for an AI solution, we've created Table 1.3 below. This table outlines the error types identified by GEMS—skill-based, rule-based, and knowledge-based—and their corresponding criteria along with potential data sources for each criterion.

Table 1.3 Operationalizing GEMS Criteria for AI Solutions

Error Type	Assessment Criteria	Operationalization for AI Solution
Skill-based errors	- Frequency of errors compared to expected given task complexity	- Track instances of errors per task complexity level
	- Time taken to complete task compared to expected given complexity	- Record time taken for task completion per skill level
	- Consistency in task performance over multiple attempts	- Analyze performance consistency across repeated attempts
	- Reaction time to unexpected events or task changes	- Measure response time to unexpected events or changes
Rule-based errors	- Frequency of rule misinterpretations or non-compliance	- Monitor instances of rule misinterpretations or non-compliance
	- Incorrect responses to specific stimuli or cues	- Log occurrences of incorrect responses to stimuli or cues
	- Percentage of correct responses to similar but distinct stimuli	- Calculate accuracy in distinguishing similar yet distinct stimuli
	- Time taken to recognize and correct errors	- Evaluate time taken to identify and rectify errors
Knowledge-based errors	- Number of logical fallacies during decision-making or problem-solving	- Detect and count logical fallacies in decision-making or problem-solving
	- Consistency with established principles or guidelines	- Assess alignment of decisions with established principles or guidelines
	- Time taken to reach a decision compared to expected given complexity	- Measure decision time relative to problem complexity and information
	- Degree of deviation from optimal outcomes or solutions	- Quantify deviation from optimal outcomes or solutions

1.6 Knowingly Violating the Rules or Gross Negligence

The GEMS framework primarily focuses on unintentional errors and their contributing factors. However, the framework can also provide insight into deliberate rule violations or gross negligence.

In the GEMS model, deliberate rule violations or gross negligence would likely fall under the "unsafe acts" category, which is associated with the level of "unsafe acts themselves". Contributing factors that could lead to deliberate rule violations or gross negligence might include:

Individual factors: These could include factors such as personal values, attitudes, beliefs, and motivations that may influence an individual's willingness to comply with rules and regulations.

Organizational factors: These could include factors such as inadequate training or supervision, conflicting goals or priorities, inadequate resources, and unclear expectations, which may create an environment where individuals are more likely to violate rules.

System factors: These could include factors such as ineffective rules and procedures, poor communication and feedback systems, and lack of accountability, which may encourage individuals to take shortcuts or bypass rules.

Cultural factors: No organization can function safely if its rules and procedures are largely ignored. One consequence of rule-breaking is a culture of complacency and disregard for rules, which requires strong leadership and positive role models. (Helmreich et al., 1999a).

It's important to note that deliberate rule violations and gross negligence may also be influenced by factors that go beyond the individual, organizational, and system levels, such as economic or political pressures, which may be addressed by looking at the broader social and cultural context in which these actions occur.

By applying the GEMS framework to analyse deliberate rule violations or gross negligence, organizations can identify the contributing factors and take steps to address them. This may involve implementing more effective training programs, improving supervision, revising procedures to make them clearer, or creating a culture that values safety and compliance.

1.7 Four Levels of Culpability (Mens Rea)

Usually, four levels of culpability (mens rea) are distinguished, used mainly in criminal law to determine criminal responsibility and the appropriate punishment for a crime. The concept of mens rea is recognized and applied in many legal systems around the world, although the specific terminology and definitions used may vary depending on the jurisdiction.

The concept of mens rea has its roots in common law, which is a legal system that originated in England and was later adopted by many countries, including the United States, Canada, Australia, and India. Common law recognizes the principle that a person should not be convicted of a crime unless they had the requisite mental state, or mens rea, at the time the crime was committed.

The concept of mens rea is also recognized in civil law systems, which are based on Roman law and are used in many countries, including France, Germany, Italy, and Japan. In civil law, the concept of intent is often used to establish liability for intentional torts, such as defamation, assault and battery.

In international law, mens rea is recognized as an important element of many crimes, particularly those defined under the Rome Statute of the International

Criminal Court (Badar, 2013). Badar has described the relevant forms of liability for its own conduct as follows (Badar, 2013):

Intent:	This is the explicit and conscious desire to commit a dangerous or illegal act.
Knowledge:	The term "knowledge" applies when a person is aware that their actions will have certain consequences, but seems to ignore this indifferently.
Recklessness:	Recklessness is the decision to carry out a certain action even though you are aware of the risks involved.
Negligence:	This is the mildest form of criminal culpability and is often encountered in the case constellations mentioned above under the GEMS model. A person commits negligence when she fails to meet a reasonable standard of behaviour for her circumstances.

In civil law, which deals with disputes between individuals or organizations and seeks compensation for the damage caused, the concept of fault is often expressed in terms of negligence; however, the concept of intent or knowledge of wrongdoing is still be relevant in certain civil law cases.

Whether and to what extent such deliberate violations of rules have legal consequences in individual cases is determined, among other things, not only by the existence of a damaging event but also by the possible lack of justification and excuses.

Overall, the focus of the legal consideration of knowing breaches of rules tends to be on the sanction and on compensation for damage.

In the context of risk minimisation and error management, the focus should not be so much on sanctions, but rather on prevention. Of particular interest here is why such breaches of the rules occur and how they can be effectively prevented in future. The reasons for such rule violations are not only inadequate attitudes or lack of preparedness with regard to safety issues, but also ignorance or misinterpretation of relevant regulations (Nerdinger et al., 2011). Ignorance or misinterpretation of safety-related regulations can be remedied through training. However, inadequate attitudes toward safety or error culture or an unwillingness to engage with it are the most difficult to come to grips with. Thus, insufficient company-risk attitudes and beliefs are considered the most dangerous category of human error.

1.8 Person-Related Error Approach

If the question is how to avoid errors or prevent or at least mitigate their harmful effects, Reason's (Reason, 2000a) distinction between person-related and system-related errors is helpful. The distinction between the two approaches is relevant for all kind of companies. This is because depending on which approach is taken will determine, on the one hand, the measures taken to promote error culture and, on the other hand, a prediction of how effective they will be in doing so.

According to the person-centered approach described by Reason (Reason, 2000a) errors are mainly caused by mental processes that deviate from the rules, such as forgetfulness, inattention, lack of motivation, carelessness, negligence and recklessness. The corresponding countermeasures are of an educational, moral, regulatory or disciplinary nature. That such an approach is conducive to a "blame culture" is obvious. This view, which is traditional in medicine, is further promoted by the fact that, from the perspective of the business organization, failure is preferred to be seen in an individual rather than, for example, in organizational culpability on the part of management (Reason, 2000a). This is legally the more comfortable legal position, not only in the Anglo-Saxon system but also in the German legal system, from the point of view of the company management.

1.9 System-Related Error Approach

With the system-based approach to error, the individual "failure" can be put into perspective by also looking at whether and to what extent the system, for example through its framework conditions or its organization, has favoured the error. It is increasingly recognized that the causes and circumstances for errors in hospitals, with or without damage consequences, are predominantly multifactorial, i.e. not only based on the "human error" of the individual (Marx, 1997). The latter are thus heirs rather than originators of the error sequence (Reason, 1995). With this systemic understanding of error, individual failure is no longer the exclusive focus of error analysis. This does not encourage a blame culture from the outset. If errors occur, the question of how and why these safety precautions did not work should be given priority.

In the systemic view of error, system defense plays a special role in error prevention. While human defectiveness continues to exist, the conditions under which humans operate can be permanently altered. Consequently, in his highly regarded article "Error in Medicine" in the journal JAMA, Leape (Leape, 1994) argues for systems thinking to promote patient safety.

The system-related view of error is to be given priority over the person-related view and is also the basis of this work. In addition to the above-mentioned promotion of a "blame culture", a major weakness of the person-related view of error is the failure to take into account that the majority of quality deficiencies e.g. but not limited in patient care are not caused by the individual, but by the system. Furthermore, focusing solely on eradicating human error in the workplace, such as through training or sanctioning, is not sufficient. This is because human errors can never be 100% eradicated. Rather, there is a need for additional efficient systems engineering approaches to error prevention.

1.10 Active and Latent Errors

In this context, Reason's division of active and latent errors is useful (Reason, 1995). Whereas in the case of active faults, undesirable events occur immediately, latent faults lie dormant in the system for a longer period until they come to light due to the occurrence of special circumstances and unleash their damaging effect. Active and latent faults differ not only in terms of the time lapse between fault and fault sequence, but both types of fault also differ in terms of the point at which the fault occurs: Either at the so-called sharp end—e.g. at the direct interface to the patient -, i.e. where the error can directly unfold its harmful effect on the patient (active error), or at another point in the system, e.g. at the management level of the hospital in corporate and organizational decisions (latent error) (Reason, 1995).

So that, among other things, organizational errors belong to the category of latent errors. Organizational and corporate culture also belong to the basic systemic causal factors of error development (Reason, 1995). Here, the industry affiliation plays a special role in the consequences of errors. If errors can lead to health damage or even death, as in the health sector, the aviation industry or the nuclear industry, the increased interest in avoiding mistakes is understandable. But all companies have an interest in avoiding mistakes, as they can make it more difficult or even endanger the achievement of corporate goals. Therefore, the tools that have been developed especially for error prevention in industries that are particularly dangerous for people, can be made usable by way of a logical first-right conclusion, as far as possible.

1.11 The Swiss-Cheese Model

How accidents or patient hazards can occur in hospitals despite existing safety precautions is very clearly illustrated by the so-called "Swiss cheese model", which is shown in the following Fig. 1.2. This model was developed by James Reason against the background of the system-oriented view, also based on the work of the Dane J. Rasmussen (Reason, 1990). For example, a whole series of safety barriers are also installed e.g. in a hospital, such as safety checklists in the operating room (team time-out). However, individual ones of these safety barriers can be breached by errors. This is the case when these barriers are as full of holes as a Swiss cheese. As a rule, the next barrier ensures that the error has no effect. Accordingly, an accident or an undesired event can only arise from a hazard if all intervening safety barriers fail, i.e. holes have been created and these holes are located exactly on an axis due to special circumstances so that a causal chain can arise.

This Swiss-cheese model can be applied to all hazards and risks, including those in the business environment. As described by Reason (Reason, 1990), organizational accidents can be characterized by the following elements:

- Shortcomings in routine processes in normal business operations.
- Latent deficiencies in the organization and its processes
- The unsafe acts committed by individuals or teams (active failures); and
- Inadequate defensive measures to protect the system from potential harm once the unsafe act has been committed.

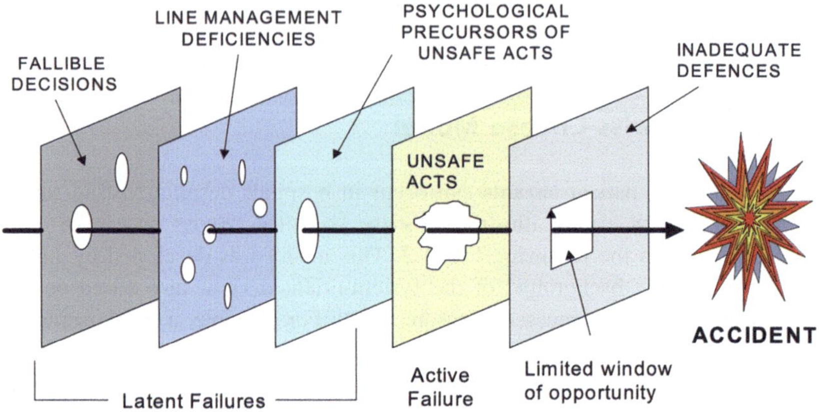

Fig. 1.2 SOAM version of the Reason Model (Eurocontrol, 2005), p. 22

1.12 Human Factors

When considering how to make HROs and other organization in general safer, human factors are at the forefront of research in addition to systems engineering. Here, human factors refer to environmental, organizational and workplace factors as well as individual and human characteristics that influence work behaviour and can therefore affect health and safety. (Health Safety Executive (HSE), 1999). Previously, the primary focus was on what human factors threaten reliability. In this respect, reference is made to the so-called dirty dozen, explained below, as an example. More recent research approaches also address the question of which human factors contribute positively to reliability, (Vogus et al., 2014).

1.13 Dirty Dozen

Originally, the so-called dirty dozen was conceptually developed by Gordon Dupont (Dupont, 1997) for the elucidation of human factors that can lead to aircraft maintenance errors and resulting accidents.

The Dirty Dozen refers to a list of twelve common human factors that can contribute to accidents and incidents in the workplace. These twelve factors include lack of communication, complacency, lack of knowledge, distraction, lack of teamwork, fatigue, lack of awareness, lack of resources, stress, pressure, lack of assertiveness and norms (Dupont, 1997).

These twelve human factors are often referred to as "dirty" because they are difficult to address and can be hard to detect.

This concept has been widely used in the aviation industry. In the meantime, this safety-relevant employee training has also been accepted in the healthcare industry and is addressed, among other things, in nursing training in the Free Hanseatic City of Hamburg under the aspect of error prevention (Behörde für Soziales, 2010).

This concept of error prevention can also be applied to other organizations, where errors may not endanger the life or health of other but can cause economic damage up to and including the insolvency of a company. Because the twelve above mentioned most common error-causing human factors can occur in any company.

1.14 SHELL-Model

The relationship between human factors and errors in the aviation industry is still an intensively researched topic in the field of safety management. Even though there are now several models, such as Domino (Bird, 1974) the Swiss Cheese (Reason, 1990), the Human Factors Analysis and Classification System (HFACS) (Wiegmann and Shappell, 2017) and the Systemic Occurrence Analysis Methodology (SOAM) (Eurocontrol, 2005).

The SHELL model remains the most widely used due to its simplicity and its ability to better emphasize the impact of human factors in accidents (Cantamessa et al., 2018). The SHELL-Model in this context refers to a safety management model that is based on the concept of layers of protection. In this model, safety is achieved by having multiple layers of protection in place, each one designed to prevent or mitigate a particular type of hazard. The SHELL model emphasizes the interfaces between a person and the other four components more than the individual effects of each component. This reflects the SHELL model's systemic approach to failure analysis. The model requires an analysis of each person's interactions with the other four components. These various interactions may contain potential sources of human error, while a mismatch between the central liveware and each of the other four components of the SHELL-Model results in a source of human error.

In the context of corporate safety, the SHELL-Model and the before mentioned Dirty Dozen are not directly related to each other. The SHELL-Model is a safety management model that can be used to design and implement safety systems, while the Dirty Dozen is a list of factors that can be used to identify and address potential safety hazards. However, both concepts can be used together as part of a comprehensive safety management approach. The SHELL-Model can help to ensure that multiple layers of protection are in place to address potential hazards, while the Dirty Dozen can be used to identify and address human factors that could contribute to safety incidents.

There are various models that illustrate the conditions under which errors can occur in complex systems. They all agree that errors emanate from manifold interactions on different levels of action, which ultimately cause damage only in their interaction. Against this background, a system structure must in any case be designed in such a way that first it is difficult for the individual to make mistakes, and that second mistakes made are "neutralized" before they can cause harm (Moray, 2018).

The SHELL-Model was originally developed as mentioned above for the aviation industry, in particular for the analysis of accidents and near misses (Molloy and O'Boyle, 2005). In particular, the cooperation in teams, e.g. in the cockpit or in the flight crew, was examined. These findings on error prevention can also be transferred to other working environments by way of a logical first-right conclusion. The appeal of the SHELL-Model may be that it can used for every kind of complex work environments and that it is particularly applicable in microsystems. These are increasingly being used to analyse team performance in high-tech work environments such as the operating room or intensive care unit (Helmreich and Musson, 2000);(Schaefer et al., 1994); (Helmreich, 2000b). So it is not very surprising that the SHELL-Model is a particularly influential model in health care for the study of medical errors and error (Sachverständigenrat für die Konzertierte Aktion im Gesundheitswesen, 2003)[4], (Molloy and O'Boyle, 2005). The SHELL-Model is also used in the business environment for failure analysis and prevention; for example, to investigate why start-up companies fail so often and which preventive measures are promising (Cantamessa et al., 2018), (Öndas and Akpinar, 2021), (Kusumaningtyas et al., 2021).

Originally the SHEL(L) -model was developed by Edwards (Edwards, 1972) later modified somewhat by Hawkins and Orlady (Hawkins and Orlady, 2017) by incorporating the liveware-liveware interface. Since then, the model has been known as SHELL. The word **SHELL** is an acronym and is made up of the first letters of four significant factors for error generation: **S**oftware, **H**ardware, **E**nvironment, **L**iveware and Liveware-Liveware Interface. According

[4] Council of Experts on Concerted Action in Health Care.

to the SHELL model, a mismatch between the human component (liveware) and the other four components contributes to human error. Therefore, these interactions must be evaluated and taken into account in all areas of the company. These factors can be the source of errors individually or through interactions (Molloy and O'Boyle, 2005). Following Fig. 1.3 clearly shows that the liveware factor and thus the human factors are of central importance.

Fig. 1.3 Shel(l) Model Molloy & O'Boyle, 2005, p. 153

The "**software**" factor encompasses all intangible aspects of a system. This includes everything that controls the system and determines how information is organized, presented and communicated to the people working in the system (Hawkins and Orlady, 1993, Hawkins and Orlady, 2017). Software includes norms of all kinds (internal or external) or standard operating procedures, customs, practices, conventions, habits, symbolism, or specific instructions from superiors and computer programs. Software also includes all types of documentation of meaningful relevant information (Wiener and Nagel, 1988). Countermeasures against software-related errors are:

- Having a robust incident response plan in place
- Regularly updating software and ensuring it is secure and up-to-date
- Conducting software testing to identify any potential vulnerabilities or weaknesses.
- Training to employees on how to use software and technology tools properly.
- Introduction and maintenance of controlled documents

Hardware includes the physical elements of the business operational system, tools, materials, buildings, vehicles, computers, conveyor belts etc. (Johnston and

McDonald, 2017); (Wiener and Nagel, 1988); (Campbell and Bagshaw, 2002). Countermeasures against hardware related errors are:

- Conducting regular inspections and maintenance of hardware to ensure it is in good working condition,
- Using high-quality hardware that meets safety standards
- Providing training to employees on how to use hardware safely and effectively

In the original SHELL model, "**environment**" primarily referred to the physical work environment, but the model has evolved.Nowadays, the environment factor also includes the organizational, political,financial, regulatory, and social variables that impact the employees (Wiener and Nagel, 1988), (Johnston and McDonald, 2017, Molloy and O'Boyle, 2005). This also include stress and fatigue: This includes the impact of stress, fatigue, and other psychological factors on individual and team performance, as well as strategies for managing and mitigating these factors. For example, tightening in hospital financing can worsen the financial situation of a hospital in such a way that nursing staff must be cut. This can cause an overload of nursing staff and promote the occurrence of errors. Consequently, the environment factor also include the level of cognitive, physical, and emotional demands placed on individuals or teams, as well as the distribution of workload among team members (workload). Furthermore, the environment factor also includes the general organizational culture, but also specific manifestations such as safety culture, which will be discussed in more detail later (see below Sect. 1.18)

In summary, the following countermeasures against environmental related errors can be mentioned:

- Conducting regular safety inspections to identify potential hazards in the workplace
- Providing adequate lighting, ventilation, and other environmental controls to ensure a safe working environment
- Providing training to employees on how to recognize and avoid environmental hazards
- Encouraging a safety culture within the organization through regular communication, training, and feedback.
- Holding employees accountable for following security policies and procedures.
- Encouraging employees to report safety concerns or incidents

- Monitoring the level of cognitive, physical, and emotional demands placed on individuals or teams, as well as the distribution of workload among team members.
- Implementing programs to manage stress and fatigue, such as providing opportunities for rest and recovery, offering stress reduction techniques, and promoting healthy lifestyle habits.

This term "**liveware**" refers to the individual human actor with all his individual characteristics. In the hospital, for example, these are, for example, the doctor or the nurse. In plant and mechanical engineering, for example, this is the engineer in mechanical construction or the commissioning engineer on the external construction site. Relevant attributes would be body characteristics, personality, communication style, motivation, risk orientation, learning style, stress tolerance, skills, knowledge, and attitude (Molloy and O'Boyle, 2005). The following countermeasures against liveware related errors can be mentioned:

- Recruiting and Retention of qualified and experience staff
- Conducting background checks on all employees who have access to sensitive information
- Training and Experience: This includes the knowledge, skills, and experience of individuals or teams, as well as the training and development opportunities provided to support their performance.
- Providing training to employees on how to work safely and effectively

"Liveware" is the system's most valuable and adaptable component (Molloy and O'Boyle, 2005). On the other hand, humans also suffer from fluctuations in performance and are also prone to error (Molloy and O'Boyle, 2005). Nevertheless, humans—which may sound paradoxical considering their error-prone nature—are one of the most important safety devices in hospitals. This is because people make the system flexible, thereby making it safer (Weick and Sutcliffe, 2007). It is questionable whether the latter can be applied without restriction to other sectors. The special feature in hospitals, such as during surgery, is the direct contact with the patient, which also requires immediate countermeasures by staff. This means that people play a special role because of their flexibility to intervene on site and not because they are superior to the system, for example because they are less prone to errors. This idea can easily be applied to all organizations with security measures or risk management systems. This is especially true when computer-based security measures require the manual intervention of an employee or the explicit decision of a human decision-maker and not exclusively that of an artificial intelligence. For example, health care workers and nurses at the so-called sharp-end monitor and control patient care in hospitals. They are of paramount importance in hospitals for identifying and potentially preventing errors (Weir et al., 2005, Woods and Doan-Johnson, 2002). On the one hand, they have a large share in, for example, the detection of physician adverse drug reactions (ADR) errors, but on the other hand, they have a significant share in the undetected dispensing errors in drug supply (Zipper, 2006).

While the SHELL-Model initially focused only on the individual actor when it came to the human factor, nowadays the **liveware-liveware interface**—the second "**L**" in the model's name-is also considered to be of central importance in the development of errors (Molloy and O'Boyle, 2005, Eurocontrol, 2005). The Liveware-Liveware Interface layer in the SHELL-Model includes the interactions and communication that occur between the human operators or personnel who work within a complex system. This layer focuses on the human factors that contribute to system safety and effectiveness, includes factors such as:

- Communication: This includes the methods and channels of communication between individuals or teams, including verbal, written, and electronic communication.
- Teamwork: This includes the collaboration and coordination of work between individuals or teams, as well as the development of shared goals and objectives.
- Leadership style and conflict resolution: Developing effective leadership practices that support communication, collaboration, and teamwork, such as setting clear expectations, providing feedback and coaching in conflict situations.

The other -non liveware—factors of the SHELL-Model, namely hardware, software and environment, must be adapted to the human factor so that they fit together for the best possible performance. However, the factors will never fit together perfectly. This is because the system is constantly changing. Therefore, the edges of the individual factors are shown unevenly in Fig. 1.3 above.

If the SHELL-Model is applied to a bank, for example, to illustrate it, the SHELL risk factors, and corresponding defense measures could be described as follows:

1. Software: The software layer includes the bank's cybersecurity systems and processes. To prevent security breaches, the bank should use state-of-the-art encryption and firewalls to protect customer data. The bank should also have a robust incident response plan in place, including regularly updating software

and ensuring it is secure and up to date, conducting software testing to identify any potential vulnerabilities or weaknesses. In addition to that the company should provide training to employees on how to use software and technology tools properly. Furthermore, to prevent security breaches, the bank should have clear policies and procedures for handling personnel and customer data.

2. Hardware: The hardware layer includes physical equipment used to control access to the bank's systems and data. To prevent security breaches, the bank should have physical security measures in place, such as surveillance cameras, access controls, and alarm systems. The bank should also have a backup power supply and redundant data storage to ensure data availability during an outage. In general, the company should conduct regular inspections and maintenance of hardware to ensure it is in good working condition, should use high-quality hardware that meets safety standards and should provide training to employees on how to use hardware safely and effectively.
3. Environment: The environment layer includes the work conditions in which the bank's employees operate. To prevent security breaches, the bank should promote a culture of security awareness and accountability. This includes holding employees accountable for following security policies and procedures, as well as encouraging employees to report any suspicious activity. In general, to improve this layer, some further defense measures include:
   - Conducting regular safety inspections to identify potential hazards in the workplace.
   - Providing adequate lighting, ventilation, and other environmental controls to ensure a safe working environment.
   - Providing training to employees on how to recognize and avoid environmental hazards.
4. Liveware: The liveware layer includes the human factors involved in the bank's operations, such as the employees and customers. and should conduct background checks on all employees who have access to sensitive information. The bank should also educate customers on how to protect their personal and financial information. In general, some defense measures for this layer include:
   - Recruiting and Retention of qualified and experience staff
   - Conducting background checks on all employees who have access to sensitive information
   - Training and Experience: This includes the knowledge, skills, and experience of individuals or teams, as well as the training and development opportunities provided to support their performance.
   - Providing training to employees on how to work safely and effectively

5. Liveware -Liveware Interface: Here are several corresponding defense measures that can be implemented to improve this layer. These include:
   - Communication training: Providing training to individuals or teams on effective communication techniques and strategies, including active listening, feedback, and conflict resolution.
   - Team building exercises: Conducting team building exercises to promote collaboration, trust, and shared goals and objectives.
   - Effective leadership: Developing effective leadership practices that support communication, collaboration, and teamwork, such as setting clear expectations, providing feedback and coaching, and promoting a positive safety culture.

By implementing the SHELL-Model's five layers of protection, a bank can significantly reduce the likelihood of a security breach and mitigate the consequences if one does occur. This will help to protect customer data and maintain the bank's reputation as a trusted institution.

Incorporating the SHELL model into the development of an AI solution can help to ensure that all relevant factors for a safe and effective system are considered. A systematic approach based on the SHELL model enables a comprehensive consideration of the interactions between the components and helps to identify and minimize potential risks and sources of error when dealing with AI.

Table 1.4 below illustrates how the criteria from the SHELL model can be operationalized for an AI solution. It outlines the layers of the model and their corresponding criteria along with potential data sources for each criterion.

Table 1.4 Operationalization of the SHELL model criteria for AI solutions: Criteria and data source overview

Layer	Criteria from SHELL Model	Objective Criteria for AI Solution
Software	- Robust incident response plan - Regularly updating software - Conducting software testing - Training on software usage	- Implementation of AI for real-time incident detection and response - AI-driven software update scheduling and vulnerability assessment - AI-based software testing for identifying vulnerabilities - AI-powered training modules for software usage
Hardware	- Regular hardware inspections and maintenance - Using high-quality hardware - Training on hardware usage	- AI-enabled predictive maintenance for hardware - AI-assisted hardware selection based on safety standards - Virtual reality (VR) training simulations for hardware safety
Environment	- Conducting safety inspections - Providing adequate lighting and ventilation - Training on hazard recognition - Promoting safety culture	- AI-driven environmental hazard detection and mitigation - AI-based optimization for environmental controls - VR safety training simulations for environmental hazards
Liveware	- Recruiting and retention of qualified staff - Conducting background checks - Training and development - Training on safe work practices	- AI-based candidate screening and recruitment - AI-driven background check systems - Personalized AI training programs for skill development - AI-powered training on safe work practices
Liveware-Liveware Interface	- Effective communication methods - Teamwork and collaboration practices - Leadership and conflict resolution strategies	- AI-enhanced communication platforms for efficient collaboration - AI-driven task coordination and project management - AI-powered conflict resolution systems for leadership and teamwork

1.15 Schein's 3-Level Model

Schein significantly shaped and disseminated the concept of organizational culture. He defines culture as the respective pattern of shared fundamental assumptions that the group has learned in dealing with its problems of external adaptation and internal integration, which has stood the test of time and is therefore considered binding (Schein, 1995).

In this context, Schein's 3-level model is often used as an illustration. The 3-level model is used to better understand a corporate culture, which, analogous to the human psyche, is only visible and consciously perceptible to a limited extent and the far greater, hidden contains partial paradigms that take a back seat to the obviously communicated rules and norms of behaviour (Schein, 2004).

At a deeper level- the third level-, it is the underlying assumptions that lead to commonly held values and norms at the next level and are eventually reflected on the surface in artifacts. The third level encompasses what is deeply believed in a community. It describes the fundamental assumptions and values that influence the culture of an organization. These assumptions and values are often implicit and unconscious and form the foundation of the culture. They influence the perceptions, decisions, and actions of employees and thus shape behaviour in the organization. The third level can sometimes be difficult to identify because it is often not explicitly articulated or communicated. However, it can be identified by observing patterns in behaviour and interaction within the organization. The underlying assumptions and values may also be expressed in stories, legends, and myths, as well as in the unwritten rules and norms of an organization.

A positive third level can foster strong employee identification with the organization and help create a shared vision and identity. A negative third level, on the other hand, can lead to conflict, misunderstanding, and poor morale.

The second level contains the values of a group and thus determines what is good and bad. Written or unwritten norms additionally determine how one behaves properly. In the first, upper level, one finds the visible culture such as behaviour, language, works, symbols, clothing, procedures, etc.: Everything is an expression of the underlying culture (Schein, 1985) (Fig. 1.4).

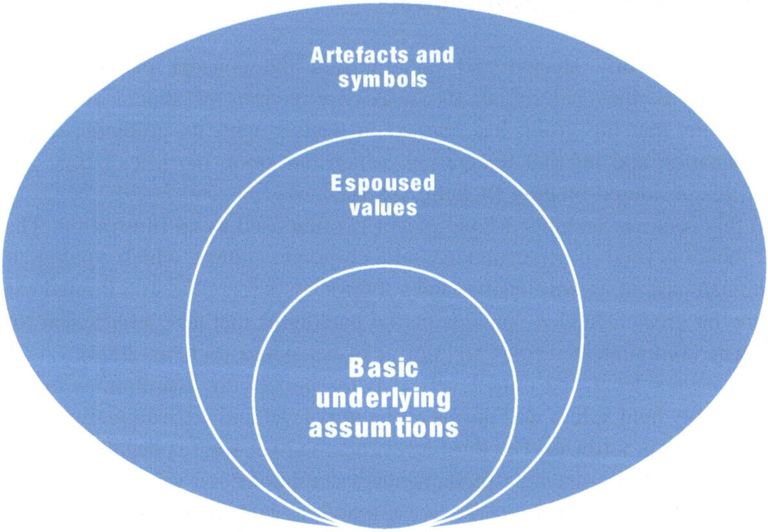

Fig. 1.4 Schein's onion layers of organizational culture, adapted from Schein (Schein, 1985)

1.16 Competing Values Framework (CVF)

There are several models that can be used to describe dimensions of an organizational culture, depending on the context and purpose of the analysis. The reason for this is that an organizational culture can be examined from many different perspectives without there being any possibility of capturing all the factors of an organizational culture and analyzing them. The question of the best theory must therefore also remain unanswered.

In this context, it is worth recalling the six blind men who come upon an elephant. Each of them touches a different part of the body and interprets the elephant from his perspective (Kieser and Walgenbach, 2003). Thus, each theory of organization has its own focus. Ultimately, an important criterion for the goodness of a theory is its empirical confirmation or non-confirmation (Kieser and Walgenbach, 2003).

Among classifications approaches the typology of Cameron and Quinn (Cameron et al., 2006) is one of the most important (Henri, 2006). The Competing Values Framework (CVF) model allows organizations to be classified according to essential core dimensions of organizational cultures. The CVF goes back to the two culture experts Kim Cameron and Robert Quinn (Cameron et al., 2006) The CVF is intended to serve as a generally applicable model for promoting successful corporate management, increasing efficiency in organizations, and developing values.

From a list of 39 performance factors for increasing efficiency in the company identified by John Campbell (Campbell, 1977) four culture types are formed in the CVF by means of two main dimensions.

The first main dimension differentiates according to efficiency criteria, which on the one hand stands for flexibility, discretion, and dynamism, and on the other hand for factors representing stability, order and control. The second main dimension, on the other hand, differentiates according to the criteria internal orientation, integration, and unity on the one hand, and on the other hand, it differentiates according to criteria that symbolize external orientation, differentiation, and rivalry.

These two main dimensions together form a 2×2 matrix with four quadrants, each of which represents several efficiency factors (see Fig. 1.5). These efficiency factors in turn represent basic assumptions, orientations, and values, which is why they also reflect corresponding four core types of organizational cultures (Cameron et al., 2006).

According to CVF, a company will be successful in the long term if it achieves extensive congruence between the dominant culture and, derived from it, leadership style, management roles, personnel management, quality management and efficiency criteria (Cameron et al., 2006). The probability of success for total quality measures is highest if they combine activities of the four culture types that are inextricably linked to the company's performance (Cameron et al., 2006). The CVF can be used to identify key quality drivers. I.e. also: Depending on which organizational culture a company can be assigned to in terms of focus, it also depends on which measures, in particular for efficient error management, are promising for the respective organizational culture.

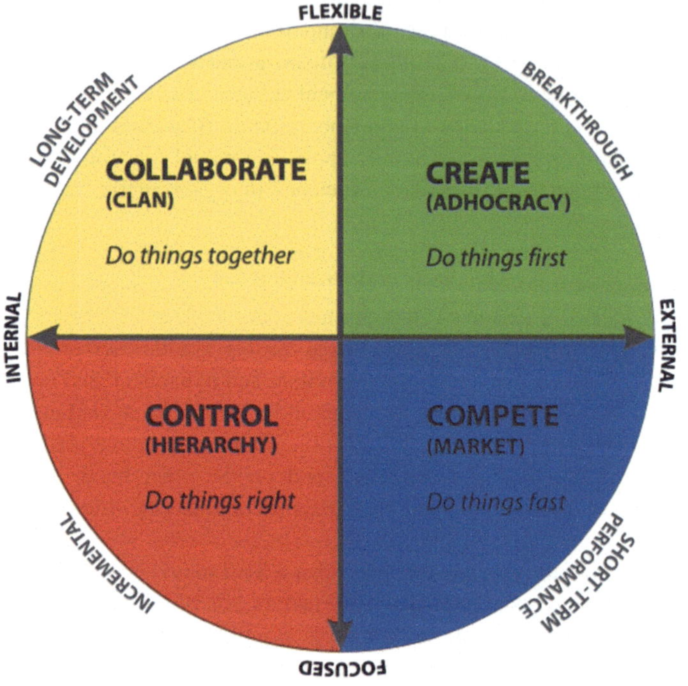

Fig. 1.5 Competing Values Framework (Cameron, 2009), page 3

1.16.1 The hierarchical organizational culture

The hierarchical organizational culture is characterized by a formalized and structured workplace (Cameron and Quinn, 1999). It focuses on stability, control, and efficiency.

Therefore, it is not surprising that Max Weber's hierarchy or bureaucracy can serve as a model for this organizational culture. In Max Weber's view, this was the ideal organizational form because it alone provided stability, efficiency, and continuity of products and services. Max Weber (Weber, 1976, pp. 561 f.) writes: "A fully developed bureaucratic mechanism behaves (…) like a machine (…) Precision, speed, unambiguity, file knowledge, continuity, discretion, uniformity, strict subordination, savings in friction, material and personal costs are increased to the optimum in strictly bureaucratic, especially: monocratic administration (…)."

1.16.2 The Market Culture

The Market Culture describes an organizational culture that functions like a market and thus keeps competition in mind to generate competitive advantage (Cameron et al., 2006). It is a competitive culture that focuses on results, performance, and goal achievement. Therefore, it is not surprising that competition and productivity are core values of such a market culture, which is essentially characterized by strong market positioning and control (Cameron et al., 2006).

1.16.3 The Clan Culture

One of the central assumptions in a clan culture is that the environment can best be shaped through teamwork, staff development and partnerships with customers. The Clan Culture is a collaborative culture focused on teamwork, cooperation, and employee satisfaction. Furthermore, the organization has the task of empowering its employees and encouraging their participation as well as their commitment and loyalty (Cameron et al., 2006)

1.16.4 Adhocracy Culture

Ad hoc cultures are "tents" rather than "palaces"; there is something temporary, specialized, and dynamic in the "ad-hoc" (Cameron et al., 2006). Characteristic of an ad hoc culture is dynamism, entrepreneurial spirit, and creative work environment (Cameron et al., 2006). Thus, an Adhocracy Culture is an innovative culture that focuses on risk-taking, experimentation and creativity. Therefore, such organizational cultures are found in industries where the goal is to develop new products and services, as well as to help shape the future through activities at the forefront of innovation leadership.

What is notable about these four core values is that they represent opposing or competing assumptions. Each dimension emphasizes a core value that is opposite to the value at the other end of the scale, e.g. flexibility versus stability, internal versus external. The dimensions therefore result in quadrants that are also diagonally competing or contradictory. The upper left quadrant identifies values that emphasize an internal, organic orientation, while the lower right quadrant identifies values that emphasize an external, controlling orientation. Similarly, the upper right quadrant identifies values that have an external, organic focus, while the lower left quadrant emphasizes internal, controlling values. These competing or opposing values in each quadrant give the model the name "Competing Values Framework" (CVF). The CVF model can be used to describe and analyze an organization's culture, as well as to determine which culture types are most appropriate for situations or strategies. It is also widely used and recognized in organizational research and practice (Helfrich et al., 2007); (O'Neill et al., 2021).

1.17 Nine Dimensions of Organizational Culture and Concept of Reconciling Corporate Culture

In this context, it is useful to use Trompenaars/Paud'Homme's (Trompenaars et al., 2004) nine dimensions of organizational culture alongside Cameron and Quinn's CVF model to describe and analyze the dimensions of organizational culture. It is important to emphasize that both models use different approaches and methods.

The CVF model focuses on four types of culture as above defined by two dimensions: Flexibility vs. Control and Internal vs. External Alignment. These dimensions are used to describe and analyze an organization's culture. Trompenaars/Paud Homme's nine dimensions of organizational culture, on the other hand, examine different aspects of an organization's culture, such as its relationship to time, its relationship to hierarchy, and its relationship to conflict. These dimensions are intended to help understand and overcome cultural differences between organizations and nations.

Although there are differences between the two models, they can be considered complementary. The CVF model provides a useful method for identifying and analyzing an organization's basic culture types, while Trompenaars/Paud Homme's nine dimensions of organizational culture can help understand specific cultural differences and challenges within an organization or between different organizations. Together, they can help develop a more comprehensive understanding of organizational culture.

In doing so, the author draws on the model of the nine dimensions of organizational culture by Trompenaars/Paud'Homme. According to this model, there are nine dimensions that describe an organizational culture (Trompenaars et al., 2004):

(1) Consistency versus Pragmatism
(2) Individualism versus group orientation
(3) Competition versus partnership orientation
(4) People centrality versus result centrality

(5) Rational versus inspirational
(6) Egalitarian versus hierarchical
(7) Internal drive versus responsiveness
(8) Stable continuity versus dynamic change
(9) Long-term stakeholder orientation versus short-term, shareholder orientation

Trompenaars/Paud'Homme argue that each dimension comes with a dilemma (Trompenaars et al., 2004). That is, in other words, stability in the company through strict structures and processes can be a strength, but also a weakness due to lack of flexibility. According to Trompenaars/Paud'Homme, the solution is to create a balance within the nine pairs of opposites as far as possible for successful corporate change. For each dimension, they offer one method for balancing (Trompenaars et al., 2004). They suggest that organizations can achieve greater cultural competence and effectiveness by understanding and reconciling the cultural dilemmas inherent in each dimension (Trompenaars et al., 2004).

Of these nine dimensions, the dimensions of competition versus partnership orientation and stable continuity versus dynamic change are particularly relevant to corporate safety and security.

Competition versus partnership orientation refers to how companies achieve results. In an achievement-oriented culture, the focus is on maximizing profits and growth, while in a partnership-oriented culture, the priority is on the safety and stability of the company. A culture of safety is particularly relevant to corporate security, as it promotes a culture focused on risk mitigation and prevention of harm.

The dimension of stable continuity versus dynamic change refers to how companies react to change and uncertainty. In a controlled environment, companies place a great emphasis on planning and control, while in an uncertain environment, flexibility and adaptability are more important. A culture that is oriented towards control and planning can help identify and minimize security risks.

To balance the competition versus partnership orientation dilemma, organizations need to find a way to promote healthy competition among employees and teams while also fostering a collaborative and cooperative work environment. This can be achieved by setting clear goals and metrics for individual and team performance, while also providing opportunities for employees to work together and share information and resources. Organizations can also create a culture that values teamwork, collaboration and provide incentives for employees who demonstrate both competitive and collaborative behaviors.

To balance the stable continuity versus dynamic change dilemma, organizations need to find a way to maintain stability and consistency while also being open to new ideas and adapting to changing market conditions. This can be achieved by establishing clear processes and procedures for decision-making and implementation, while also empowering employees to suggest new ideas and innovations. Organizations can also create a culture that values learning, experimentation and provide incentives for employees who demonstrate both a commitment to stability and a willingness to adapt and change.

Overall, balancing these dilemmas requires a nuanced and context-specific approach, as the appropriate balance will vary depending on the specific needs and goals of the organization. By recognizing and addressing these dilemmas, organizations can improve their ability to navigate the complex and dynamic landscape of corporate safety and security.

In the context of this paper, it is of particular interest how HRO deals with the aforementioned dilemmas. According to Trompenaars/Paud'Homme's nine dimensions of organizational culture, there are several characteristics that make HROs particularly effective:

Consistency versus Pragmatism: HROs tend to prioritize consistency over pragmatism, meaning they apply consistent rules and procedures regardless of individual or situational differences. This helps ensure that everyone is working to the same high standards and reduces the likelihood of errors.

Group Orientation versus Individualism: HROs typically prioritize group orientation over individualism, meaning they place a high value on teamwork and collaboration. This helps ensure that everyone is working together towards the common goal of ensuring safety and reliability.

Partnership versus Competition: HROs tend to prioritize partnership over competition, meaning they work collaboratively with other organizations and stakeholders to ensure safety and reliability. This helps ensure that everyone is aligned towards the common goal of safety, rather than competing against each other.

People Centrality versus Result Centrality: HROs place a high value on people centrality, meaning they prioritize the safety and well-being of their employees and stakeholders over other concerns. This helps ensure that everyone is motivated to maintain high levels of safety and reliability.

Rational versus Inspirational: HROs typically have a more rational culture, meaning they prioritize objectivity and rationality over emotional reactions or inspiration. This allows them to assess and respond to situations based on objective data and analysis, rather than being swayed by emotions or personal biases.

Egalitarian versus Hierarchical: HROs tend to have a more egalitarian culture, meaning they minimize power differentials and prioritize collaboration and teamwork. This helps ensure that everyone can contribute to the organization's goals and that decisions are made based on expertise rather than hierarchy.

Internal Drive versus Responsiveness: HROs tend to have a strong internal drive culture, meaning they prioritize self-regulation and self-discipline to maintain high levels of safety and reliability. At the same time, they remain responsive to changing circumstances and are constantly monitoring and adjusting their systems and processes to ensure safety.

Stable Continuity versus Dynamic Change: HROs tend to have a stable continuity culture, meaning they prioritize consistency and reliability in their systems and processes. At the same time, they are open to dynamic change when necessary to improve safety and reliability.

Long-term Stakeholder Orientation versus Short-term, Shareholder Orientation: HROs tend to have a long-term stakeholder orientation, meaning they prioritize the safety and well-being of all stakeholders over short-term financial gains. This helps ensure that they are able to maintain their reputation and credibility over the long term.

Overall, HROs are characterized by a strong culture of safety, reliability, and attention to detail, which is supported by a range of cultural dimensions that prioritize teamwork, objectivity, self-regulation, and long-term planning.

1.18 Safety Culture

There are numerous definitions of safety culture. In Germany, Aktionsbündnis Patientensicherheit (Aktionsbündnis Patientensicherheit (APS), 2016)) uses a hospital-specific definition in the context of hospital clinical risk management, according to which safety culture describes the way safety is organized in the context of patient care and thus reflects the attitudes, beliefs, perceptions, values, and behaviours of managers and employees regarding the safety of patients, employees, and the organization. This definition appears to be influenced by the British Health and Safety Commission (HSC) definition that safety culture is the result of individual and group values, attitudes, competencies, and patterns of behaviour that determine the commitment, style, and competence of the organization's health and safety programs (Booth, 1993).

Safety culture can be defined pursuant to the Advisory Committee on Safety of Nuclear Installations (ACSNI) definition as the result of individual and group values, attitudes, competencies, and behaviours that determine the commitment, style, and competence of the organization's safety program (Health Safety Executive (HSE), 1999).

According to Reason, a safe culture is the result of several interdependent subcultures, each of which can be socially shaped to a certain degree. (Reason, 1998, Reason, 2000b).

First and foremost, this includes the informed culture. This is a culture in which those who manage and use the system have all the current information about human, technical, organizational, and environmental factors that affect the safety of the system as a whole (Reason, 1998). This explains the importance of a safety information system in which critical incidents, near misses, or other safety-related events are collected, analysed, and lessons learned are shared to prevent future failures (Reason, 1998). For Reason an informed culture *is* a safety culture in most important respects (Reason, 1998).

Against this background, an error reporting system or CIRS is an indispensable component of error management. However, a prerequisite for this is a reporting (Reason, 1998). This reporting culture presupposes that employees do not have to fear punishment if they openly report errors. An effective reporting culture depends on how the organization deals with blame and punishment (Reason, 2016). A just culture encourages and even rewards employees when they provide important safety-related information—but at the same time, clear lines must be drawn between acceptable and unacceptable behavior (Reason, 2016).

The systemic accident analysis methodology supports the principles of a just culture in two ways. First, it inherently shifts the focus of an investigation away from the "active errors" of operational personnel to the latent conditions that are more deeply rooted in the organization and provide the context for the event. Secondly, and more importantly in my view, when involving human actors, language should be used that avoids blame as much as possible. Even terms such as 'unsafe acts', used in Professor James Reason's original model of organizational accidents (Reason, 1990, Reason, 1991), might suggest that the person's actions or omissions were deliberately unsafe, which is clearly not true in most cases (Eurocontrol, 2005).

A characteristic feature of this just culture is that the company openly communicates the point at which an action or omission requiring sanctions is present and will be pursued accordingly. Sanctioning serious behaviour is indispensable if the company does not want to lose its credibility (Reason, 1998). However, it should be mentioned that the greatest challenge in practice is to define a boundary line that, on the one hand, encourages employees to report their own or other people's errors and, on the other hand, does not give the company the impression in dealing with errors that the company is too tolerant of errors and thus counteracts the propagated safety culture. Against this background, however, criminal offenses and reckless behaviour must be consistently pursued and sanctioned without having a lasting impact on the safety culture. For the sanctioned party, like everyone else, could not trust the organization to be lenient and simply accept this without action in the case of such blatant violations of safety.

Consistently all proposals for just cultures advocate a clear distinction between acceptable and unacceptable behaviour (Sidney and Dekker, 2009). But therein lies the big problem. Because it is precisely around negligence that there is a lot of leeway on the part of the decision-makers, be it superiors, company management, supervisory authorities or, and finally the courts. What is negligence? "*Negligence is a conduct that falls below the standard required as normal in the community. It applies to a person who fails to use the reasonable level of skill expected of a person engaged in that particular activity, whether by omitting to do something that a prudent and reasonable person would do in the circumstances or by doing something that no prudent or reasonable person would have done in the circumstances. To raise a question of negligence, there needs to be a duty of care on the person, and harm must be caused by the negligent action. In other words, where there is a duty to exercise care, reasonable care must be taken to avoid acts or omissions which can reasonably be foreseen to be likely to cause harm to persons or property. If, as a result of a failure to act in this reasonably skillful way, harm/injury/damage is caused to a person or property, the person whose action caused the harm is negligent*" (Global Aviation Information Network (GAIN) Working Group E, 2004, p. 6).

The assessment of whether and to what extent a person can be accused of negligent conduct depends on numerous factors. Nevertheless, the numerous indeterminate legal terms make it difficult to clearly predict the decision-making process, not only for courts but also for corporate decision-makers, who are advised, at least internally, to report critical incidents or errors to the compliance organization in good time in view of compliance obligations. This enables the compliance organization to review critical cases and take appropriate protective measures. The compliance organization thus has an extraordinary role to play with in the company, especially to make clear statements concerning acceptable and unacceptable behaviour.

Interestingly, Reason does not explicitly speak of a trust culture as a subculture of a safety culture. "*What is needed is a just culture, an atmosphere of trust in which people are encouraged, even rewarded, for providing essential safety-related information-but in which they are also clear about where the line must be drawn between acceptable and unacceptable behaviour*" (Reason, 2016, p. 195).

Rather, he sees the just culture as an atmosphere of trust. In my opinion, this equation should be rejected. A just culture and a trust culture are related concepts, with a just culture being a necessary foundation for a trust culture.

A just culture is an environment in which employees take responsibility while feeling assured that their mistakes will not automatically result in punishment, if they act within the framework of applicable rules and standards.

A trust culture, on the other hand, is built upon a just culture and requires a high level of trust between employees and the organization. In a trust culture, employees can communicate openly and honestly without fear of retaliation. They feel confident in sharing their ideas and concerns, and they trust their colleagues and leaders to support them in achieving shared goals (Fig. 1.6).

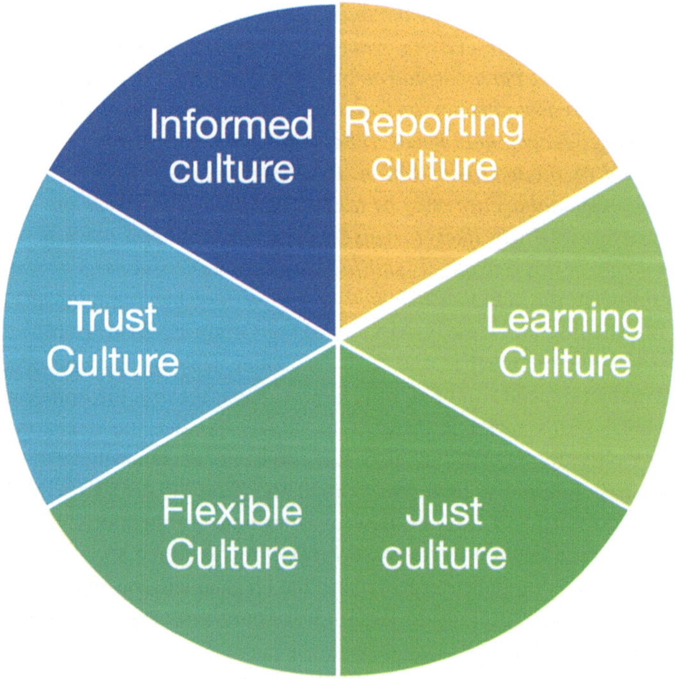

Fig. 1.6 Six Elements of the safety culture

1.19 Safety Climate

There are numerous definitions of safety culture or safety climate, especially in the Anglo-American language area. In this respect, reference is made to the work of Guldenmund (Guldenmund, 2000), which contains an extensive synopsis of definitions of "safety culture" and "safety climate". The terms safety culture and safety climate are also sometimes used synonymously. Wachter (Wachter, 2010), for example, understands safety culture as a working climate that emphasizes teamwork, clear communication, and openness in the event of errors, both toward other medical staff and toward patients (Wachter, 2010).

Safety climate originally propagated by Zohar (Zohar, 1980). Zohar's approach concentrated upon the perceptions of employees, defining organizational climate as the "perceptions held by employees about aspects of their organizational environment, summarized over individual employees". The culture defines the frame within which the climate operates.

Hudson (Hudson, 2001) regrets that Zohar (Zohar, 1980), did not use the concept of climate as a cultural description; the changing perceptions could then have been seen as the "weather" in the context of the overall climate. This criticism is not justified; the appeal of the term climate is that climate, such as mindful organizing, is measurable as opposed to culture.

The difficulty of differentiating between the two terms may be because climate and culture of an organization are inextricably linked. Schein (Schein, 1992) understands climate as a preceding culture. Based on this understanding of the term, safety climate would be safety culture in the making.

Guldenmund (Guldenmund, 2000) follows Schein's 3-level model and refers to the 2nd layer of safety culture as "supporting values": These refer to the safety-specific attitudes of organizational members that embody the safety climate. Here, Guldenmund distinguishes four broad groups to which the security-specific attitudes relate: Hardware, Management Systems, People, and Behaviour. While the safety climate embodies the second layer of Guldenmund's (Guldenmund, 2000), the core consists of "basic assumptions" that are taken for granted and tacitly and unconsciously shared by the entire organization. At the same time, these assumptions are not specifically relevant to safety, but apply generally. The outer 3rd layer consists of artifacts; i.e., it is the outward expression of the safety culture. These include, for example, protective equipment (e.g., X-ray protective apron, face mask, hygienic gloves) or behaviour (e.g., use of safety equipment, performance of safety inspections).

Cooper (Cooper, 2000) also distinguishes between safety culture and safety climate. According to him, the term "safety culture" refers to behavioural aspects (i.e., what do people do) and situational aspects of the organization (i.e., what does the organization have). While the term "safety climate" captures psychological characteristics of employees (i.e., how do people feel)-referring to values, attitudes, and perceptions of employees regarding safety within an organization. Cooper, like Guldenmund, sees the safety climate as a visibility of safety-related values, attitudes, and perceptions of employees.

In this paper, the terms safety climate and safety culture are not used synonymously. This is also supported by the fact that, applying Guldemund's safety culture concept in Schein's tradition, safety culture simply encompasses all three layers of organizational culture (see I.18). According to Vogus and Sutcliffe (Vogus and Sutcliffe, 2007) the developers of the Mindful Organizing Scale (MOS), the safety climate embodies the "visible sign of life" of collective care or mindfulness through the implementation of safety-related measures.

1.20 High Reliability Organizations (HROs).

The safety culture concept has its origins in HRO. This is because, according to Reason (Reason, 2000a), HROs are characterized as organizations by being, on the one hand, complex, internally dynamic, and intermittently suspending and intensely interactive. On the other hand, they perform demanding tasks under considerable time pressure. At the same time, they manage to perform these demanding activities with a low number of critical events and to ensure the absence of catastrophic failures over several years.

At first glance, typical business organizations may not seem comparable to High Reliability Organizations (HROs) like nuclear power plants, nuclear-powered aircraft carriers, air traffic control centers, hospitals, or firefighting units. However, through logical reasoning, this concept can be applied to all enterprises because safety, in the broadest sense, is important for every company.

Perhaps due to perceptions of an increasingly volatile, uncertain, complex and ambiguous (VUCA) world, researchers are now thinking more about the benefits that the principles of high reliability offer other organizations, particularly in terms of increased resilience (O'Neill et al., 2021). This idea is appealing in principle, and initial research findings show a strong, significant relationship between collective mindfulness, as measured by the Mindful Organizing Scale (Weick and Sutcliffe, 2007) and objective measures of performance (O'Neill et al., 2021).

Preliminary analyses suggest that mindfulness is particularly important for the performance of teams pursuing ambitious, high-risk strategies (O'Neill et al., 2021, Buranapin et al., 2023).

The Anglo-American HRO literature does not know the term error culture. Nevertheless, aspects with which some authors rewrite error culture can be assigned to the term organizational mindfulness or the synonym collective mindfulness. Organizational mindfulness is described by Weick and Sutcliffe as the ability of an organization to organize itself in such a way that it can recognize unexpected negative events in good time and initiate the necessary defensive measures or restore the organization's ability to function as quickly as possible (Weick and Sutcliffe, 2007).

Collective mindfulness has five interrelated central characteristics (Weick et al., 1999), (Weick and Sutcliffe, 2007):

(1) Preoccupation with failure means that organizations consistently deal with possible, near or actual failures, as they may provide evidence of safety-related hazards.
(2) Reluctance to simplify interpretations is about questioning established and simplifying perceptual categories and patterns of interpretation as well as previously confirmed expectations. In this way, systematic attention to unexpected events and their discovery is achieved or maintained.
(3) Sensitivity to operations describes the interaction and exchange of information about human and system factors that affect system safety.
(4) The pursuit of resilience (commitment to resilience) is a central feature of organizational mindfulness. Resilience is focused on ensuring an organization's ability to exist and survive by identifying, remediating, containing, and mitigating failures. Resilience can be defined as the degree to which a system to is able to recover or return to (or close to) its original state after a perturbation (Hansson and Helgesson, 2003).
(5) Deference to expertise means that in crisis situations, decisions are shifted to decentralized organizational levels to a person or persons without regard to their organizational rank, where the expertise and experiential knowledge is available. In other words, decision-making competencies are shifted to experts on a situational basis.

Mindful organizing, on the other hand, represents a process and characterizes the way organizational members, especially those in the front line or at the co-called sharp end, perform their function (Vogus and Sutcliffe, 2012). The main difference between mindful organizing and individual mindfulness is that mindful organizing is not an intrapsychic process that takes place in the minds of individuals (Morgeson and Hofmann, 1999). Instead, it is an emergent, collective process that becomes visible in the actions and interactions of organizational members (Vogus and Sutcliffe, 2007).

Organizational mindfulness and mindful organizing are not mutually exclusive; rather, they are mutually dependent. For example, according to Vogus et. al (Vogus et al., 2014), mindful organizing provides information about the extent to which an organization has engaged with characteristic details of emerging threats and rapidly developed capabilities to act on them (Weick and Sutcliffe, 2007),(Weick and Sutcliffe, 2001),(Weick et al., 1999). Both mindfulness aspects are necessary for strategic and operational reliability of HRO; nonetheless, mindful organizing is most characteristic of HRO (Vogus et al., 2014).

Compared to Reason's concept of safety, Vogus & Sutcliff's concept of mindful organizing can be better operationalized.

1.21 Error Management

If the human error rate has to be accepted realistically, the question of effective error detection and error prevention arises. The focus here must be primarily on the people working in an organization. This is because human error and not technical failure poses the greatest threat to system safety, even in a hospital (Reason, 1995). In this context, the Institute of Medicine's report To Err Is Human, (Institute of Medicine (US) Committee on Quality of Health Care in America, 2000), is worth remembering. This was a turning point for the US healthcare system. The report dramatically focused on patient safety and subsequently led to hereditary improvements in patient care (Bates and Gawande, 2000).

In the health care industry, for example, experience from the field of HRO is drawn upon in this regard. In this context, special mention should be made of error management at airlines for training pilots and crew members. Special measures have been developed for this purpose, including Crew Resource Management (CRM) training. The content of CRW has been developed over the years into error management (Helmreich et al., 1999a). Furthermore, specific team training is recommended to make hospitals safer through team performance (Wilson et al., 2005). While error management in HROs such as aviation and the nuclear industry is long established, proven, and indispensable, it is surprising that there is still no widespread risk or error management in hospitals in Germany (Zipper, 2006, Härter and Koch-Gromus, 2022). There are numerous reasons for this. For example, the introduction of error management involves overcoming psychological hurdles and investing financial resources that are not immediately apparent but only pay off in the long term (Zipper, 2006).

Helmreich understands error management as the elimination of conditions that cause errors, the establishment of rules of conduct to prevent or mitigate errors, and the training of employees in their use (Helmreich, 2000a). Helmreich thus advocates system-based error management. This is because such a system is not only focused on the individual employee, but also looks at the team, the work tasks, the workplace and the institution (Reason, 2016)

According to Hoffmann und Rohe (Hoffmann and Rohe, 2010), error management means identifying and reporting critical events, investigating them with the aim of avoiding such and similar events in the future, and planning, implementing, and evaluating appropriate measures to prevent critical events and errors. The latter definition is used as a basis for this work, since it seems more practicable due to the concrete process steps shown.

The primary goal of error management is to avoid errors to increase safety. In this context, it is implicit that errors can still occur. Secondarily, errors must be absorbed, i.e. neutralized, as early as possible in their development phase. And thirdly, the consequences of errors must be mitigated as far as possible (Helmreich et al., 1999b). These three error prevention measures form three lines of defence called the troika of error management (Helmreich et al., 1999b). The first line of defence is error prevention. The second line of defence is neutralizing incipient errors as early as possible, and the third line of defence is mitigating negative consequences of errors committed. Fig. 1.7 illustrates the error management troika (Helmreich et al., 1999b), p. 28).

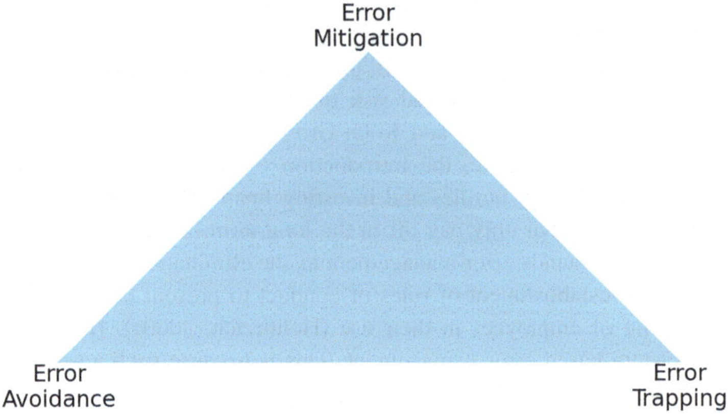

Fig. 1.7 Error Management Troika

Even if in principle an unconditional adoption of error management measures by from HROs to other sectors is not sensible, the following **six step approach to establish error management** should generally make sense. It has proved its worth in the aviation and can be used not only in the hospital environment (Helmreich and Musson, 2000, Helmreich, 2000), but can also be used as a model for the establishment of error management on other industries:

In the first step, an analysis of the status quo and an assessment with historical depth must be carried out; this includes information on the organization, its standards, and personnel. This is followed in the second step by the diagnosis, which also considers the confidential error reports and survey results in addition to any team observations as well as details of near misses and adverse events. Third, latent errors must be addressed through appropriate changes in organizational culture and professional cultures. This includes communicating clear performance levels and using a non-punitive approach to errors, but this does not apply to voluntary violations of safety rules. Fourth, adequate training must be provided on teamwork, error theories, and the limits of human performance. Fifth, a feedback culture must be established, and interpersonal and technical performance must be strengthened. In the sixth and final step, error management must be firmly anchored in the organization through recurring training and data collection.

1.22 Error Culture and Error Management Culture

In the search for a generally valid definition of error culture, it is striking that in the Anglo-Saxon language area, in comparison with the term safety culture, the term error culture is almost not to be found at all. In Comparison with the term "error culture the concept of "safety culture" is indeed prevalent in organizational and safety research, particularly in healthcare and high-risk industries. The emphasis on safety culture often includes discussions around minimizing errors, learning from mistakes, and creating environments where safety is a priority. One reason for this could be that the term 'error culture' is potentially misleading. While safety is clearly a desirable goal for an organization and its safety culture, error cannot be a goal. Instead, it is more practical to focus on error climate and error management, referring to this as an "error management culture."

The Financial Conduct Authority (FCA) describes an error management culture as an organizational culture where errors are actively communicated within the organization and employees dare to admit mistakes because this is considered human (Authority Financial Conduct (FCA), 2018). Within such an error management culture errors are quickly identified, analyzed and corrected and knowledge is actively shared within the organization, with a focus on learning and taking effective improvement measures (Authority Financial Conduct (FCA), 2018).

This also promotes acceptance among all those involved, as it puts the focus on what it is primarily about: creating and maintaining a climate in which blame culture is not encouraged, but where mistakes are learned from and sustainable.

There are different definitions of error culture, depending on the point of view or the scientific discipline. In the context of system safety, error culture is often understood as a culture that allows and encourages disclosure of errors or incidents (Institute of Medicine (US) Committee on Quality of Health Care in America, 2000);(Eiff, 2007);(Brügge, 2007). Similarly, Bauer (Bauer et al., 2004) defines error culture as consisting of two components: On the one hand, the assessment of the importance of errors in the company and, on the other hand, the handling of the occurrence of errors. Siebert (Siebert, 2014), on the other hand, understands error culture as an attitude that cultivates safety in the care of the sick and injured with conviction and through action, and can be equated with safety culture. In this respect, the terms "error culture" and "safety culture" are used synonymously. However, the equation of error culture and safety culture must be rejected. An error culture primarily supports the identification of security gaps to be able to subsequently eliminate or mitigate their risks within the framework of error management. Safety culture, on the other hand, highlights all aspects of an organizational culture that have an influence on risk-increasing or risk-minimizing attitudes and behaviour.

These definitions show that there are very different understandings of what constitutes the core of the concept of error culture and which dimensions are constitutive for an error culture. This can also be seen in the following example from the healthcare industry. Löber (Löber, 2012) developed his own error culture concept for the hospital sector, which includes a synthesis of different error culture concepts. According to Löber, error culture as a sub-construct of corporate culture is the product of individual and collective values, attitudes, perceptions, competencies, and behavioural patterns that determine the extent, type, and depth of organizational engagement with internal errors (Löber, 2012). His error culture concept will not be discussed further here. Nevertheless, Löber's assumption that safety culture is part of a constructive error culture seems at least questionable (Löber, 2012). Because the error culture is part of the safety culture and not the other way around. This is primarily because the top priority is patient safety.

There are indeed arguments that the error culture should be understood not only as part of the safety culture, but also as an expression of the "Stable continuity versus dynamic change" dimension of organizational culture according to Trompenaars/Paud'Homme (Trompenaars et al., 2004). This is supported by the fact that a pronounced error culture requires a certain openness to change and experimentation. Employees must be able to generate and implement new ideas without fear of making mistakes. This requires a culture that views mistakes not as failure, but as part of the learning process. Such a culture can help employees be more open to change and willing to develop and implement new ideas.

Error culture has to be considered a subculture of the broader corporate culture. The overall corporate culture of an organization encompasses its values, beliefs, norms, and practices, while the error culture specifically relates to how the organization deals with mistakes, errors, and failures.

An organization's error culture can have a significant impact on its performance, as it influences how employees and leaders respond to errors and whether they view them as opportunities for learning and improvement or as sources of blame and punishment (Van Dyck et al., 2005). Therefore, it's important for organizations to cultivate a positive error culture within their broader corporate culture to promote learning, innovation, and continuous improvement.

Error culture and collective mindfulness are closely related and can be seen as complementary aspects. A positive error culture that encourages employees to openly report and learn from errors can help increase collective mindfulness in the organization. If employees feel safe to report their mistakes and know that their observations will be taken seriously, they will be more willing to proactively look for potential mistakes and make sure they do not happen again. On the other hand, collective mindfulness can also help to improve the error culture. An organization with a high level of collective mindfulness can proactively identify and prevent mistakes before they occur, which can help to increase employees' trust in the organization. When employees see their organization working mindfully and proactively to prevent errors, they are more likely to openly report and accept errors when they occur.

In summary, error culture and collective mindfulness can be seen as two sides of the same coin. A positive error culture can help increase collective mindfulness and, conversely, high collective mindfulness can help promote a positive error culture. An organization that successfully integrates both aspects is likely to be able to create a safe, effective and learning environment where employees are able to realize their full potential. Error management culture represents a synthesis of both concepts, emphasizing proactive error handling and learning within an organization embedded within an adequate error management system.

In practical sense it makes smore sense to speak about error management culture instead of error culture.

1.23 The Mindful Organizing Scale (MOS)

The recording of the safety culture is an important component of error management. This is because a vulnerability analysis enables the organization to avoid the occurrence of errors at an early stage. This requires a reliable and valid measurement method. However, measuring safety culture requires measurements at all three levels of organizational culture from different perspectives using complex and imaginative methods of assessment and analysis; questionnaires or similar measurement methods are not suitable for this purpose (Glendon and Stanton, 2000). In comparison, it is easier and less costly to measure the safety climate with questionnaires and especially with appropriate employee surveys.

That this is possible has already been successfully demonstrated in the medical field. Nurses are the largest occupational group in hospitals and thus play the largest role in ensuring patient safety in quantitative terms alone. On the other hand, they also play an outstanding qualitative role in identifying and potentially preventing errors (Weir et al., 2005); (Woods and Doan-Johnson, 2002). Therefore, it makes sense to use nurses as a relevant target group for measurements of the safety climate in a hospital. With various questionnaires developed in the USA, the "safety climate" can be recorded and measured. These include, for example, the "Hospital Survey on Patient Safety Culture" (Blegen et al., 2009);

(Sorra and Dyer, 2010) and "Safety Attitudes Questionnaire" (Sexton et al., 2006).

Another safety climate questionnaire used in this work is the Mindfulness (formerly Safety) Organizing Scale (MOS) developed by Vogus & Sutcliffe (Vogus and Sutcliffe, 2007) (Vogus and Sutcliffe, 2012) MOS is based on the systemic failure approach and is based on detailed case studies of HRO's (Vogus and Sutcliffe, 2007, Vogus and Sutcliffe, 2012). MOS provides a scale for measuring mindful organizing. Based on this, conclusions can be drawn about the collective mindfulness and thus the error culture of the organization.

In the meantime, MOS has been further strengthened in its reliability and validity (Ausserhofer et al., 2013). This also applies to the Spanish Version (Renecle et al., 2020), Italian (Magnano et al., 2017) and German version (Ausserhofer et al., 2013), of the MOS data collection questionnaire (Ausserhofer et al., 2012), whose nine items are accordingly as follows:

MOS Item 1) We have a clear picture of the talents and skills/abilities (expertise) of our individual team members.

MOS Item 2) We talk to each other about mistakes and how we can learn from them.

MOS Item 3) We share our professional knowledge and skills and therefore know who in this department has particular expertise and experience.

MOS Item 4) We also discuss alternative approaches in relation to our routine activities.

MOS Item 5) When handing off to the following caregiver, it is common to discuss what to look for.

MOS Item 6) When attempting to solve a problem, we utilize the existing professional skills of our team members.

MOS Item 7) We take time to identify activities that must not fail under any circumstances.

MOS item 8) When mistakes have happened, we discuss how we could have prevented them.

MOS Item 9) When a critical situation arises with a patient, we assure to resolve it quickly by using our professional skills.

Since the MOS questionnaire is aimed at humans, it cannot be used by artificial intelligence. To make the MOS questionnaire usable for an artificial intelligence system, the questions need to be transformed into objective test criteria that are aligned with the underlying concepts. This process involves identifying the key concept and constructs that are being measured by the questionnaire and then creating objective measures that can be used to assess these constructs. These objective measures should be designed to be independent of human interpretation and judgment, so that they can be accurately measured and compared across different contexts and populations. These objective measures can be used to train and test artificial intelligence systems, allowing them to assess and make decisions based on the same criteria that human experts use.

The nine items of the MOS data collection questionnaire that address aspects of mindful organizing correspond to the five processes of collective mindfulness as shown in Table 1.5 below. In addition, this table structure helps to categorize and identify specific metrics along with their potential data sources, which can then be used to measure and improve upon different aspects of organizational processes and effectiveness by an AI solution.

Table 1.5 based on Five dimensions of collective mindfulness and corresponding MOS items (Sutcliffe and Vogus, 2007), p. 48, extended by objective test criteria

Category	MOS items	Metric	Data Source
Deal with Failure	MOS Item 5) When handing off to the following caregiver, it is common to discuss what to look for.	Number of reported failures	Incident reporting systems, customer complaints, Quality Control (QC) logs
	MOS Item 7) We take time to identify activities that must not fail under any circumstances.	Percentage of failures analyzed and addressed	Incident reporting systems, resolution tracking
		Time taken to analyze and address failures	Incident reports, resolution logs
		Effectiveness of solutions to address failures	Stakeholder feedback, performance metrics
Questioning Simplistic Interpretations	MOS Item 4) We also discuss alternative approaches in relation to our routine activities.	Frequency of questioning by team members	Meeting transcripts, notes
		Number of different perspectives considered	Decision-making logs, meeting records
		Percentage of decisions made after multiple perspectives	Decision-making logs
		Effectiveness of decisions made after multiple perspectives	Performance metrics, assessments
Sensitivity to Operational Processes	MOS item 1) We have a clear picture of the talents and skills/abilities (professional competencies) of our individual team members.	Number of reported process deviations	Process deviation logs, incident reporting systems
	MOS-Item 3) We exchange our professional knowledge and skills and therefore know who in this department has special expertise and experience.	Percentage of process deviations analyzed and addressed	Incident reporting systems, resolution tracking
		Time taken to analyze and address process deviations	Incident reports, resolution logs
		Effectiveness of solutions to address process deviations	Stakeholder feedback, performance metrics
Striving for Resilience	MOS Item 2) We talk to each other about mistakes and how we can learn from them.	Frequency of proactive measures to prevent failures/deviations	Preventive maintenance, risk assessments records
	MOS item 8) When mistakes have happened, we discuss how we could have prevented them.	Number of backup or redundancy systems in place	Inventory systems, system configurations
		Time taken to recover from failures/deviations	Incident reports, resolution logs
		Effectiveness of recovery solutions	Stakeholder feedback, performance metrics
Pay Attention to Subject Matter Expertise	MOS Item 6) When attempting to solve a problem, we utilize the existing professional skills of our team members.	Number of incidents related to lack of expertise	Incident reporting systems
	MOS Item 9) When a critical situation arises, we assure to resolve it quickly by using our professional skills.	Percentage of team members with relevant expertise	HR records, skill databases
		Frequency of seeking advice from experts	Team communication logs, meeting records
		Effectiveness of solutions based on expert advice	Stakeholder feedback, performance metrics

In addition to the use of objective assessment criteria, it makes sense to include the factor of professional experience. This is suggested by the results of an employee survey using the MOS questionnaire, which was expanded to include the aspect of professional experience (Becker, 2016). The analyses show the following correlations (Becker, 2016):

- The more professionally experienced employees are, the more likely they are to talk to each other about mistakes and how they can learn from them.
- The more experienced the employees are, the more likely they are to consider alternative approaches to their routine activities.
- The more experienced employees are, the more likely they are to use the existing technical skills of their team members when trying to solve a problem.
- The more experienced employees are, the more likely they are to take time to identify activities that must not fail under any circumstances.

1.24 Active Shaping of Error Culture

Let us now explore the question of how an error culture can be actively shaped. While it is difficult to change the safety-specific attitudes of organizational members that embody the safety climate through persuasion, the path through safety-promoting organizational structures, practices, controls, and policies seems more promising (Reason, 1998). In other words, error management changes error culture. This is because actions shaped by organizational controls can lead to corresponding thinking and believing (Reason, 1998).

Nonetheless, this is not a cause—effect relationship, but rather the two appear to influence each other. The Health Foundation (The Health Foundation, 2011) e.g. generally speaks of a complex interrelationship between the following factors: safety culture, safety climate, implemented initiatives (*e.g. improve patient safety protocols and procedures, enhance communication and collaboration among healthcare staff, implement new technologies or systems to streamline processes and reduce errors, provide training and education programs for staff members, promote a culture of continuous improvement and learning*), employee outcomes and patient outcomes. Some factors appear to be particularly important for the successful establishment of new approaches to patient safety: First, the organizational innovations must be validated by significant improvements; second, the affected project members must be involved in learning activities to promote their innovations and ensure understanding of them in the organization; and third, there must be a psychologically safe climate in the organization that promotes a climate of openness (Tucker et al., 2007)

Nevertheless, the relationship between safety culture and increased patient safety still requires further scientific investigation (DiCuccio, 2015).

1.25 Prosocial Motivation and Emotional Ambivalence

Vogus et. al. have initiated a discussion in this context by pointing out the particular importance of two success factors in the HRO context that can make people more receptive to the interests of others and drive the organization to highly reliable performance: Prosocial Motivation and Emotional Ambivalence (Vogus et al., 2014). Prosocial motivation refers to the desire to help others or to seek benefits for others, and not by the prospect of getting rewards or avoiding punishment (Grant, 2008, Eisenberg et al., 1985). Emotional ambivalence, on the other hand, refers to the simultaneous experience of positive and negative emotions such as hope and doubt (Koch, 1987).

Prosocial behaviour encompasses a wide range of voluntary actions that benefit others and are recognized as valuable by society (Eisenberg and Spinrad, 2014). In corporate terms, these behaviours can be performed by shareholders, management, a supervisor, an employee, a group or the organization itself, and they can relate to an individual, a group, an organization, a community or a broader societal goal. Prosocial motivation fits harmoniously into system-related error approach and its basic motivation does not promote a blame culture and is solution-oriented.

According to Vogus et al. (Vogus et al., 2014), prosocial motivation and emotional ambivalence make people in HROs special, enabling them to sustain levels of extraordinary effort and empowering them to engage in required open-minded thinking. According to that job design must not disregard these two factors, but rather promote them. For example, the introduction of routine work processes to reduce complexity should be avoided. Rather, they argue, it is more promising to design work in complex and contradictory ways to create tension that promotes emotional ambivalence. In other words, the feeling of deceptive security among the actors is to be avoided at all costs. The emotional ambiguity must not lead to a blockade. This is ensured by empowering employees to resolve this ambiguity in the interests of corporate reliability and corporate resilience. A vital error management culture is essential for that.

It remains to be seen what research findings on prosocial motivation and emotional ambivalence will emerge over time that can be made useful to companies in general to increase organisational resilience. A recent study based on affective event theory (AET) succeeds in establishing the positive link between workplace awe and prosocial behaviour of employees via prosocial intention (Meng and Wang, 2023). AET assumes that the cognitive processing of work events triggers affective reactions, which in turn affect the person's attitude and behaviour (Weiss and Cropanzano, 1996). Workplace awe has significantly a positive influence on prosocial motivation of employees. To inspire and promote awe, organizations can actively assume social responsibility towards internal and external stakeholders (Hu and Meng, 2022). E.g. organizations can design employee engagement initiatives that aim to evoke feelings of awe in the workplace. This could include organizing team-building activities in natural settings, arranging visits to inspirational locations, or hosting guest speakers who can share awe-inspiring stories and experiences. By fostering awe among employees, organizations can enhance their sense of purpose and commitment to the company's mission. Externally, organizations should adopt ethical practices (e.g., respecting and promoting human rights, investing in local community development, environmental protection measures and development, and offering high-quality products or services).

1.26 Risk Management Systems

It is important to emphasize in advance that management systems and organizations are not directly comparable, as they represent different concepts. A management system is a structured method to manage and improve an organization. For example, such a system may be a quality management system, an environmental management system, or an information security management system (International Organization for Standardization (ISO), 2024b). Establishing a management system is a conscious decision by the organization to make its business processes more effective and efficient. An organization, on the other hand, is a group of people working together to achieve common goals. An organization can have different goals depending on whether it is a nonprofit organization, a business, or a government agency. Management systems are a tool that organizations can use to achieve their goals and improve their processes. An organization can use multiple management systems at the same time to improve different aspects of its business. Integrative management systems are recommended. This allows companies to connect different tools, processes, and departments to create synergies, reduce redundancies and improve overall performance.

Depending on the situational context, the definition of a management system could vary. The research will consider a management system as "*the methods by which an organization plans, operates, and controls activities to meet goals and objectives by utilizing the resources of money, people, equipment, materials, and information*" (Glans, 1968, p. 3).

To strengthen corporate resilience, it is essential to establish a management system. A management system is designed to provide a structured and systematic method for controlling, monitoring, and improving an organization's processes and performance. A key aspect of risk management is to identify, assess, and address potential risks to the organization to minimize or eliminate them. By implementing a robust management system, organizations can enhance their ability to anticipate and mitigate risks, thereby improving overall resilience and ensuring sustained operational success.

An effective management system includes risk-based thinking and thus also supports the organization's risk management. Risk-based thinking means that risks and opportunities for the organization are identified, and appropriate measures are taken to minimize risks and exploit opportunities. This helps ensure that the organization can achieve its goals and successfully implement its strategies. In addition, management systems may contain specific requirements for risk management, as shown below for ISO 31000:2018 and COSO ERM Integrated framework:

1.26.1 ISO Standard 31000:2018

Since the end of 2008 ISO standard 31000 has created a valid standard about risk management. Risk management means coordinated activities to direct and control an organization regarding risk (International Organization for Standardization (ISO), 2018a). At present, well over 170 countries are united in these organizations, which lends considerable weight to the standards and definitions developed by ISO (International Organization for Standardization (ISO), 2024a). Comparable to ISO is the International Electrotechnical Commission (IEC), which is primarily active in the fields of electrics and electronics (International Electrotechnical Commission (IEC), 2024). Also worth mentioning is the International Telecommunication Union (ITU), which is a specialized agency of the United Nations and the only organization that deals officially and worldwide with technical aspects of telecommunications including standardization (International Telecommunication Union (ITU), 2024).

ISO standard 31000:2018 sets out principles to help achieve the purpose of risk management, namely the creation and protection of values (International Organization for Standardization (ISO), 2018a). In doing so, the principles are intended to provide a basis for how to deal with risks and should therefore be considered when developing the framework and processes of a risk management system (International Organization for Standardization (ISO), 2018a). Thus, in compliance with the principles, effective risk management should be integrated, structured, comprehensive, tailored, inclusive, and dynamic (International Organization for Standardization (ISO), 2018a). In addition, the best available information should be used, human and cultural factors should be considered, and continuous improvement of risk management should take place (International Organization for Standardization (ISO), 2018a). ISO 31000:2018 also has the advantage of providing recommendations that can or must be adapted to specific organizations rather than prescribing requirements (International Organization for Standardization (ISO), 2018a).

ISO standard 31000:2018 sets out principles to help achieve the purpose of risk management, namely the creation and protection of values. These principles provide a basis for how to deal with risks and should therefore be considered when developing the framework and processes of a risk management system.

Now, we delve deeper into the components and processes as outlined by ISO 31000:2018, which are central to implementing a robust risk management system within an organization.

ISO 31000:2018 Components:

The ISO 31000:2018 outlines eight risk management principles that serve as a foundation for effective risk management practices (International Organization for Standardization (ISO), 2018a). These principles include integration, structure, comprehensive approach, customization, inclusion, human and cultural factors, continuous improvement, and timely decision-making (International Organization for Standardization (ISO), 2018a).

The Risk Framework, as per the ISO standard (International Organization for Standardization (ISO), 2018a), is a comprehensive set of elements that establish the basis and organizational procedures for constructing, executing, observing, revising, and perpetually enhancing risk management across the organization. These elements encompass understanding the organization and its context, instituting a risk management policy, integrating risk management into the organization's operations, confirming that risk management is a fundamental part of decision-making, and constant improvement of the risk management framework.

The ISO 31000:2018 risk management process consists of the following stages:

The risk management process according to ISO 31000:2018 includes several important steps to ensure that risks are effectively identified, assessed and addressed. A key component is communication and consultation, where all relevant stakeholders are involved in the process to consider and address their views, concerns and expectations.

The next step is to define the scope, context and criteria to ensure that risks can be appropriately identified and assessed. This includes defining the framework and assessment measures required for risk assessment.

The risk identification process identifies potential events, situations or circumstances that could affect an organization's ability to achieve its objectives. This is followed by risk assessment, in which the probability and consequences of the identified risks and other relevant attributes are analyzed to determine the level of risk.

This is followed by risk evaluation, where the results of the risk assessment are compared with the defined criteria to determine the significance of the risks and inform risk treatment decisions. Risk treatment involves developing and implementing strategies to modify the risks, considering options such as avoiding, transferring, reducing or retaining the risk.

The process also includes monitoring and review to ensure that risk management remains continuously effective and relevant, and to identify areas for improvement. Finally, all activities, results and decisions related to risk management are recorded and communicated in the documentation and reporting step to support accountability and informed decision making.

These steps are based on the guidelines of the International Organization for Standardization (ISO 31000:2018) (International Organization for Standardization (ISO), 2018a).

Even if ISO 31000:2018 do not have any legal effect and could only achieve this through legislative activities, their global significance is considerable through contractual references in international trade. Overall, ISO certification plays an important role in national and international business transactions, as it enables standardization of processes and quality standards that are recognized by companies around the world.

Overall, we can say that management systems are an important expression of risk management and help to minimize the organization's risks and continuously improve its performance, ultimately strengthening resilience. Resilience and HRO are two concepts that are closely related in the field of organizational and risk management. HROs have developed a set of organizational characteristics and behaviors that allow them to consistently deliver safe and reliable performance, even in high-pressure situations (high reliability). Resilience, on the other hand, refers to an organization's ability to adapt and recover from unexpected events or disruptions. Resilient organizations can absorb shocks, maintain essential functions, and quickly return to normal operations. HROs are often seen as highly reliable and resilient organizations. This is because they have developed a set of organizational characteristics and behaviors that enable them to quickly recognize and respond to unexpected events or disruptions. These characteristics include a strong safety culture, clear communication channels, effective teamwork, and a focus on continuous learning and improvement.

Organizations with risk management systems and HROs have some similarities:

(1) Focus on risk management: Both approaches have a strong focus on risk management and are designed to identify, assess, and mitigate potential risks and hazards at an early stage.
(2) Proactive stance: Both have a proactive stance to minimize potential risks before they become problems.
(3) System orientation: both are system-oriented and integrate risk management into all aspects of their business processes.
(4) Continuous improvement: Both approaches have a strong focus on continuous improvement to ensure that potential risks and vulnerabilities are continuously identified and addressed.
(5) Employee involvement: Both involve their employees in the risk management process and create a culture where safety and reliability has a high priority.

On the other side there are remarkable differences concerning flexibility and adaptability: HRO‘s are very flexible and can respond quickly to changes in their environment to minimize risk and maintain safety and reliability. A company that is focusing on risk management systems solely shares obviously also their weaknesses; e.g. the main focus on control may lead to inflexibility in risk response (also see below Sect. 1.26.3 Key weaknesses of risk management systems).

Overall, we can say that organizations that essentially rely on risk management systems to avoid or mitigate risk, and HROs share common characteristics that focus on proactive risk management, system-oriented approach, employee engagement, and continuous improvement. These characteristics help organizations succeed in high-risk, potentially catastrophic environments. But nevertheless, enormous failures of these risk management systems occur in numerous spectacular insolvencies, e.g. Enron (Macey, 2008), Lehman Brothers (Wiggins and Metrick, 2015), Barings Bank (Bhalla, 1995), WorldCom (Lyke and Jickling, 2002), and MF Global (Holzhauer, 2015) or Wirecard (Teichmann et al., 2023).These cases show that there is a need to take a closer look at risk management systems to identify and minimize their structural weaknesses. In this way, the reliability and resilience of the company can be effectively improved by means of risk management systems.

1.26.2 COSO ERM Integrated Framework

In addition to ISO 31000:2018, there is another globally significant risk management system: The COSO ERM framework (Simkins and Fraser, 2010). The COSO ERM Integrated Framework is developed by the COSO organization, a joint initiative of five professional associations, including the American Institute of Certified Public Accountants (AICPA) and the Institute of Internal Auditors (IIA) (Committee of Sponsoring Organizations of the Treadway Commission (COSO), 2017). The COSO ERM Integrated Framework is built upon the foundation of the COSO Internal Control Framework but extends its reach to provide a comprehensive approach to risk management across the entire organization (The Committee of Sponsoring Organizations (COSO), 2013).

The COSO-ERM framework consists of five interconnected components and various underlying principles that guide organizations in developing a robust risk management strategy (Committee of Sponsoring Organizations of the Treadway Commission (COSO), 2017). These components are:

(1) Governance and Culture: Establishes a strong governance structure and risk-aware culture, focusing on board oversight, organizational ethics, values, risk appetite, and stakeholder roles and responsibilities.
(2) Strategy and Objective-Setting: Integrates risk management into strategic planning and objective-setting, involving principles such as evaluating risk in strategy formulation, setting business objectives considering risk appetite, and developing risk tolerance thresholds.
(3) Performance: Involves identifying, assessing, prioritizing, and responding to risks, including principles of risk identification, assessment, prioritization, response, and reporting on risk, culture, and performance.
(4) Review and Revision: Ensures continuous improvement in risk management through regular review and revision of processes, including reviewing risk and performance, pursuing improvements, and modifying practices based on lessons learned.
(5) Information, Communication, and Reporting: Focuses on the effective flow of risk-related information throughout the organization, leveraging information and technology, communicating risk information, and reporting to relevant stakeholders.

Together, these components and their underlying principles offer a comprehensive approach to enterprise risk management, allowing organizations to more effectively identify, assess, and mitigate risks (Committee of Sponsoring Organizations of the Treadway Commission (COSO), 2017).

The COSO framework was developed in response to a series of financial reporting scandals in the 1980s, such as the collapse of Enron and WorldCom, which highlighted the need for stronger internal controls and corporate governance (International Organization for Standardization (ISO), 2018a). It was created to address the deficiencies in internal control systems and provide organizations with a standardized framework for mitigating risks, enhancing transparency, and improving overall organizational performance (Moeller, 2007). The primary objective of the COSO framework is to help organizations effectively manage risks, achieve operational efficiency, and ensure reliable financial reporting (Healy and Palepu, 2003). It provides a comprehensive approach to internal controls, encompassing various components and principles that guide organizations in establishing and maintaining an adequate control environment (Simkins and Fraser, 2010). The COSO ERM Framework addresses a broader spectrum of risks and is designed to help organizations proactively manage those risks to achieve their strategic objectives (Lam, 2014).

Both the COSO ERM Framework and ISO 31000:2018 provide valuable guidance for risk management, but the choice between them depends on factors like organizational context, geographical scope, and the level of detail and structure needed for specific risk management efforts (Turnbull, 1999). Some organizations may choose to align with both frameworks to benefit from their respective strengths (National Institute of Standards and Technology (NIST), 2018). The COSO ERM Framework is often used by organizations in the United States and is widely recognized for its emphasis on integrating risk management with strategic planning and execution (Committee of Sponsoring Organizations of the Treadway Commission (COSO), 2017). ISO 31000:2018 is an international standard and is applied globally (Hubbard, 2020). It is used by organizations worldwide and is not specific to any region or industry (Power, 2007).

It is important to note that there are also other significant risk management frameworks that are preferred in different industries or countries. Some examples are the Turnbull Report in the UK, the NIST Cybersecurity Framework in the US, and the AS/NZS 4360:2004 standard in Australia (Beasley et al., 2014). The selection of the appropriate risk management system depends on the specific requirements, regulatory framework, and corporate culture (Kaplan and Mikes, 2012).

1.26.3 Key Weaknesses of Risk Management Systems

Traditional risk management systems, while sharing similarities with HROs, exhibit key weaknesses. These systems often concentrate on past events, hindering responsiveness to new or evolving risks. They emphasize control, which may lead to inflexibility in risk response. Risk management often operates in hierarchies, potentially disengaging employees from decision-making, impacting safety and reliability. Technical focus often overshadows the crucial human and cultural factors, as seen in standards like ISO 31000:2018. A predominant focus on mistake avoidance overlooks the importance of a learning culture for organizational resilience.

Studies have shown that organizations relying heavily on traditional risk management systems have faced challenges in adapting to rapidly changing environments (Rice and Sheffi, 2005). For example, the 2008 financial crisis exposed the limitations of traditional risk management in many financial institutions (Farrell and Gallagher, 2015).

AI can significantly enhance the effectiveness of risk management practices in ISO 31000:2018 and the COSO ERM Framework. AI develops predictive models for process deviation analysis and automates incident detection and response, optimizing recovery strategies. It tailors risk mitigation strategies using real-time data and employs Natural Language Processing (NLP) for sentiment analysis in decision-making. AI-driven tools assess decision inclusivity and continuously monitor operational processes for deviations. AI tracks Key Performance Indicators (KPIs) to evaluate recovery solutions and assesses decision-making processes to identify logical fallacies.

While AI offers significant advantages, its implementation in frameworks like ISO 31000:2018 and COSO ERM would not be straightforward. Challenges include the complexity of integrating AI into existing risk management processes, ensuring the reliability of AI predictions, and addressing ethical concerns related to automated decision-making (Turing, 1950, Moor, 2006). Moreover, researchers such as Bostrom have highlighted the potential risks of AI systems surpassing human intelligence, leading to unforeseen consequences (Bostrom, 2014). Additionally, the work of Floridi delves into the concept of "informational structural realism," shedding light on the intricate relationship between AI, information, and reality (Floridi, 2016). Furthermore, recent studies by Mittelstadt et al. emphasize the importance of transparency and accountability in AI systems, particularly in high-stakes domains such as risk management (Mittelstadt et al., 2016).

1.27 AI in Promoting Error Culture and Error Management

To assess AI's role in building and maintaining corporate resilience, it's essential to understand AI's capabilities. AI is the capability of machines to perform tasks that typically require human intelligence, such as problem-solving, decision-making, language comprehension, and learning(Russell and Norvig, 2010). The definition of AI is fluid, evolving alongside technological advancements (Collins et al., 2021); (Russell and Norvig, 2010)

AI can significantly bolster an error management system in various ways. For instance, AI systems can process and analyze large datasets to identify potential error sources, which is crucial for resilience based on the business model. These systems can evaluate error frequency and severity, aiding in prioritizing remedial actions. Furthermore, AI can suggest solutions and diagnose problems, facilitating proactive error resolution. AI systems can adapt processes and systems based on learned errors, enhancing future error prevention.

However, implementing AI in error management systems poses challenges. Issues such as data privacy, the need for large datasets for effective machine learning, and potential biases in AI algorithms are significant concerns (Bostrom and Yudkowsky, 2014). Moreover, the integration of AI into existing systems requires substantial investment and skilled personnel, which may not be feasible for all organizations (Haenlein and Kaplan, 2019).

AI can analyze large volumes of data from various sources to identify risk patterns (Russell and Norvig, 2010). It detects and responds to risks promptly and uses predictive analytics to forecast potential risks and their impact (Russell and Norvig, 2010). AI provides analytical insights for risk management and automates risk assessments and compliance checks. It refines risk assessment models for accuracy and conducts risk assessments tailored to individual characteristics. As AI continues to evolve, future research should focus on developing more sophisticated AI models that can adapt to diverse organizational contexts, addressing ethical and privacy concerns, and ensuring the transparency and explanation of AI systems and their abilities (Wiener, 1960, Bostrom, 2014).

Practical application of AI in promoting error culture and management faces challenges such as the need for continuous updating of AI algorithms, potential resistance from employees, and the challenge of interpreting complex AI outputs (Davenport and Ronanki, 2018).

AI offers numerous advantages and disadvantages for companies, public institutions, and citizens. On 9th December 2023 the Council presidency and the European Parliament's negotiators reached a provisional agreement on the proposal on harmonized rules on AI, the so-called artificial intelligence act (AIA). The proposal of AIA includes concrete proposals for regulating AI use in research and business.

Pursuant to Article 3 (1) of the AIA an "*AI system' means a machine-based system that is designed to operate with varying levels of autonomy and that may exhibit adaptiveness after deployment, and that, for explicit or implicit objectives, infers, from the input it receives, how to generate outputs such as predictions, content, recommendations, or decisions that can influence physical or virtual environments*".

Recital 6 of the draft AIA explains the main features of the definition in more detail. It clarifies that the definition does not apply to simpler, conventional software systems or programming approaches that are based on rules established by natural persons for the automatic execution of processes. The Commission was also tasked with developing guidelines for the application of the definition of an AI system. (Council of the European Union (Council), 2024).

The final AIA text was formally approved by the European Parliament on 13 March 2024 and formal approved by the Council on 21 May 2024.

The AIA will enter into force twenty days after its publication in the Official Journal and will be fully applicable 24 months after entry into force, with the exception of the following provisions: Prohibitions on unauthorized practices, which will apply six months after entry into force; codes of conduct (nine months after entry into force); rules for general AI including governance (12 months after entry into force); and obligations for high-risk systems (36 months after entry into force) (European Parliament, 2024).

The Artificial Intelligence Act follows the approach of the EU Commission's existing White Paper on Artificial Intelligence, in which AI applications are divided into four categories. The classification is based on the potential risk associated with the area of application of artificial intelligence. The risk groups are divided into an unacceptable risk, high risk and (high-risk AI systems), a low or minimal risk. The higher the risk, the stricter the regulations (European Commission, 2020, European Commission, 2024) (Fig. 1.8).

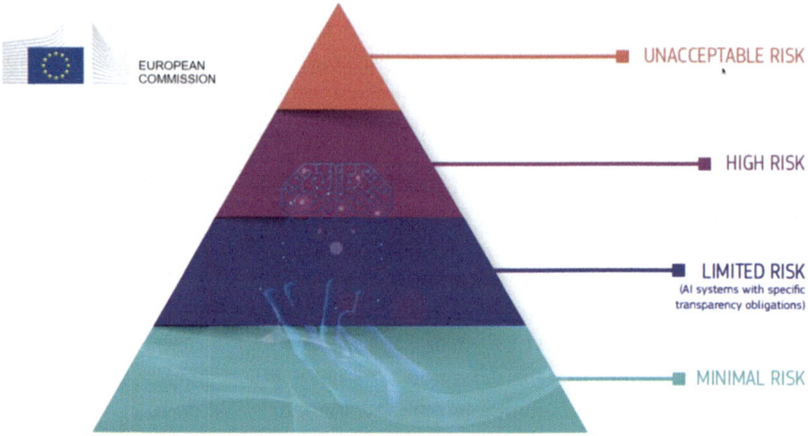

Fig. 1.8 4 levels of risk in AI (European Commission, 2024)

Interestingly, the European Commission's white paper on Artificial Intelligence emphasizes security, while the potential for using AI to enhance corporate resilience is overlooked. For companies, the benefits of using AI are primarily seen in the development of new products and services to strengthen their competitive position (European Commission, 2020). All AI systems considered a clear threat to the safety, livelihoods and rights of people will be banned, from social scoring by governments to toys using voice assistance that encourages dangerous behavior.

AI systems identified as high-risk include AI technology used in: Critical infrastructures (e.g. transport), that could put the life and health of citizens at risk; educational or vocational training, that may determine the access to education and professional course of someone's life (e.g. scoring of exams); safety components of products (e.g. AI application in robot-assisted surgery); employment, management of workers and access to self-employment (e.g. CV-sorting software for recruitment procedures); essential private and public services (e.g. credit scoring denying citizens opportunity to obtain a loan); law enforcement that may interfere with people's fundamental rights (e.g. evaluation of the reliability of evidence); migration, asylum and border control management (e.g. verification of authenticity of travel documents); administration of justice and democratic processes (e.g. applying the law to a concrete set of facts) (European Commission, 2020, European Commission, 2024).

High-risk AI systems will be subject to strict obligations before they can be put on the market (European Commission, 2020, European Commission, 2024): adequate risk assessment and mitigation systems; high quality of the datasets feeding the system to minimize risks and discriminatory outcomes; logging of activity to ensure traceability of results; detailed documentation providing all information necessary on the system and its purpose for authorities to assess its compliance; clear and adequate information to the user; appropriate human oversight measures to minimize risk; high level of robustness, security and accuracy.

All remote biometric identification systems are considered high risk and subject to strict requirements. The use of remote biometric identification in publicly accessible spaces for law enforcement purposes is, in principle, prohibited (European Commission, 2020, European Commission, 2024).

Narrow exceptions are strictly defined and regulated, such as when necessary to search for a missing child, to prevent a specific and imminent terrorist threat or to detect, locate, identify, or prosecute a perpetrator or suspect of a serious criminal offence (European Commission, 2020, European Commission, 2024). Those usages are subject to authorization by a judicial or other independent body and to appropriate limits in time, geographic reach and the data bases searched (European Commission, 2020, European Commission, 2024).

Limited risk refers to AI systems with specific transparency obligations. When using AI systems such as chatbots, users should be aware that they are interacting with a machine so they can take an informed decision to continue or step back (European Commission, 2020, European Commission, 2024).

Minimal or no risk AI, such as video games or spam filters, can be freely utilized under the AI Act, encompassing the majority of AI systems in use within the EU (European Commission, 2020, European Commission, 2024).

AI systems with limited risk must adhere to transparency standards, particularly in applications like chatbots, where users should be informed they are interacting with AI.

Considering the European legislation, it is reasonable to assume that AI systems that support risk management systems in error management will generally fall under the minimal or no risk category. The integrated use of AI systems in critical infrastructure as part of an automated error management or risk management system requires a thorough review before market approval.

Even if AI systems that support risk management systems in error management are not generally classified as high risk, it is nevertheless recommended that such error or risk management-related AI systems fulfill the following seven safety features (National Institute of Standards and Technology (NIST), 2023):

1. Adequate risk assessment and mitigation systems.
2. High quality of the datasets feeding the system.
3. Logging of activity to ensure traceability of results.
4. Detailed documentation providing all information necessary on the system and its purpose for authorities or third persons (e.g. auditors) to assess its compliance.
5. Clear and adequate information to the user.
6. Appropriate human oversight measures to minimize risk.
7. High level of robustness, security and accuracy.

1.28 Organization and Management of the Information Process in Business Management

Section 1.28 takes an in-depth look at the organization and management of the information process in operational management. Particular attention is paid to the quality of the data sets that feed the AI systems in error or risk management. The integrity and precision of data are paramount, as they directly influence the performance and accuracy of AI applications. To maximize the effectiveness of AI systems, it is recommended that companies ensure their data sets are of high quality. This necessitates a rigorous process of review and cleansing to ensure data is accurate, up-to-date, and relevant. Additionally, it is crucial to eliminate any bias in the data sets that could skew the outcomes of AI analyses. By maintaining high-quality data sets, organizations can empower their AI systems to make informed and reliable decisions, which is a fundamental aspect of successful information management in an operational setting.

1.28.1 Integration of Technology Assessment Frameworks in Corporate Strategies

Understanding and evaluating technologies before implementing an AI system is a strategic imperative for businesses. This process ensures effective leverage of technology to achieve goals and remain competitive in today's rapidly evolving landscape. A technology assessment framework at the beginning can help define the strategic lenses through which subsequent technologies are viewed and evaluated. A structured approach to technological adoption that is aligned with corporate strategies is essential. Information processes, when optimized, enable organizations to navigate complex environments and adapt to technological changes swiftly. Vigilant monitoring and regular self-assessment are essential for organizational development and adaptation.

Santos et al. provide a comprehensive analysis of the role of technology assessment frameworks in corporate strategy, emphasizing their critical function in enabling organizations to effectively navigate the complexities of technological advancements. These frameworks serve as essential tools for executives and strategists to forecast technology trends, assess the potential impacts of new technologies, and integrate these insights into strategic planning (Santos et al., 2015). Key Components of Technology Assessment Frameworks are Trend Analysis and Forecasting, Risk Assessment and Management, Resource Allocation, Stakeholder Analysis, Feedback Mechanism, Strategic Implementation of Technology Assessment (Santos et al., 2015).

Santos et al. discuss how technology assessment frameworks incorporate methods for trend analysis and forecasting that help organizations anticipate future technology developments. These methods include Delphi techniques, scenario planning, and predictive analytics, which allow companies to prepare strategic responses to anticipated changes in the technology landscape (Santos et al., 2015).

A significant aspect covered by Santos et al. is the framework's capability to evaluate and manage the risks associated with the adoption of new technologies (Santos et al., 2015). This involves assessing not only the technological and financial risks but also considering the broader social, ethical, and regulatory implications. Effective risk management ensures that potential issues are identified and mitigated before full-scale implementation.

The frameworks detailed by Santos et al. facilitate informed decision-making regarding the allocation of resources. By providing a structured approach to evaluate the viability and strategic value of new technologies, companies can make more informed investment decisions, ensuring that resources are allocated to initiatives that align with long-term strategic goals (Santos et al., 2015).

Santos et al. conclude by suggesting that as technology continues to evolve at an unprecedented rate, the need for dynamic and adaptable technology assessment frameworks becomes increasingly critical. They advocate for the ongoing development of these frameworks to include more advanced analytical tools and broader integrative capabilities, ensuring that organizations can remain competitive and resilient in a rapidly changing technological landscape.

1.28.2 Feedback Mechanisms and Stakeholder Engagement

Technology assessment frameworks also incorporate stakeholder analysis to gauge the potential impacts of new technologies on various internal and external stakeholders. Santos et al. highlight how understanding stakeholder perspectives can guide the development of technology strategies that are not only innovative but also socially responsible and widely accepted. Santos et al. emphasize the inclusion of robust feedback mechanisms within these frameworks. These mechanisms ensure continuous learning and adaptation by incorporating feedback from various phases of technology implementation back into the strategic planning process. Robust feedback mechanisms create a culture of responsiveness and resilience, facilitating iterative innovation. The dynamics of feedback loops encourage a symbiotic relationship between organizational stakeholders and information systems. Innovative approaches, such as sentiment analysis and natural language processing, are explored for their potential to enhance strategic decision-making and organizational agility (Baker, 1995).

1.28.3 AI in Strategic Decision-Making

AI offers transformative insights that markedly enhance strategic decision-making capabilities (Ao et al., 2010). AI's potential in decision-making processes is vast, providing tools that can analyze large datasets rapidly and with high accuracy. However, this growing reliance on AI also brings forth critical ethical questions and potential biases that need addressing to ensure these technologies are used responsibly. Multidisciplinary approaches are recommended to ensure the responsible deployment of AI technologies. The integration of AI into critical decision-making processes raises substantial ethical concerns, particularly regarding biases that AI systems may inherit from their training data or developers. These biases can lead to skewed outcomes that favor one demographic over another, inadvertently perpetuating existing inequalities.

To combat these issues, there is a strong advocacy for explainable AI (XAI)—AI systems designed with transparency in mind, where decisions made by machines can be understood and traced by human operators. This approach not only helps in identifying and correcting biases but also builds trust among stakeholders by clarifying how decisions are derived.

To ensure the responsible deployment of AI technologies, a multidisciplinary approach is essential. This involves collaboration across fields such as ethics, law and computer science. Ethics: To weave moral considerations into the fabric of AI technologies; law: To ensure compliance with international and local regulations concerning data use; computer Science: To advance the technical robustness of AI systems.

As businesses increasingly integrate artificial intelligence (AI) into their operations, the need for explainable AI (XAI) becomes imperative to foster trust and ensure transparency. However, this need must be balanced with the equally crucial requirement to protect sensitive data and proprietary algorithms. Below, we explore strategies to achieve this balance, ensuring that businesses can leverage the benefits of XAI without compromising their competitive edge or confidentiality.

Companies can adopt XAI strategies that offer enough insights into AI decisions to build user trust and compliance without compromising on the details of the underlying data or proprietary models. This approach involves providing explanations that are useful and sufficient for users to understand the AI's decisions, focusing on outcomes rather than the intricacies of the model's workings.

Access to explanations can be tiered according to the user's role and their need to know. System operators, for example, may receive detailed explanations necessary for system maintenance and troubleshooting, while end-users might only access high-level insights. This method ensures that sensitive details are only available to those who require them for their operational roles.

To secure sensitive information, techniques such as encryption and anonymization can be employed. These methods protect data while allowing the AI to perform necessary operations, ensuring that personal or proprietary data is not exposed during the AI's decision-making processes. This is crucial for maintaining privacy and security against external threats.

Developing robust legal frameworks and ethical guidelines is vital for governing what should be disclosed through XAI. These guidelines can help define the boundaries of transparency, focusing on compliance with data protection laws, intellectual property rights, and specific industry regulations. This framework helps in aligning XAI implementations with legal and ethical standards.

Implementing comprehensive audit trails can facilitate the tracking of decisions made by AI systems without revealing sensitive data or algorithms. Audit trails are crucial for regulatory compliance and accountability, providing a verifiable means to assess the AI's operations without compromising proprietary information.

There is a persistent risk that detailed explanations could enable competitors or malicious entities to reverse-engineer AI systems. It is essential to carefully manage the level of detail that is publicly shared to mitigate this risk. Navigating the balance between adhering to stringent data protection laws and maintaining a competitive advantage is challenging. Companies must carefully strategize to protect their proprietary information while complying with regulations.

1.28.4 Implementing AI for Error Minimization

The integration of AI enables new strategies for error minimization. AI's application within specific risk management frameworks like ISO 31000 and COSO ERM enhances risk assessment capabilities, integrates risk data analytics, and improves the dynamic management of risks. This makes these frameworks more adaptive and effective, demonstrating AI's role in transforming risk management practices. In the following two practical examples are shown: One from the healthcare sector and the other one from manufacturing Sector.

In the healthcare industry, the integration of AI-driven analytics has yielded remarkable outcomes in improving patient care and outcomes. For instance, a study published in the Journal of the American College of Cardiology showcased how AI-powered predictive analytics transformed cardiovascular care (Bhavnani et al., 2017). By analyzing vast datasets, AI algorithms accurately predicted patient health trajectories, enabling clinicians to intervene preemptively and personalize treatment plans. This proactive approach significantly reduced misdiagnoses, minimized adverse events, and ultimately enhanced patient outcomes. The seamless integration of AI-driven analytics into healthcare operations exemplifies the potential of AI to revolutionize traditional practices and optimize patient care.

The next case study from manufacturing sector demonstrates the practical implementation and benefits of leveraging Digital Twin technology in manufacturing operations. Digital Twin technology is a cutting-edge concept in the realm of digital innovation, particularly in industries like manufacturing, healthcare, and transportation. Essentially, a Digital Twin is a virtual representation or mirror image of a physical object, process, or system (Kritzinger et al., 2018). It's not merely a static model but a dynamic simulation that mirrors the real-world entity in real-time or near-real-time, incorporating data from sensors, the Internet of Things (IoT) devices, and other sources (Kritzinger et al., 2018).

A global manufacturing firm embraced Digital Twin technology to optimize its production processes and mitigate operational risks (Biesinger et al., 2019). By creating dynamic virtual replicas of its production lines, the company simulated various production scenarios and identified potential vulnerabilities before they impacted the physical operations. Through real-time data analysis and predictive modeling, the Digital Twin technology enabled proactive risk management, ensuring uninterrupted production, and minimizing downtime. This strategic application of Digital Twin technology not only enhanced operational efficiency but also aligned with the principles of the COSO ERM framework, fostering a culture of risk-awareness and resilience within the organization (Tao et al., 2018).

1.28.5 AI Technology and Corporate Social Responsibility

Corporate Social Responsibility (CSR) plays a vital role in the responsible management of environmental and corporate information systems. Potter and Doris note that ethical considerations are increasingly critical in the deployment of AI technologies, calling for greater transparency and accountability in their development (Potter and Doris, 2024). As organizations incorporate new technologies into their operations, it is crucial to consider the ethical implications and societal consequences. Building a culture of ethical and responsible innovation involves integrating ethical considerations into the design, development, and deployment of new technologies. This approach not only mitigates risks but also enhances societal acceptance and promotes long-term resilience.

1.28.6 Anticipatory Governance

For organizational resilience in the face of rapid technological changes Anticipatory governance, as discussed by Guston, is crucial (Guston, 2014). Anticipatory governance is defined as a wide-ranging capacity anchored in society that can respond to various inputs to steer emerging knowledge-based technologies while this is still possible (Guston, 2008). Guston emphasizes that a proactive stance in technology management allows organizations to better anticipate and manage potential risks associated with new technological advancements. This strategic approach enhances organizational adaptability and success by aligning governance practices with the pace of technological innovation.

1.28.7 Global Information Governance

To navigate jurisdictional conflicts and data sovereignty issues, various international treaties and multilateral agreements have been proposed. These initiatives aim to promote interoperability and address the challenges posed by global information governance. Here are some key initiatives:

The General Data Protection Regulation (GDPR) implemented by the European Union (EU), is one of the most comprehensive data protection regulations globally. It aims to harmonize data protection laws across EU member states and governs the processing and movement of personal data. GDPR requires organizations to implement appropriate technical and organizational measures to ensure a level of security appropriate to the risk. This requirement underscores the GDPR's focus on ensuring the security and integrity of personal data.

Convention on Cybercrime (Budapest Convention): The Budapest Convention, adopted by the Council of Europe, is the first international treaty addressing crimes committed via the internet and other computer networks. It facilitates international cooperation among member states in combating cybercrime, including offenses related to data breaches, fraud, and hacking. According to Kizza (Kizza et al., 2013) the Budapest Convention provides a legal framework for international cooperation in investigating and prosecuting cybercrimes, including offenses related to unauthorized access to computer systems and data.

1.29 Conclusion

The theory section, which spans Sects. 1.1 to 1.28 explores the diverse aspects of error culture, safety, and risk management in different organizational contexts and provides deep insights into the mechanisms of error occurrence, its prevention, and the frameworks that support organizational resilience. The first chapters explore key concepts related to error culture, distinguish between safety and security, and highlight the importance of understanding human error and its consequences in different industries. The critical role of error reporting systems and the impact of human error on high technology systems are introduced and form the basis for a deeper exploration of error management strategies. As it progresses, the focus shifts to a systemic view of error analysis, emphasizing the importance of distinguishing between person- and system-related errors and the concepts of active and latent errors. This approach underscores the need to address systemic errors and organizational culture to mitigate errors rather than placing blame on individuals. The examination of the Swiss Cheese model, human factors, and the SHELL model delves deeper into the complexity of errors and the need for comprehensive safety management that incorporates environmental, organizational, and workplace factors. It also introduces the concept of

High Reliability Organizations (HROs), emphasizing their success in maintaining safety and reliability through the principles of collective mindfulness and prosocial motivation. The following chapters focus on the influence of organizational culture on safety culture, introducing models such as Schein's 3-level model, the Competing Values Framework, and Trompenaars/Paud'Homme's nine dimensions. These models shed light on how organizational culture influences safety practices and the importance of promoting a just, informed, and trust-based culture for effective error management and safety promotion. It goes on to discuss the distinction between safety culture and safety climate, the importance of error management culture, and the impact of collective mindfulness on organizational safety. A shift towards proactively dealing with errors, learning from errors, and embedding these practices into an appropriate error management system is advocated to improve organizational performance and safety. The final sections highlight the role of risk management systems such as ISO 31000:2018 and the COSO ERM Integrated Framework in promoting proactive risk management and continuous improvement. The theory section highlights the critical importance of a holistic approach to understanding and managing failures, emphasizing the interplay between human factors, organizational culture, and risk management systems. A case is made for promoting a culture of safety and resilience, leveraging technological advances such as AI to support these efforts, and finally improving organizational performance and reliability through proactive error management and safety culture promotion.

Section 1.27 delves into the significant support that AI can provide to error management systems, as well as the potential risks associated with its implementation, particularly in the context of the Artificial Intelligence Act (AIA) in the European Union. The section begins by outlining how AI can enhance error management systems by processing large datasets to identify error sources, evaluating error frequency and severity, suggesting solutions, and adapting processes based on learned errors. However, it also highlights challenges such as data privacy concerns, the need for substantial investment and skilled personnel, and potential biases in AI algorithms. Furthermore, it discusses the AIA and its implications for regulating AI use in research and business. The AIA categorizes AI applications into four groups based on the level of risk associated with them: unacceptable risk, high risk, low risk and minimal risk. High-risk AI systems, which include those in critical infrastructure, safety components of products, human resource management and law enforcement, are subject to strict requirements before they can be placed on the market. These include appropriate risk assessment, high quality data sets and human oversight measures. AI systems that are classified as minimal or no risk, such as video games or spam filters, on the other hand, have fewer regulatory requirements. Nevertheless, it is recommended that even AI systems that support risk management in the event of errors comply with certain safety features to ensure their effectiveness and compliance. Overall, the importance of understanding AI's capabilities and limitations in promoting error culture and management is underscored, while also highlighting the regulatory framework proposed by the AIA to address potential risks associated with AI deployment. Section 1.28 underscores the critical importance of organization and management in the information process within business management, particularly in the realm of operational management. The quality and integrity of data sets that fuel AI systems for error and risk management are emphasized as key factors influencing the performance and accuracy of AI applications. It is imperative for companies to prioritize maintaining high-quality data through thorough review, cleansing, and the elimination of bias to empower AI systems for making informed decisions. Furthermore, the integration of technology assessment frameworks into corporate strategies is highlighted as a strategic imperative for businesses aiming to effectively leverage technology and remain competitive in today's dynamic landscape. By optimizing information processes and aligning technological adoption with corporate strategies, organizations can enhance their ability to adapt to technological changes and drive organizational development.

2 Development and Application of an Integrated Audit Approach to Identify the Weaknesses of the Risk Management Systems ISO 31000 and COSO ERM Framework in Capturing the Error Culture, Which has the Potential for Operationalization through AI

2.1 Methodology for Literature Research on Error Management in HROs and AI Transformation of MOS

This chapter outlines the methodology employed for conducting literature research to support the Working Hypothesis with the supporting four Sub-Hypotheses:

1) Error management approaches developed for High Reliability Organizations (HRO) can be largely transferred to all other business enterprises and organizations subject to risk management systems.
2) MOS has the potential to be transferred into an AI solution in order to sustainably promote error culture and error management in the organization.
3) The error culture can be measured and operationalized by an AI system.
4) The risk management systems ISO 31000:2018 and COSO ERM Integrated Framework show significant weaknesses on the field of human factors that can be mitigated by MOS criteria, operationalized by an AI system.

The research will be conducted through a systematic literature review. This approach involves a comprehensive and structured examination of existing literature to gather relevant information and evidence that supports or refutes the Working Hypothesis and its supporting four Sub-Hypotheses. The review will

H. Becker, *Using Artificial Intelligence (AI) to Minimize Errors in Business Enterprise Management*, https://doi.org/10.1007/978-3-658-47243-6_2

focus on academic journals, conference proceedings, and authoritative publications in the fields of organizational management, risk management, AI in business, and error management.

Data will be collected using specific keywords and phrases related to HROs, error management, knowledge-based systems, and AI transformation. The search will be refined to include only peer-reviewed articles and reputable sources. The analysis will involve categorizing the literature based on relevance to the Working Hypothesis and its supporting four Sub-Hypotheses, summarizing key findings, and critically evaluating the evidence to draw conclusions.

Criteria for including literature in the review will be based on the publication date (preferably within the last 10 years), relevance to the before mentioned hypothesis, and the credibility of the source. Exclusion criteria will involve outdated sources, non-peer-reviewed articles, and literature not directly related to the Working Hypothesis and Sub-Hypotheses.

The expected outcome of this research is a comprehensive understanding of the current state of knowledge regarding error management in HROs and the potential for AI transformation of knowledge-based systems like MOS. The findings will provide insights into the applicability and effectiveness of these approaches in various organizational contexts.

2.2 Methodology for Comparing ISO 31000 and COSO ERM Frameworks

This section outlines the methodology used to compare the ISO 31000 and the COSO ERM Integrated framework. The comparison is structured around a matrix that evaluates both standards against a set of predefined criteria.

2.2.1 Criteria

The first step involves defining the criteria for comparison. These criteria are selected based on their relevance and importance in assessing the effectiveness and comprehensiveness of each standard in risk management. The criteria encompass various aspects of organizational culture, organizational responsiveness, error culture, and the interaction of people within a system. An integrated approach that considers all of these aspects enables a holistic assessment and improvement of organizational processes and performance. It is essential to understand both macro- and micro-level factors in order to effectively manage and continuously improve an organization.

2.2.1.1 Competing value framework

Depending on which organizational culture a company can be assigned to in terms of focus, it also depends on which measures, in particular for efficient error management, are promising for the respective organizational culture. **Reconciling two risk related dimensions of corporate culture**: Competition versus partnership orientation dilemma (TC 1.1) and stable continuity versus dynamic change are the most relevant elements of the VCF in this context (TC 1.2).

2.2.1.2 MOS Items

Deal with failure (TC 2.1)

- Number of reported failures within a given period (TC 2.1.1)
- Percentage of reported failures that were analysed and addressed (TC 2.1.2)
- Time taken to analyse and address failures (TC 2.1.3)
- Effectiveness of the solutions implemented to address failures (TC 2.1.4)

Questioning simplistic interpretations (TC 2.2)

- Frequency of questioning by team members during meetings or discussions (TC 2.2.1)
- Number of different perspectives considered when making decisions (TC 2.2.2)
- Percentage of decisions made after considering multiple perspectives (TC 2.2.3)
- Effectiveness of decisions made after considering multiple perspectives (TC 2.2.4)

Sensitivity to operational processes (TC 2.3)

- Number of reported process deviations within a given period (TC 2.3.1)
- Percentage of process deviations that were analysed and addressed (TC 2.3.2)
- Time taken to analyse and address process deviations (TC 2.3.3)
- Effectiveness of the solutions implemented to address process deviations (TC 2.3.4)

Striving for resilience (TC 2.4)

- Frequency of proactive measures taken to prevent failures or process deviations (TC 2.4.1)
- Number of backup or redundancy systems in place (TC 2.4.2)
- Time taken to recover from failures or process deviations (TC 2.4.3)
- Effectiveness of the solutions implemented to recover from failures or process deviations (TC 2.4.4)

Pay attention to subject matter expertise (TC 2.5)

- Number of reported incidents related to lack of expertise within a given time period (TC 2.5.1)
- Percentage of team members with relevant expertise or qualifications (TC 2.5.2)
- Frequency of seeking advice or guidance from team members with relevant expertise (TC 2.5.3)
- Effectiveness of the solutions implemented based on advice or guidance from team members with relevant expertise (TC 2.5.4)

2.2.1.3 GEMS Criteria

Skill-based errors (slips and oversights) (TC 3.1)

- Frequency of certain errors compared to the expected number of errors given the task complexity and individual skill level (TC 3.1.1)
- Time taken to complete a task compared to the expected time given the task complexity and individual skill level (TC 3.1.2)
- Consistency in performing the task correctly over multiple attempts (TC 3.1.3)
- Reaction time to unexpected events or changes in the task (TC 3.3.4)

Rule-based errors (errors of confusion and recognition) (TC 3.2)

- Number of times a rule was misinterpreted or not followed correctly (TC 3.2.1)
- Frequency of incorrect responses to specific stimuli or cues (TC 3.2.2)
- Percentage of correct responses to similar but distinct stimuli or cues (TC 3.2.3)
- Time taken to recognize and correct an error (TC 3.2.4)

Knowledge-based errors (errors of reasoning and judgment) (TC 3.3)
Objective assessment criteria for knowledge-based actions could include

- Number of logical fallacies committed during decision-making or problem-solving (TC 3.3.1)
- Consistency of decision-making with established principles or guidelines (TC 3.3.2)
- Time taken to reach a decision compared to the expected time given the complexity of the problem and available information (TC 3.3.3)
- The degree of deviation from optimal outcomes or solutions (TC 3.3.4)

2.2.1.4 SHELL criteria

In SHELL model, safety is achieved by having multiple layers of protection in place, each one designed to prevent or mitigate a particular type of hazard. All the five layers of protection are:

Software (TC 4.1)

- Having a robust incident response plan in place (TC 4.1.1)
- Regularly updating software and ensuring it is secure and up-to-date (TC 4.1.2)
- Conducting software testing to identify any potential vulnerabilities or weaknesses (TC 4.1.3)
- Training to employees on how to use software and technology tools properly (TC 4.1.4)

Hardware (TC 4.2)

- Conducting regular inspections and maintenance of hardware to ensure it is in good working condition (TC 4.2.1)
- Using high-quality hardware that meets safety standards (TC 4.2.2)
- Providing training to employees on how to use hardware safely and effectively (TC 4.2.3)

Environment (TC 4.3)

- Conducting regular safety inspections to identify potential hazards in the workplace (TC 4.3.1)
- Providing adequate lighting, ventilation, and other environmental controls to ensure a safe working environment (TC 4.3.2)
- Providing training to employees on how to recognize and avoid environmental hazards (TC 4.3.3)
- Encouraging a safety culture within the organization through regular communication, training, and feedback (TC 4.3.4)
- Holding employees accountable for following security policies and procedures (TC 4.3.5)
- Encouraging employees to report safety concerns or incidents (TC 4.3.6)
- Monitoring the level of cognitive, physical, and emotional demands placed on individuals or teams, as well as the distribution of workload among team members (TC 4.3.7)
- Stress and Fatigue includes the impact of stress, fatigue, and other psychological factors on individual and team performance, as well as strategies for managing and mitigating these factors; e.g. stress and fatigue management: Implementing programs to manage stress and fatigue, such as providing opportunities for rest and recovery, offering stress reduction techniques, and promoting healthy lifestyle habits (TC 4.3.8)

Liveware (TC 4.4)

- Recruiting and Retention of qualified and experienced staff (TC 4.4.1)
- Conducting background checks on all employees who have access to sensitive information (TC 4.4.2)
- Training and Experience: This includes the knowledge, skills, and experience of individuals or teams, as well as the training and development opportunities provided to support their performance (TC 4.4.3)
- Providing training to employees on how to work safely and effectively (TC 4.4.4)

Liveware-Liveware Interface (TC 4.5)

- Communication includes the methods and channels of communication between individuals or teams, including verbal, written, and electronic communication (TC 4.5.1)

- Teamwork includes the collaboration and coordination of work between individuals or teams, as well as the development of shared goals and objectives (TC 4.5.2)
- Leadership style and conflict resolution: Developing effective leadership practices that support communication, collaboration, and teamwork, such as setting clear expectations, providing feedback and coaching in conflict situations (TC 4.5.3)

2.2.1.5 Dirty Dozen

The additional inclusion of the test criteria using the Dirty Dozen (Dupont, 1997) is not necessary, as each source of error can be attributed to the SHELL model:

Lack of communication: This can be attributed to the Liveware-Liveware component, which includes the people involved in the system and their communication processes. Communication breakdowns can arise from various factors, including inadequate training or equipment, language barriers, or misaligned objectives.

Complacency: This can be attributed to the Liveware component, which includes the cognitive and psychological aspects of human performance. Complacency can arise when individuals become overconfident or complacent in their abilities, leading to errors or accidents.

Lack of knowledge: This can be attributed to the Liveware components. The Liveware component includes the knowledge, skills, and training of the people involved in the system.

Distraction: This can be attributed to the Liveware and Environment components. Distractions can arise from a variety of sources, such as noisy or cluttered environments, competing demands or tasks, or personal issues that affect attention or focus.

Lack of teamwork: This can be attributed to the Liveware and Liveware interactions components. Effective teamwork requires clear communication, mutual trust and respect, and a shared sense of purpose and goals. When these factors are lacking, teamwork can break down and errors can occur.

Fatigue: This can be attributed to the Liveware component and Environment components. Fatigue can result from a variety of factors, such as long working hours, sleep deprivation, or physical or mental strain. It can affect cognitive and motor performance and increase the risk of errors or accidents.

Lack of awareness: This can be attributed to the Liveware components. Lack of awareness can result from various factors, such as insufficient information or training, inadequate situational awareness, or complacency.

Lack of resources: This can be attributed to the Environment component, which includes the physical and organizational factors that can affect performance. Lack of resources can include inadequate staffing or insufficient funding or support.

Stress and pressure: These can be attributed to the Liveware and Environment components. Stress and pressure can arise from a variety of sources, such as high workload, time pressure, or high stakes. They can affect cognitive and emotional performance and increase the risk of errors or accidents.

Lack of assertiveness: This can be attributed to the Liveware and Liveware interactions components. Assertiveness is an important communication skill that allows individuals to express their concerns or opinions effectively. When individuals lack assertiveness, they may be hesitant to speak up or challenge assumptions, leading to errors or accidents.

Lack of norms: The source of error "lack of norms" can be attributed to the Software component of the SHELL model. Norms are the written or unwritten rules, customs, and practices that guide behavior within a group or organization. When there is a lack of norms, it can lead to confusion, misunderstandings, and inconsistencies in behavior. This can result in errors or accidents, especially in complex systems where teamwork and coordination are critical. All test criteria are consolidated in the following Table 2.1.

2.2.2 Matrix and Scale

After defined the 56 criteria, the table is created with the two standards as column headings and the criteria as row headings. The fist column names the correlating concept.

The matrix is then filled in, rating each criterion on how the two standards treat it. A scale of 1 to 5 is used, where 1 means that the criterion is not addressed in the standard and 5 means that the criterion is addressed in detail.

1 Does not apply at all
2 Does not apply in part
3 Neither
4 Partly true
5 Fully applicable

Table 2.1 Test criteria

Test criteria (TC)	Sub criteria
TC 1.1: Competition versus partnership orientation dilemma	-
TC 1.2: Stable continuity versus dynamic change	
TC 2.1: Deal with failure	Number of reported failures within a given period (TC 2.1.1) Percentage of reported failures that were analyzed and addressed (TC 2.1.2) Time taken to analyze and address failures (TC 2.1.3) Effectiveness of the solutions implemented to address failures (TC 2.1.4)
TC 2.2: Questioning simplistic interpretations	Frequency of questioning by team members during meetings or discussions (TC 2.2.1) Number of different perspectives considered when making decisions (TC 2.2.2) Percentage of decisions made after considering multiple perspectives (TC 2.2.3) Effectiveness of decisions made after considering multiple perspectives (TC 2.2.4)
TC 2.3: Sensitivity to operational processes	Number of reported process deviations within a given period (TC 2.3.1) Percentage of process deviations that were analyzed and addressed (TC 2.3.2) Time taken to analyse and address process deviations (TC 2.3.3) Effectiveness of the solutions implemented to address process deviations (TC 2.3.4)
TC 2.4: Striving for resilience	Frequency of proactive measures taken to prevent failures or process deviations (TC 2.4.1) Number of backup or redundancy systems in place (TC 2.4.2) Time taken to recover from failures or process deviations (TC 2.4.3) Effectiveness of the solutions implemented to recover from failures or process deviations (TC 2.4.4)
TC 2.5: Pay attention to subject matter expertise	Number of reported incidents related to lack of expertise within a given time period (TC 2.5.1) Percentage of team members with relevant expertise or qualifications (TC 2.5.2) Frequency of seeking advice or guidance from team members with relevant expertise (TC 2.5.3) Effectiveness of the solutions implemented based on advice or guidance from team members with relevant expertise (TC 2.5.4)
TC 3.1: Skill-based errors (slips and oversights)	Frequency of certain errors compared to the expected number of errors given the task complexity and individual skill level (TC 3.1.1) Time taken to complete a task compared to the expected time given the task complexity and individual skill level (TC 3.1.2) Consistency in performing the task correctly over multiple attempts (TC 3.1.3) Reaction time to unexpected events or changes in the task (TC 3.1.4)
TC 3.2: Rule-based errors (errors of confusion and recognition)	Number of times a rule was misinterpreted or not followed correctly (TC 3.2.1) Frequency of incorrect responses to specific stimuli or cues (TC 3.2.2) Percentage of correct responses to similar but distinct stimuli or cues (TC 3.2.3) Time taken to recognize and correct an error (TC 3.2.4)
TC 3.3: Knowledge-based errors (errors of reasoning and judgment)	Number of logical fallacies committed during decision-making or problem-solving (TC 3.3.1) Consistency of decision-making with established principles or guidelines (TC 3.3.2) Time taken to reach a decision compared to the expected time given the complexity of the problem and available information (TC 3.3.3) The degree of deviation from optimal outcomes or solutions (TC 3.3.4)
TC 4.1: Software	Having a robust incident response plan in place (TC 4.1.1) Regularly updating software and ensuring it is secure and up-to-date (TC 4.1.2) Conducting software testing to identify any potential vulnerabilities or weaknesses (TC 4.1.3) Training to employees on how to use software and technology tools properly (TC 4.1.4)
TC 4.2: Hardware	Conducting regular inspections and maintenance of hardware to ensure it is in good working condition (TC 4.2.1) Using high-quality hardware that meets safety standards (TC 4.2.2) Providing training to employees on how to use hardware safely and effectively (TC 4.2.3)
TC 4.3: Environment	Conducting regular safety inspections to identify potential hazards in the workplace (TC 4.3.1) Providing adequate lighting, ventilation, and other environmental controls to ensure a safe working environment (TC 4.3.2) Providing training to employees on how to recognize and avoid environmental hazards (TC 4.3.3) Encouraging a safety culture within the organization through regular communication, training, and feedback (TC 4.3.4) Holding employees accountable for following security policies and procedures (TC 4.3.5) Encouraging employees to report safety concerns or incidents (TC 4.3.6) Monitoring the level of cognitive, physical, and emotional demands placed on individuals or teams, as well as the distribution of workload among team members (TC 4.3.7) Stress and Fatigue includes the impact of stress, fatigue, and other psychological factors on individual and team performance, as well as strategies for managing and mitigating these factors; e.g. stress and fatigue management: Implementing programs to manage stress and fatigue, such as providing opportunities for rest and recovery, offering stress reduction techniques, and promoting healthy lifestyle habits (TC 4.3.8)
TC 4.4: Liveware	Recruiting and Retention of qualified and experienced staff (TC 4.4.1) Conducting background checks on all employees who have access to sensitive information (TC 4.4.2) Training and Experience: This includes the knowledge, skills, and experience of individuals or teams, as well as the training and development opportunities provided to support their performance (TC 4.4.3) Providing training to employees on how to work safely and effectively (TC 4.4.4)
TC 4.5: Liveware-Liveware Interface	Communication includes the methods and channels of communication between individuals or teams, including verbal, written, and electronic communication (TC 4.5.1) Teamwork includes the collaboration and coordination of work between individuals or teams, as well as the development of shared goals and objectives (TC 4.5.2) Leadership style and conflict resolution: Developing effective leadership practices that support communication, collaboration, and teamwork, such as setting clear expectations, providing feedback and coaching in conflict situations (TC 4.5.3)

The ratings are based on an in-depth analysis of the content and emphasis of each standard on the respective criteria.

The final step involves interpreting the results of the comparison matrix. This includes analyzing the differences and similarities between the two standards, assessing their strengths and weaknesses.

Comparison of the Risk Management Systems ISO 31000:2018 and COSO ERM Framework with regard to their Ability to Capture the Error Culture

3

3.1 Competing Value Framework (CVF)

Table 3.1 Competition versus partnership orientation dilemma: ISO 31000:2018 and COSO ERM Framework

Criteria (TC 1.1)	ISO 31000:2018	COSO ERM Framework
Competition versus partnership orientation dilemma.	5	4

COSO ERM Framework (4—Partly true):

The COSO ERM framework provides guidance on managing risks associated with competition and partnership but primarily focuses on internal processes, controls, and governance. It places significant emphasis on internal control environments and may not offer as comprehensive guidance for external competitive forces or fostering partnerships. While it does recognize the importance of addressing external factors, such as competitive pressures, it might not provide as detailed guidance on handling partnership orientation or stakeholder relationships. The COSO ERM framework's strength lies in providing a structured internal approach to risk management, which is important but might not fully address the partnership orientation aspect.

H. Becker, *Using Artificial Intelligence (AI) to Minimize Errors in Business Enterprise Management*, https://doi.org/10.1007/978-3-658-47243-6_3

ISO 31000:2018 (5—Fully applicable):

ISO 31000:2018 is highly applicable to managing the competition versus partnership orientation dilemma. It takes a more holistic and adaptable approach to risk management, which includes both internal and external factors. ISO 31000 emphasizes the importance of considering external competitive forces and stakeholder relationships in risk management. It recognizes that organizations operate in dynamic environments where competition and partnerships play a vital role. The framework's flexibility allows organizations to tailor their risk management processes to address competition and partnership challenges effectively. ISO 31000's focus on aligning risk management with strategic objectives makes it well-suited for organizations navigating the complexities of competition and partnership orientation.

In summary, the COSO ERM Framework is partly true (4) in addressing the competition versus partnership orientation dilemma, as it primarily focuses on internal aspects of risk management. In contrast, ISO 31000:2018 is fully applicable (5) because of its adaptability and holistic approach that considers both internal and external factors, making it suitable for managing the challenges posed by competition and partnership orientation in a dynamic business environment. ISO 31000:2018 is rated as fully applicable (5) because it holistically considers external competitive forces and stakeholder relationships, emphasizing the need for adaptability and stakeholder engagement in risk management processes. COSO ERM, rated partly true (4), also emphasizes stakeholder relationships but does not focus as strongly on external competitive forces, making it slightly less comprehensive in this regard (Table 3.1).

Table 3.2 Stable continuity versus dynamic change: ISO 31000:2018 and COSO ERM Framework

Criterion (TC 1.2)	ISO 31000:2018	COSO ERM Framework
Stable continuity versus dynamic change.	5	1

COSO ERM Framework (1—Does not apply at all):

The COSO framework is traditionally focused on providing a structured approach to risk management that suits stable continuity more than dynamic change. It places a heavy emphasis on internal controls, processes, and governance. While it recognizes the importance of adapting to changing circumstances, it may not be as inherently flexible or adaptable as ISO 31000 when it comes to addressing the challenges posed by dynamic change. The COSO framework's strength lies in providing a solid foundation for established processes and organizations that prioritize stability, making it less suitable for rapid or disruptive changes.

ISO 31000:2018 (5—Fully applicable):

ISO 31000 is ideally suited to address both stable continuity and dynamic change. It is inherently adaptable and designed to be applicable in different contexts. As stated in ISO 31000:2018 (E), "Risk management is dynamic and anticipates, detects, acknowledges and responds to changes and events in an appropriate and timely manner" (ISO 31000:2018(E), section 4, page 3).

ISO 31000's flexibility allows organizations to tailor their risk management processes to the specific needs and challenges presented by dynamic change.

Its focus on a risk-based approach and continual improvement aligns perfectly with managing risks in a dynamic environment, making it fully applicable.

In summary, the COSO ERM Framework is less suited for addressing dynamic change (1), as its traditional focus is on stability and established processes. In contrast, ISO 31000:2018 is highly applicable (5) in both stable and dynamic contexts due to its inherent flexibility and adaptability, allowing organizations to effectively manage risks regardless of the circumstances they face (Table 3.2).

ISO 31000:2018 is rated as fully applicable (5) due to its strong emphasis on adaptability and dynamic change in risk management practices. In contrast, COSO ERM is rated not applicable (1) as it focuses more on stability and control within governance practices, lacking the same level of emphasis on dynamic change (Fig. 3.1).

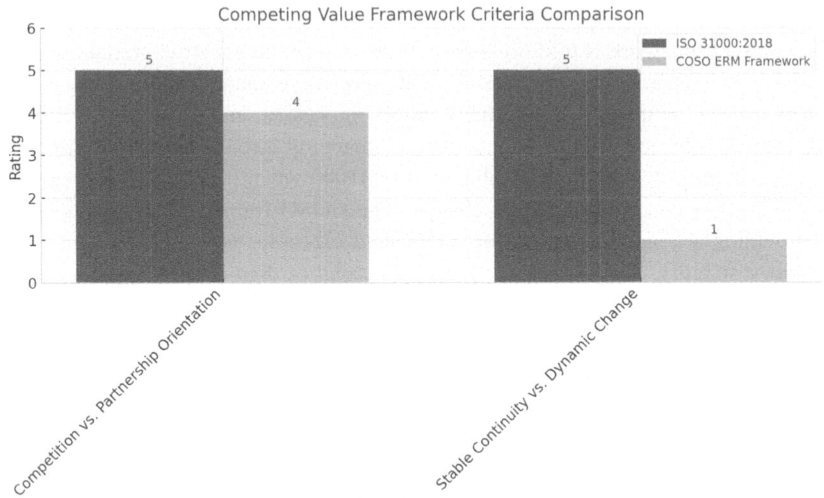

Fig. 3.1 Bar chart comparing the ISO 31000:2018 and COSO ERM Framework for Competing Value Framework Criteria

3.2 MOS Criteria

3.2.1 MOS: Deal with Failure

Table 3.3 Number of reported failures within a given time period: ISO 31000:2018 and COSO ERM Framework

Criterion (TC 2.1.1)	ISO 31000:2018	COSO ERM Framework
Number of reported failures within a given time period.	3	4

COSO ERM Framework (4—Partly true):

The COSO framework provides guidance for identifying, assessing, and managing risks, including those related to reported failures. It emphasizes the importance of internal controls and processes to prevent and detect failures. COSO encourages organizations to have robust internal reporting mechanisms to track and report failures promptly. However, its focus is more on internal control environments, which may not directly address the number of reported failures. While COSO ERM helps establish a risk-aware culture and internal controls, it may not provide extensive guidance on external reporting or how to reduce the actual number of failures within a given period.

ISO 31000:2018 (3—Neither):

ISO 31000 provides a high-level risk management framework that is applicable to various risks, including failures. However, it does not specifically focus on the number of reported failures within a given period. ISO 31000 offers guidance on risk assessment and treatment, but it does not prescribe specific measures or actions for reducing the number of reported failures. Organizations can use ISO 31000 as part of their broader risk management efforts to improve their risk posture, which might indirectly contribute to reducing failures. However, it does not directly address this criterion.

In summary, The COSO ERM Framework is partly true (4) in addressing the number of reported failures, as it provides guidance on internal controls and reporting mechanisms but may not directly focus on reducing the number of failures. On the other hand, ISO 31000:2018 is neither (3) applicable nor inapplicable to this specific criterion, as it offers a general risk management framework that organizations can adapt to address various types of risks, including failures, but it does not provide specific guidance on reducing their number within a given period. Organizations should complement ISO 31000 with additional measures tailored to their specific needs for managing and reducing failures. COSO ERM is rated higher (4) than ISO 31000:2018 (3) because it places a strong emphasis on internal controls and monitoring mechanisms which facilitate detailed reporting of failures. ISO 31000:2018, while comprehensive, focuses more broadly on risk management processes and less on the specific internal controls for failure reporting (Table 3.3).

Table 3.4 Percentage of reported failures that were analyzed and addressed: ISO 31000:2018 and COSO ERM Framework

Criterion (TC 2.1.2)	ISO 31000:2018	COSO ERM Framework
Percentage of reported failures that were analyzed and addressed.	3	4

COSO ERM Framework (4—Partly true):

The COSO framework emphasizes the importance of analyzing and addressing reported failures as part of its risk management process. It encourages organizations to have robust internal reporting mechanisms and processes for incident analysis.

COSO provides guidance on internal controls and monitoring, which can help organizations in analyzing and addressing failures. However, its focus is primarily on internal controls and may not provide extensive guidance on external reporting or the percentage of reported failures.

While COSO ERM helps establish a risk-aware culture and internal controls, it may not directly address the specific metric of the percentage of reported failures that were analyzed and addressed.

ISO 31000:2018 (3—Neither):

ISO 31000 offers a high-level risk management framework that can be applied to various risks, including reported failures. However, it does not specifically focus on determining or improving the percentage of reported failures that are analyzed and addressed.

ISO 31000 provides guidance on risk assessment and treatment, which are relevant to managing reported failures. Still, it does not prescribe specific measures or actions to calculate or enhance the percentage of failures addressed.

Organizations can use ISO 31000 as part of their broader risk management efforts, which might indirectly contribute to improving the handling of reported failures. However, it does not provide a direct framework for this specific metric.

In summary, the COSO ERM Framework is partly true (4) in addressing the percentage of reported failures that are analyzed and addressed. It promotes the importance of analyzing and addressing failures but may not provide specific metrics or guidelines for calculating this percentage. ISO 31000:2018 is neither (3) applicable nor inapplicable to this specific criterion, as it offers a general risk management framework that organizations can adapt to various risk types, including failures, but it does not provide specific guidance on determining or improving the percentage of reported failures addressed. Organizations should complement these frameworks with additional measures and metrics tailored to their specific needs for analyzing and addressing failures (Table 3.4).

Table 3.5 Time taken to analyze and address failures: ISO 31000:2018 and COSO ERM Framework

Criterion (TC 2.1.3)	ISO 31000:2018	COSO Framework
Time taken to analyze and address failures.	3	4

COSO ERM Framework (4—Partly true):

The COSO framework emphasizes the importance of analyzing and addressing reported failures as part of its risk management process. It encourages organizations to have robust internal reporting mechanisms and processes for incident analysis.

COSO provides guidance on internal controls and monitoring, which can help organizations in analyzing and addressing failures. However, its focus is primarily on internal controls and may not provide extensive guidance on external reporting or the percentage of reported failures.

While COSO ERM helps establish a risk-aware culture and internal controls, it may not directly address the specific metric of the percentage of reported failures that were analyzed and addressed.

ISO 31000:2018 (3—Neither):

ISO 31000 offers a high-level risk management framework that can be applied to various risks, including reported failures. However, it does not specifically focus on determining or improving the percentage of reported failures that are analyzed and addressed.

ISO 31000 provides guidance on risk assessment and treatment, which are relevant to managing reported failures. Still, it does not prescribe specific measures or actions to calculate or enhance the percentage of failures addressed.

Organizations can use ISO 31000 as part of their broader risk management efforts, which might indirectly contribute to improving the handling of reported failures. However, it does not provide a direct framework for this specific metric.

In summary, the COSO ERM Framework is partly true (4) in addressing the percentage of reported failures that are analyzed and addressed. It promotes the importance of analyzing and addressing failures but may not provide specific metrics or guidelines for calculating this percentage. ISO 31000:2018 is neither (3) applicable nor inapplicable to this specific criterion, as it offers a general risk management framework that organizations can adapt to various risk types, including failures, but it does not provide specific guidance on determining or improving the percentage of reported failures addressed. Organizations should complement these frameworks with additional measures and metrics tailored to their specific needs for analyzing and addressing failures (Table 3.5).

Table 3.6 Effectiveness of the solutions implemented to address failures: ISO 31000:2018 and COSO ERM Framework

Criterion (TC 2.1.4)	ISO 31000:2018	COSO ERM Framework
Effectiveness of the solutions implemented to address failures.	4	4

COSO ERM Framework (4—Partly true):

The COSO framework provides guidance on identifying, assessing, and mitigating risks, including those related to failures. It encourages organizations to establish robust internal controls and processes to address failures effectively.

COSO ERM emphasizes the importance of monitoring and evaluating the effectiveness of controls, which can help organizations assess the impact of implemented solutions.

However, COSO may not provide specific measures for determining the effectiveness of solutions or a structured framework for evaluating the success of risk mitigation strategies.

While COSO offers valuable guidance for managing failures, it may require organizations to supplement it with additional performance metrics and evaluation methods to assess the effectiveness of implemented solutions more comprehensively.

ISO 31000:2018 (4—Partly true):

ISO 31000 offers a general risk management framework that can be adapted to address various risks, including failures. It encourages organizations to assess the effectiveness of risk treatment measures.

ISO 31000 promotes a continuous improvement approach, which aligns with evaluating the effectiveness of solutions. It emphasizes the need for ongoing monitoring and assessment.

However, like the COSO framework, ISO 31000 does not provide specific metrics for measuring the effectiveness of solutions or a prescriptive framework for conducting such evaluations.

While ISO 31000 supports a systematic approach to risk management and improvement, organizations may need to develop their own methods for assessing the effectiveness of implemented solutions in the context of specific failures.

In summary, both the COSO ERM Framework and ISO 31000:2018 are partly true (4) in addressing the effectiveness of solutions implemented to address failures. They both provide guidance on risk management and emphasize monitoring and assessment. However, neither framework prescribes specific metrics or a comprehensive framework for evaluating the success of risk mitigation strategies. Organizations may need to complement these frameworks with their own performance measurement and evaluation methodologies to assess the effectiveness of solutions fully (Table 3.6) (Fig. 3.2).

Here is the bar chart for the "Deal with Failure" category, comparing ISO 31000:2018 and COSO ERM Framework across various criteria:

- Number of reported failures within a given time period
- Percentage of reported failures that were analyzed and addressed
- Time taken to analyze and address failures
- Effectiveness of the solutions implemented to address failures

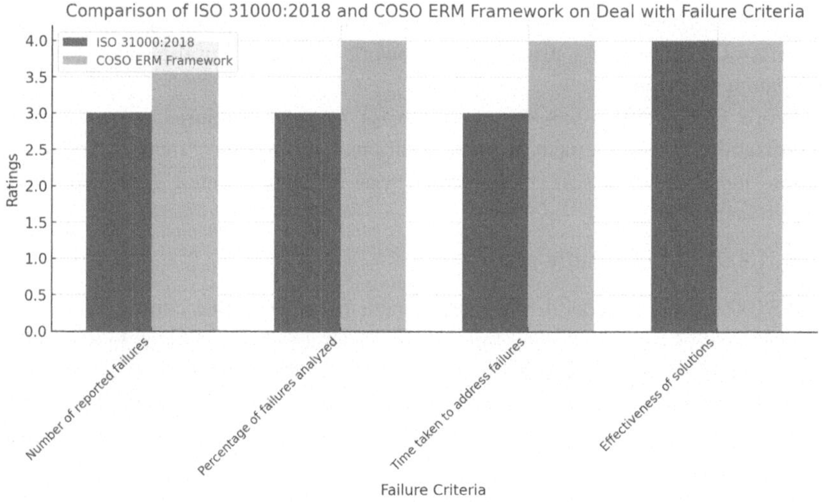

Fig. 3.2 Bar chart comparing the ISO 31000:2018 and COSO ERM Framework for Deal with Failure criteria

The COSO ERM Framework generally shows higher ratings in this category, indicating a stronger alignment with the criteria related to dealing with failure.

3.2.2 MOS: Questioning Simplistic Interpretations

Table 3.7 Frequency of questioning by team members during meetings or discussions: ISO 31000:2018 and COSO ERM Framework

Criterion (TC 2.2.1)	ISO 31000:2018	COSO ERM Framework
Frequency of questioning by team members during meetings or discussions.	4	4

COSO ERM Framework (4—Partly true):

The COSO framework provides guidance on identifying, assessing, and mitigating risks, including those related to failures. It encourages organizations to establish robust internal controls and processes to address failures effectively.

COSO ERM emphasizes the importance of monitoring and evaluating the effectiveness of controls, which can help organizations assess the impact of implemented solutions.

However, COSO may not provide specific measures for determining the effectiveness of solutions or a structured framework for evaluating the success of risk mitigation strategies.

While COSO offers valuable guidance for managing failures, it may require organizations to supplement it with additional performance metrics and evaluation methods to assess the effectiveness of implemented solutions more comprehensively.

ISO 31000:2018 (4—Partly true):

ISO 31000 offers a general risk management framework that can be adapted to address various risks, including failures. It encourages organizations to assess the effectiveness of risk treatment measures.

ISO 31000 promotes a continuous improvement approach, which aligns with evaluating the effectiveness of solutions. It emphasizes the need for ongoing monitoring and assessment.

However, like the COSO framework, ISO 31000 does not provide specific metrics for measuring the effectiveness of solutions or a prescriptive framework for conducting such evaluations.

While ISO 31000 supports a systematic approach to risk management and improvement, organizations may need to develop their own methods for assessing the effectiveness of implemented solutions in the context of specific failures.

In summary, both the COSO ERM Framework and ISO 31000:2018 are partly true (4) in addressing the effectiveness of solutions implemented to address failures. They both provide guidance on risk management and emphasize monitoring and assessment. However, neither framework prescribes specific metrics or a comprehensive framework for evaluating the success of risk mitigation strategies. Organizations may need to complement these frameworks with their own performance measurement and evaluation methodologies to assess the effectiveness of solutions fully (Table 3.7).

Table 3.8 Number of different perspectives considered when making decisions: ISO 31000:2018 and COSO ERM Framework

Criterion (TC 2.2.2)	ISO 31000:2018	COSO ERM Framework
Number of different perspectives considered when making decisions.	4	4

COSO ERM Framework (4—Partly True):

While the framework does not prescribe a specific number of perspectives to be considered, it encourages a holistic view of decision-making that incorporates diverse viewpoints, which contributes to more informed and balanced decisions. The framework's principles support the consideration of multiple perspectives, fostering a comprehensive and integrated risk management approach.

ISO 31000:2018 (4—Partly True):

Similarly, ISO 31000:2018 encourages organizations to engage a variety of stakeholders and consider different viewpoints when making decisions. The framework emphasizes risk assessment and treatment across a broad organizational context, supporting the integration of multiple perspectives into the decision-making process. Although it does not provide specific guidelines on the exact number of perspectives to be included, it stresses the importance of inclusive decision-making that promotes effective risk management.

In summary, they both promote an inclusive and broad approach to decision-making that supports comprehensive risk management, emphasizing stakeholder engagement and the integration of diverse viewpoints. Therefore, the rating of four out of four is appropriate for both frameworks, as they both inherently support this principle but do not prescribe a fixed number of perspectives (Table 3.8)

Table 3.9 Percentage of decisions made after considering multiple perspectives: ISO 31000:2018 and COSO ERM Framework

Criterion (TC 2.2.3)	ISO 31000:2018	COSO ERM Framework
Percentage of decisions made after considering multiple perspectives.	4	4

COSO ERM Framework (4—Partly true):

The COSO framework promotes a risk-aware culture and emphasizes the importance of considering various perspectives when making risk-related decisions.

COSO encourages organizations to engage with different stakeholders, including internal and external parties, to identify and assess risks comprehensively.

While COSO provides guidance on considering multiple perspectives, it may not offer explicit instructions or metrics for quantifying the percentage of decisions made after considering multiple viewpoints.

However, the framework's principles and practices inherently support the idea of incorporating diverse perspectives into risk management decisions, making it partly true in this context.

ISO 31000:2018 (4—Partly true):

ISO 31000 also encourages organizations to consider a wide range of perspectives when making risk-related decisions. It emphasizes the importance of stakeholder engagement and consultation.

ISO 31000 provides a general framework for risk management, including the consideration of various viewpoints. However, it does not offer specific metrics or guidelines for quantifying the percentage of decisions made after considering multiple perspectives.

The framework's principles align with the idea of incorporating different perspectives into the risk management process, but organizations may need to develop their own methods for assessing and measuring the extent to which they consider multiple viewpoints.

In summary, both the COSO ERM Framework and ISO 31000:2018 are partly true (4) in addressing the criterion of the percentage of decisions made after considering multiple perspectives. They emphasize the importance of diverse viewpoints and stakeholder engagement but do not provide specific metrics for quantifying the percentage of such decisions. Instead, they lay the foundation and principles for organizations to adopt practices that promote a more comprehensive and inclusive decision-making process, leaving the specific measurement to the discretion of individual organizations (Table 3.9).

Table 3.10 Effectiveness of decisions made after considering multiple perspectives: ISO 31000:2018 and COSO ERM Framework

Criterion (TC 2.2.4)	ISO 31000:2018	COSO ERM Framework
Effectiveness of decisions made after considering multiple perspectives.	4	4

COSO ERM Framework (4—Partly true):

The COSO framework promotes the consideration of various perspectives when making risk-related decisions. It encourages organizations to engage with different stakeholders to identify and assess risks comprehensively.

COSO emphasizes the importance of a risk-aware culture and internal controls that facilitate effective decision-making. However, it may not offer explicit instructions or metrics for assessing the effectiveness of decisions made after considering multiple viewpoints.

While the COSO framework provides a strong foundation for inclusive decision-making, it may not provide a structured framework for measuring the effectiveness of decisions in practice.

Organizations using COSO can establish processes for post-decision evaluations to assess the impact of considering multiple perspectives, but the framework itself does not provide specific guidance on this aspect.

ISO 31000:2018 (4—Partly true):

ISO 31000 encourages organizations to consider a wide range of perspectives when making risk-related decisions. It emphasizes the importance of stakeholder engagement and consultation.

The framework provides a general risk management structure that supports effective decision-making, but it does not offer specific metrics or guidelines for measuring the effectiveness of decisions made after considering multiple viewpoints.

ISO 31000's principles align with the idea of incorporating different perspectives into the risk management process, but organizations may need to develop their own methods for assessing and measuring the effectiveness of decisions in practice.

Like COSO, ISO 31000 leaves the specific measurement of decision effectiveness to the discretion of individual organizations.

In summary, both the COSO ERM Framework and ISO 31000:2018 are partly true (4) in addressing the criterion of the effectiveness of decisions made after considering multiple perspectives. They emphasize the importance of diverse viewpoints and stakeholder engagement in decision-making but do not provide specific metrics or guidelines for measuring decision effectiveness. Instead, they provide a foundational framework that supports inclusive decision-making, with the measurement of effectiveness left to the discretion and practices of individual organizations (Table 3.10) (Fig. 3.3).

Here is the bar chart for the "Questioning Simplistic Interpretations" category, comparing ISO 31000:2018 and COSO ERM Framework across various criteria:

- Frequency of questioning by team members during meetings or discussions
- Number of different perspectives considered when making decisions
- Percentage of decisions made after considering multiple perspectives
- Effectiveness of decisions made after considering multiple perspectives

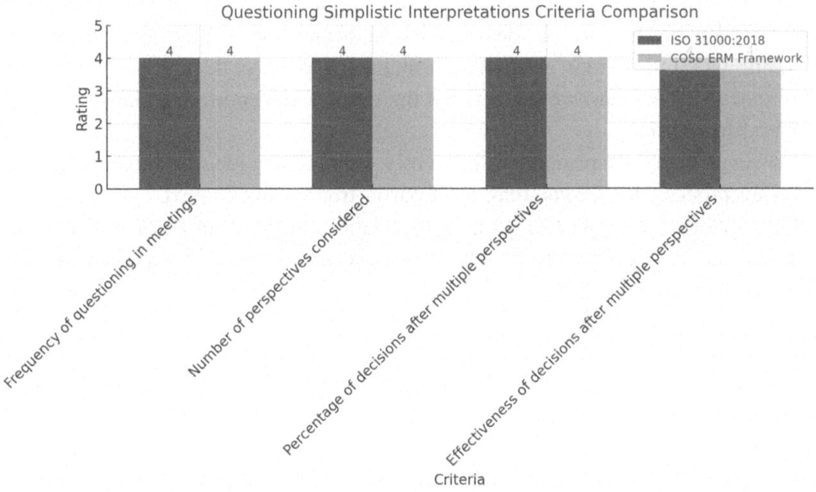

Fig. 3.3 Bar chart comparing the ISO 31000:2018 and COSO ERM Framework for Questioning Simplistic Interpretations Criteria

Both frameworks show similar ratings for all questioning simplistic interpretations criteria.

3.2.3 MOS: Sensitivity to Operational Processes

Table 3.11 Number of reported process deviations within a given period: ISO 31000:2018 and COSO ERM Framework

Criterion (TC 2.3.1)	ISO 31000:2018	COSO ERM Framework
Number of reported process deviations within a given time period.	3	4

COSO ERM Framework (4—Partly true):

The COSO framework emphasizes the importance of identifying and managing risks, including process deviations. It encourages organizations to establish robust internal controls and monitoring processes.

COSO promotes a risk-aware culture and effective internal reporting mechanisms, which can lead to the identification and reporting of process deviations.

While COSO provides guidance on managing process deviations, it may not offer specific benchmarks or targets for the number of reported deviations within a given time period.

However, COSO's principles inherently support the idea of monitoring and reporting process deviations, making it partly true in this context.

Organizations can use COSO as a foundation and customize their risk management and monitoring processes to measure the number of reported process deviations effectively.

ISO 31000:2018 (3—Neither):

ISO 31000 offers a general risk management framework that includes the management of process deviations. It encourages organizations to assess risks and take appropriate actions.

However, ISO 31000 does not provide specific metrics or guidelines for measuring the number of reported process deviations within a given time period.

The framework's focus is on risk assessment, treatment, and continuous improvement, rather than specifying quantitative measures for process deviation reporting.

While ISO 31000 supports a systematic approach to risk management, organizations may need to develop their own methods and performance indicators for measuring the number of reported process deviations.

In summary, the COSO ERM Framework is partly true (4) in addressing the criterion of the number of reported process deviations within a given time period. It provides guidance on risk management and monitoring, which indirectly supports measuring process deviations. In contrast, ISO 31000:2018 is neither (3) applicable nor inapplicable to this specific criterion, as it offers a general risk management framework but does not provide specific metrics or guidelines for measuring process deviations. Organizations may need to customize and complement these frameworks with their own measurement and monitoring processes to effectively assess the number of reported process deviations (Table 3.11).

Table 3.12 Percentage of process deviations that were analyzed and addressed: ISO 31000:2018 and COSO ERM Framework

Criterion (TC 2.3.2)	ISO 31000:2018	COSO ERM Framework
Percentage of process deviations that were analyzed and addressed.	3	4

COSO ERM Framework (4—Partly true):

The COSO ERM framework emphasizes the importance of identifying and managing risks, including process deviations. It promotes the establishment of robust internal controls, monitoring processes and reporting systems. These elements are critical to the effective identification and management of process deviations.

The principles of COSO ERM support the creation of a risk-aware culture within organizations, which facilitates the identification, reporting and analysis of process deviations. Effective internal reporting systems ensure that deviations are identified and dealt with in a timely manner. By emphasizing the need to analyze and address risks, COSO ensures that process deviations are dealt with systematically.

Although COSO ERM provides comprehensive guidance on managing process deviations and performing risk analysis, it lacks specific metrics or guidelines for calculating the percentage of process deviations analyzed and resolved. Therefore, organizations must develop their own specific metrics and processes based on the COSO principles to effectively meet this criterion.

Chapter 7 of the COSO ERM Framework, which focuses on control activities, emphasizes the importance of risk mitigation activities and describes how these activities are implemented at all levels of the organization. This supports the analysis and remediation of process deviations and strengthens monitoring and reporting, which contributes to the continuous improvement of internal controls.

The rating of 4 (partly true) is justified because COSO ERM provides a solid foundation for identifying, analyzing and addressing process deviations, although it does not provide specific metrics for calculating the percentage. The principles of COSO fundamentally support these activities, enabling organizations to develop their own metrics and processes to effectively meet this criterion.

ISO 31000:2018 (3—Neither):

ISO 31000 offers a general risk management framework that includes the management of process deviations. It encourages organizations to assess risks and take appropriate actions.

However, ISO 31000 does not provide specific metrics or guidelines for measuring the percentage of process deviations that were analyzed and addressed.

The framework's focus is on risk assessment, treatment, and continuous improvement, rather than specifying quantitative measures for process deviation analysis.

While ISO 31000 supports a systematic approach to risk management, organizations may need to develop their own methods and performance indicators for measuring the percentage of process deviations that were analyzed and addressed.

In summary, the COSO ERM Framework is partly true (4) in addressing the criterion of the percentage of process deviations that were analyzed and addressed. It provides guidance on risk management and monitoring, which indirectly supports measuring process deviations' analysis and addressing. In contrast, ISO 31000:2018 is neither (3) applicable nor inapplicable to this specific criterion, as it offers a general risk management framework but does not provide specific metrics or guidelines for measuring the percentage of process deviations analyzed and addressed. Both frameworks emphasize the importance of operational processes in risk management. However, COSO ERM Framework provides more detailed guidance on control activities related to these processes, justifying a higher score. Organizations may need to customize and complement these frameworks with their own measurement and monitoring processes to effectively assess this aspect of risk management (Table 3.12).

Table 3.13 Time taken to analyze and address process deviations: ISO 31000:2018 and COSO ERM Framework

Criterion (TC 2.3.3)	ISO 31000:2018	COSO Framework
Time taken to analyze and address process deviations.	3	4

COSO ERM Framework (4—Partly true):

The COSO framework emphasizes the importance of promptly identifying and managing risks, including process deviations. It encourages organizations to establish efficient internal controls, monitoring processes, and reporting mechanisms.

COSO promotes a risk-aware culture and effective internal reporting mechanisms, which can lead to the prompt identification and reporting of process deviations, contributing to a timely response.

While COSO provides guidance on managing process deviations and risk assessments, it may not offer specific benchmarks or targets for the time taken to analyze and address these deviations.

However, COSO's principles inherently support the idea of timely response and resolution of process deviations, making it partly true in this context.

Organizations can use COSO as a foundation and customize their risk management and monitoring processes to improve the timeliness of analyzing and addressing process deviations.

ISO 31000:2018 (3—Neither):

ISO 31000 offers a general risk management framework that includes the management of process deviations. It encourages organizations to assess risks and take appropriate actions.

However, ISO 31000 does not provide specific metrics or guidelines for measuring the time taken to analyze and address process deviations.

The framework's focus is on risk assessment, treatment, and continuous improvement, rather than specifying quantitative measures for process deviation analysis timelines.

While ISO 31000 supports a systematic approach to risk management, organizations may need to develop their own methods and performance indicators for measuring the timeliness of analyzing and addressing process deviations.

In summary, the COSO ERM Framework is partly true (4) in addressing the criterion of the time taken to analyze and address process deviations. It provides guidance on risk management and monitoring, which indirectly supports improving the timeliness of addressing deviations. In contrast, ISO 31000:2018 is neither (3) applicable nor inapplicable to this specific criterion, as it offers a general risk management framework but does not provide specific metrics or guidelines for measuring the time taken to analyze and address process deviations. Organizations may need to customize and complement these frameworks with their own measurement and monitoring processes to effectively assess the timeliness of addressing process deviations (Table 3.13).

Table 3.14 Effectiveness of the solutions implemented to address process deviations: ISO 31000:2018 and COSO ERM Framework

Criterion (TC 2.3.4)	ISO 31000:2018	COSO ERM Framework
Effectiveness of the solutions implemented to address process deviations.	4	4

COSO ERM Framework (4—Partly true):

The COSO framework promotes the identification and management of risks, including process deviations. It encourages organizations to establish effective internal controls, monitoring processes, and reporting mechanisms.

COSO emphasizes the importance of a risk-aware culture and effective internal reporting mechanisms, which can contribute to the effectiveness of solutions implemented to address process deviations.

While COSO provides guidance on managing process deviations and risk assessments, it may not offer specific metrics or guidelines for directly measuring the effectiveness of these solutions.

However, COSO's principles inherently support the idea of effective solutions by promoting a systematic approach to risk management.

Organizations can use COSO as a foundation and customize their risk management and monitoring processes to assess the effectiveness of the solutions implemented to address process deviations.

ISO 31000:2018 (4—Partly true):

ISO 31000 offers a general risk management framework that includes the management of process deviations. It encourages organizations to assess risks and take appropriate actions.

However, ISO 31000 does not provide specific metrics or guidelines for measuring the effectiveness of solutions implemented to address process deviations.

The framework's focus is on risk assessment, treatment, and continuous improvement, which indirectly supports the idea of effective solutions.

Like COSO, ISO 31000 supports a systematic approach to risk management, and organizations may need to develop their own methods and performance indicators for assessing the effectiveness of solutions implemented to address process deviations.

In summary, both the COSO ERM Framework and ISO 31000:2018 are partly true (4) in addressing the criterion of the effectiveness of solutions implemented to address process deviations. They emphasize the importance of identifying and managing risks, including process deviations, but do not provide specific metrics or guidelines for directly measuring solution effectiveness. Instead, they lay the foundation for organizations to adopt practices that promote effective solutions by focusing on risk management processes and controls. Organizations should complement these frameworks with their own methods for assessing the effectiveness of solutions tailored to their specific needs and contexts (Table 3.14) (Fig. 3.4).

Here is the bar chart for the "Sensitivity to Operational Processes" category, comparing ISO 31000:2018 and COSO ERM Framework across various criteria:

- Number of reported process deviations within a given time period
- Percentage of process deviations that were analyzed and addressed
- Time taken to analyze and address process deviations
- Effectiveness of the solutions implemented to address process deviations

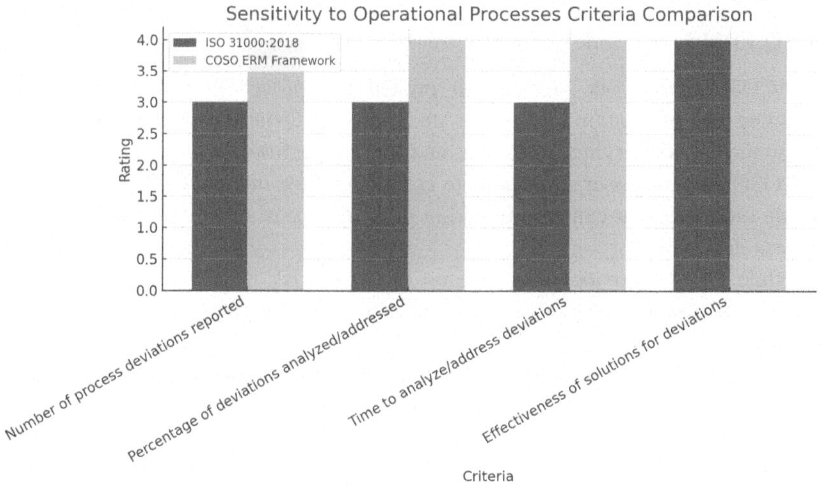

Fig. 3.4 Bar chart comparing the ISO 31000:2018 and COSO ERM Framework for Sensitivity to Operational Processes Criteria

The COSO ERM Framework demonstrates higher ratings across all criteria in this category, suggesting a stronger alignment with operational process sensitivity.

3.2.4 MOS: Striving for Resilience

Table 3.15 Frequency of proactive measures taken to prevent failures or process deviations: ISO 31000:2018 and COSO ERM Framework

Criterion (TC 2.4.1)	ISO 31000:2018	COSO ERM Framework
Frequency of proactive measures taken to prevent failures or process deviations.	4	4

COSO ERM Framework (4—Partly true):

The COSO framework promotes a proactive approach to risk management, including the prevention of failures and process deviations. It emphasizes the importance of identifying, assessing, and mitigating risks.

COSO encourages organizations to establish robust internal controls and monitoring processes that can help in taking proactive measures to prevent failures or process deviations.

While COSO provides guidance on proactive risk management, it may not offer specific metrics or guidelines for measuring the frequency of these proactive measures.

However, COSO's principles inherently support the idea of taking proactive steps to reduce risks, making it partly true in this context.

Organizations can use COSO as a foundation and customize their risk management processes to measure the frequency of proactive measures more comprehensively.

ISO 31000:2018 (4—Partly true):

ISO 31000 also encourages organizations to adopt a proactive approach to risk management. It emphasizes the importance of risk assessment and treatment, which includes proactive measures to prevent failures or process deviations.

The framework provides a general risk management structure that supports proactive risk mitigation. However, it does not provide specific metrics or guidelines for measuring the frequency of these proactive measures.

ISO 31000's principles align with the idea of taking proactive steps to manage risks, but organizations may need to develop their own methods and performance indicators for assessing the frequency of such measures.

Like COSO, ISO 31000 promotes a systematic approach to risk management, and organizations can use it as a basis for incorporating proactive measures into their risk management practices.

In summary, both the COSO ERM Framework and ISO 31000:2018 are partly true (4) in addressing the criterion of the frequency of proactive measures taken to prevent failures or process deviations. They both emphasize the importance of proactive risk management but do not provide specific metrics or guidelines for measuring the frequency of such measures. Instead, they lay the foundation for organizations to adopt practices that promote proactive risk mitigation by focusing on risk assessment, treatment, and control processes. Organizations should complement these frameworks with their own methods for measuring the frequency of proactive measures tailored to their specific needs and contexts (Table 3.15).

Table 3.16 Number of backup or redundancy systems in place: ISO 31000:2018 and COSO ERM Framework

Criterion (TC 2.4.2)	ISO 31000:2018	COSO ERM Framework
Number of backup or redundancy systems in place.	3	3

COSO ERM Framework (3—Neither):

The COSO framework primarily focuses on providing guidance for risk management, internal controls, and governance practices. It does touch upon the importance of identifying and mitigating risks, including those related to systems and processes.

While COSO encourages organizations to assess and manage risks comprehensively, it does not provide specific guidance or metrics for determining the number of backup or redundancy systems to have in place.

COSO's principles inherently support the idea of risk mitigation, but the framework does not delve into the specifics of redundancy systems.

Organizations may use COSO as a foundational framework to consider risk factors that could necessitate backup or redundancy systems, but the framework itself does not prescribe the number or type of such systems.

ISO 31000:2018 (3—Neither):

ISO 31000 offers a general risk management framework that organizations can adapt to various risk types, including the need for backup or redundancy systems.

However, ISO 31000 does not provide specific guidance or metrics for determining the number of backup or redundancy systems to have in place.

The framework's primary focus is on risk assessment, treatment, and continuous improvement, rather than specifying the details of technical infrastructure, such as redundancy systems.

Like COSO, ISO 31000 encourages organizations to incorporate risk management principles into their decision-making processes, but it does not offer specific directives regarding backup or redundancy systems.

In summary, both the COSO ERM Framework and ISO 31000:2018 are neither (3) applicable nor inapplicable to the criterion of the number of backup or redundancy systems in place. These frameworks provide foundational guidance for risk management, but they do not address the specifics of technical infrastructure, including the quantification of backup or redundancy systems. Decisions about the number and type of redundancy systems should be based on industry best practices, specific organizational needs, and the technical expertise of IT and operational teams, rather than relying solely on these risk management frameworks (Table 3.16).

Table 3.17 Time taken to recover from failures or process deviations: ISO 31000:2018 and COSO ERM Framework

Criterion (TC 2.4.3)	ISO 31000:2018	COSO Framework
Time taken to recover from failures or process deviations.	3	3

COSO ERM Framework (3—Neither):

The COSO framework primarily focuses on risk management, internal controls, and governance practices. While it emphasizes identifying and mitigating risks, it doesn't provide specific guidance or metrics for measuring the time taken to recover from failures or process deviations.

COSO's principles do inherently support the idea of prompt response and recovery, as part of effective risk management. However, it doesn't provide explicit recommendations on recovery timeframes.

Organizations using COSO can align their internal control and risk management practices to minimize downtime and recovery times, but the framework itself doesn't directly address this aspect.

The time taken to recover from failures or process deviations often involves technical, operational, and IT considerations that are beyond the scope of COSO's governance-oriented framework.

Measuring recovery times is typically a function of an organization's operational policies and procedures, rather than something explicitly addressed by COSO.

ISO 31000:2018 (3—Neither):

ISO 31000 offers a general risk management framework that encourages organizations to assess risks and take appropriate actions. While it promotes a proactive approach to risk management, it doesn't specifically address the measurement of recovery times.

The framework's primary focus is on risk assessment, treatment, and continuous improvement, rather than prescribing recovery timeframes.

ISO 31000 can inform an organization's risk management practices, which could indirectly influence recovery times. However, it doesn't provide specific guidelines for quantifying or managing recovery time.

Recovery time is often dependent on the nature of the failure, the organization's IT infrastructure, operational processes, and other technical considerations. These aspects are typically addressed through IT and operational standards rather than through ISO 31000.

As such, ISO 31000 is neither applicable nor inapplicable to this specific criterion.

In summary, both the COSO ERM Framework and ISO 31000:2018 are neither (3) applicable nor inapplicable to the criterion of the time taken to recover from failures or process deviations. These frameworks provide guidance on risk management and governance practices but do not address the specifics of technical infrastructure or operational recovery times. Recovery time is typically managed through technical and operational standards and procedures that organizations develop separately from these risk management frameworks (Table 3.17).

Table 3.18 Effectiveness of the solutions implemented to recover from failures or process deviations: ISO 31000:2018 and COSO ERM Framework

Criterion (TC 2.4.4)	ISO 31000:2018	COSO ERM Framework
Effectiveness of the solutions implemented to recover from failures or process deviations.	3	3

COSO ERM Framework (3—Neither):

The COSO framework primarily focuses on providing guidance for risk management, internal controls, and governance practices. While it emphasizes identifying and mitigating risks, it doesn't provide specific guidance or metrics for measuring the effectiveness of solutions implemented to recover from failures or process deviations.

COSO's principles do inherently support the idea of effective risk response and recovery, as part of comprehensive risk management. However, it doesn't provide explicit recommendations on assessing the effectiveness of recovery solutions.

Organizations using COSO can align their internal control and risk management practices to minimize downtime and enhance recovery efforts, but the framework itself doesn't directly address this aspect.

Assessing the effectiveness of recovery solutions typically involves technical, operational, and IT considerations that are beyond the scope of COSO's governance-oriented framework.

Measuring the effectiveness of recovery solutions often depends on specific performance indicators and operational standards that organizations develop separately from COSO.

ISO 31000:2018 (3—Neither):

ISO 31000 offers a general risk management framework that encourages organizations to assess risks and take appropriate actions, which may include the development of recovery solutions. However, it doesn't specifically address the measurement of the effectiveness of these solutions.

The framework's primary focus is on risk assessment, treatment, and continuous improvement, rather than prescribing specific measures for evaluating the effectiveness of recovery solutions.

ISO 31000 can inform an organization's risk management practices, which could indirectly influence the effectiveness of recovery solutions. However, it doesn't provide detailed guidance on assessing recovery solution effectiveness.

Evaluating the effectiveness of recovery solutions often involves technical, operational, and performance considerations that are typically addressed through separate operational standards and procedures.

As such, ISO 31000 is neither applicable nor inapplicable to this specific criterion.

In summary, both the COSO ERM Framework and ISO 31000:2018 are neither (3) applicable nor inapplicable to the criterion of measuring the effectiveness of the solutions implemented to recover from failures or process deviations. While these frameworks provide guidance on risk management and governance practices, they do not address the specifics of technical infrastructure or operational effectiveness measurement. The effectiveness of recovery solutions is typically assessed through performance indicators and operational standards developed separately by organizations and tailored to their specific needs and contexts (Table 3.18) (Fig. 3.5).

The bar chart above displays the comparison between ISO 31000:2018 and COSO ERM Framework for the "Striving for Resilience" category, which includes:

- Frequency of proactive measures taken to prevent failures or process deviations
- Number of backup or redundancy systems in place
- Time taken to recover from failures or process deviations
- Effectiveness of the solutions implemented to recover from failures or process deviations

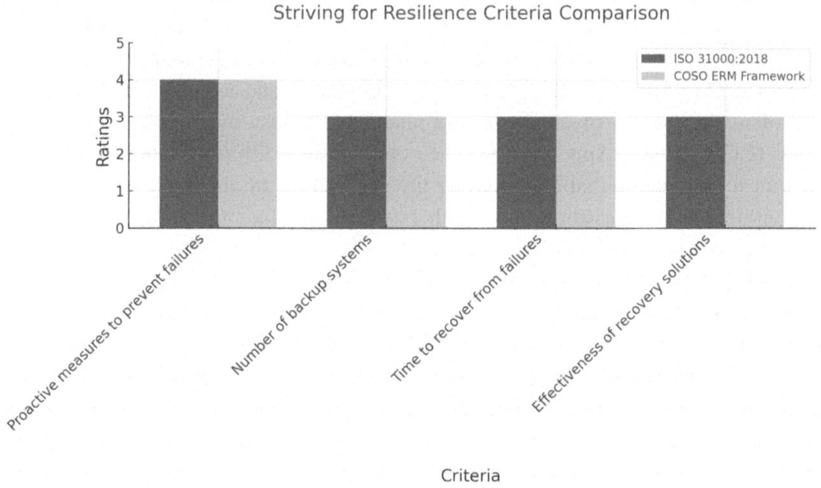

Fig. 3.5 Bar chart comparing the ISO 31000:2018 and COSO ERM Framework for Striving for Resilience Criteria

Both frameworks have similar ratings across these criteria, indicating a consistent approach in promoting resilience in organizations.

3.2.5 MOS: Pay Attention to Subject Matter Expertise

Table 3.19 Number of reported incidents related to lack of expertise within a given time period: ISO 31000:2018 and COSO ERM Framework

Criterion (TC 2.5.1)	ISO 31000:2018	COSO ERM Framework
Number of reported incidents related to lack of expertise within a given time period.	3	3

COSO ERM Framework (3—Neither):

The COSO framework primarily focuses on risk management, internal controls, and governance practices. While it emphasizes the importance of identifying and mitigating risks, it doesn't provide specific guidance or metrics for measuring the number of reported incidents related to a lack of expertise. Various organizational functions or operating units support the business through specialized capabilities, such as risk management, finance, controller, product/service quality management, technology, compliance, legal, human resources and others (COSO ERM, Appendix B) They provide guidance and assessment of internal control in their areas of expertise and share and assess overarching issues and trends (COSO ERM, Appendix B). They continuously inform the organization of relevant requirements that change over time (e.g., new or amended laws and regulations in various jurisdictions). Such business-enabling functions are referred to as the second line of defense, while the frontline staff perform their control activities (COSO ERM, Appendix B). COSO's principles do inherently support the idea that a lack of expertise can be a risk factor, and it promotes a risk-aware culture. However, it doesn't offer explicit recommendations on measuring incidents related to expertise gaps. Organizations using COSO ERM can incorporate expertise-related risk factors into their risk assessments and risk management practices. However, the framework itself doesn't directly address this specific aspect of expertise-related incidents. Measuring and addressing incidents related to a lack of expertise often involve HR policies, training programs, and specific expertise development initiatives, which are typically managed separately from COSO's governance-oriented framework. While COSO can provide a context for understanding and mitigating risks related to expertise, the measurement of incidents would depend on organizational-specific data collection and analysis.

ISO 31000:2018 (3—Neither):

ISO 31000 offers a general risk management framework that encourages organizations to assess risks and take appropriate actions, which may include addressing risks related to a lack of expertise. However, ISO 31000 does not provide specific guidance or metrics for measuring the number of reported incidents related to expertise gaps within a given time period. The framework's primary focus is on risk assessment, treatment, and continuous improvement, rather than prescribing specific measures for monitoring expertise-related incidents. ISO 31000 can inform an organization's risk management practices and the identification of expertise-related risks. Still, the actual measurement and management of incidents related to expertise are typically addressed through HR and talent management processes. As such, ISO 31000 is neither applicable nor inapplicable to this specific criterion.

In summary, both the COSO ERM Framework and ISO 31000:2018 are neither (3) applicable nor inapplicable to the criterion of measuring the number of reported incidents related to a lack of expertise within a given time period. These frameworks provide guidance on risk management and governance practices but do not address the specifics of expertise-related incident measurement. The tracking and management of incidents related to expertise are typically handled through HR, training, and talent management processes, which are managed separately from these risk management frameworks (Table 3.19).

Table 3.20 Percentage of team members with relevant expertise or qualifications: ISO 31000:2018 and COSO ERM Framewor

Criterion (TC 2.5.2)	ISO 31000:2018	COSO ERM Framework
Percentage of team members with relevant expertise or qualifications.	2	2

COSO ERM Framework (2—Does not apply in part):

The COSO framework primarily focuses on risk management, internal controls, and governance practices. While it emphasizes the importance of identifying and mitigating risks, it doesn't provide specific guidance or metrics for measuring the percentage of team members with relevant expertise or qualifications.

COSO's principles do inherently support the idea that a team with relevant expertise is crucial for effective risk management, but it doesn't offer explicit recommendations on measuring the percentage of such team members.

However, COSO does emphasize the need for a competent workforce to manage risks effectively, and this indirectly supports the importance of having team members with the right expertise.

Organizations using COSO can incorporate expertise-related considerations into their risk assessments and risk management practices. Still, the framework itself doesn't directly address this specific aspect of team expertise.

Measuring the percentage of team members with relevant expertise or qualifications is typically a function of HR policies, recruitment, and talent management practices, which are typically managed separately from COSO's governance-oriented framework.

ISO 31000:2018 (2—Does not apply in part):

ISO 31000 offers a general risk management framework that encourages organizations to assess risks and take appropriate actions, which may include considering the expertise of team members. However, ISO 31000 does not provide specific guidance or metrics for measuring the percentage of team members with relevant expertise or qualifications. The framework's primary focus is on risk assessment, treatment, and continuous improvement, rather than prescribing specific measures for monitoring team expertise. ISO 31000 can inform an organization's risk management practices and the consideration of team expertise. Still, the actual measurement and management of team members' qualifications and expertise are typically addressed through HR and talent management processes. As such, ISO 31000 is in a similar position as COSO and does not directly address this specific criterion.

In summary, both the COSO ERM Framework and ISO 31000:2018 do not fully apply in part (2) to the criterion of measuring the percentage of team members with relevant expertise or qualifications. While they emphasize the importance of a competent workforce for effective risk management, they do not provide specific guidelines or metrics for quantifying team expertise. The measurement and management of team members' qualifications and expertise are typically handled through HR, recruitment, and talent management processes, which are managed separately from these risk management frameworks (Table 3.20).

Table 3.21 Frequency of seeking advice or guidance from team members with relevant expertise: ISO 31000:2018 and COSO ERM Framework

Criterion (TC 2.5.3)	ISO 31000:2018	COSO ERM Framework
Frequency of seeking advice or guidance from team members with relevant expertise.	4	4

COSO ERM Framework (4—Partly true):

The COSO framework primarily focuses on risk management, internal controls, and governance practices. While it doesn't provide specific metrics for the frequency of seeking advice from experts, it inherently promotes collaboration and knowledge sharing.

COSO encourages a risk-aware culture and effective internal reporting mechanisms, which can indirectly support the idea of seeking advice or guidance from team members with relevant expertise.

While COSO doesn't prescribe the frequency, it promotes a systematic approach to risk management that includes consulting experts when needed.

Organizations using COSO can align their risk management practices encouraging the regular seeking of advice from experts. However, the framework itself doesn't provide quantitative measures for this specific aspect.

The frequency of seeking advice from team members with relevant expertise often depends on an organization's specific risk culture and operational needs, which can be influenced by COSO's principles.

ISO 31000:2018 (4—Partly true):

ISO 31000 offers a general risk management framework that encourages organizations to assess risks and take appropriate actions, which may include seeking advice from experts.

The framework doesn't provide specific metrics for the frequency of seeking advice but promotes a proactive approach to risk management that aligns with the idea of consulting experts when needed.

ISO 31000 can inform an organization's risk management practices and the consideration of expert advice. However, the actual frequency of seeking advice from team members with relevant expertise is typically determined by organizational culture and specific risk assessment processes.

While ISO 31000 doesn't prescribe the frequency, it provides the conceptual foundation for organizations to incorporate expertise-driven decision-making into their risk management practices.

The frequency of seeking advice from experts often varies depending on the organization's industry, risk profile, and risk management maturity, which ISO 31000 can help shape.

In summary, both the COSO ERM Framework and ISO 31000:2018 are partly true (4) in addressing the criterion of the frequency of seeking advice or guidance from team members with relevant expertise. While they don't provide specific metrics, they promote a risk-aware culture and a systematic approach to risk management that encourages consulting experts when needed. The actual frequency of seeking advice depends on an organization's risk culture and specific operational needs, which can be influenced by these frameworks' principles. Organizations can use these frameworks to emphasize the importance of expert advice within their risk management practices (Table 3.21).

Table 3.22 Effectiveness of the solutions implemented based on advice or guidance from team members with relevant expertise: ISO 31000:2018 and COSO ERM Framework

Criterion (TC 2.5.4)	ISO 31000:2018	COSO ERM Framework
Effectiveness of the solutions implemented based on advice or guidance from team members with relevant expertise.	4	4

ISO 31000:2018 (4—Partly true):

ISO 31000 offers a general risk management framework that encourages organizations to assess risks and take appropriate actions, which may include implementing solutions based on expert advice.

The framework doesn't provide specific metrics for measuring the effectiveness of such solutions, but it promotes a proactive approach to risk management that aligns with the idea of leveraging expertise.

ISO 31000 can inform an organization's risk management practices and the integration of expert guidance into its decision-making processes. However, the actual effectiveness of solutions implemented based on expert advice is determined by the organization's ability to execute these recommendations.

While ISO 31000 doesn't prescribe how to measure effectiveness, it provides the conceptual foundation for organizations to incorporate expertise-driven decision-making into their risk management practices.

The effectiveness of solutions based on expert advice often varies depending on the organization's industry, risk profile, and the quality of the advice received, which ISO 31000 can help shape.

COSO ERM Framework (4—Partly true):

The COSO ERM Framework provides a structured approach to enterprise risk management, focusing on integrating risk management with the organization's overall strategy and performance. Relevant aspects include:

The COSO ERM Framework emphasizes the integration of risk management practices with the organization's strategic planning and performance management. It encourages the involvement of team members with relevant expertise in this process.

The framework outlines five components and seventeen principles that support effective risk management. These components include internal control environment, risk assessment, control activities, information and communication, and monitoring activities. Expert advice is often integrated into these components to enhance risk management effectiveness.

COSO ERM highlights the importance of involving knowledgeable individuals in risk assessment and management activities. This ensures that the solutions developed are informed by relevant expertise.

Similar to ISO 31000, the COSO ERM Framework does not provide specific metrics for measuring the effectiveness of solutions implemented based on expert advice. The framework focuses on creating an environment where expert guidance is valued and integrated into decision-making processes.

The actual effectiveness of solutions depends on the organization's ability to implement and execute recommendations effectively. COSO ERM supports this by providing a comprehensive structure but leaves the measurement of effectiveness to the organization's discretion.

In summary, both the COSO ERM Framework and ISO 31000:2018 are partly true (4) in addressing the criterion of the effectiveness of solutions implemented based on advice or guidance from team members with relevant expertise. While they don't provide specific metrics for measuring effectiveness, they encourage a risk-aware culture and a systematic approach to risk management that supports leveraging expertise. The actual effectiveness of solutions depends on the organization's ability to integrate expert guidance effectively, which these frameworks can help facilitate. Organizations should use these frameworks to emphasize the importance of expert advice within their risk management practices and develop their own methods for assessing solution effectiveness (Table 3.22).

Here is the bar chart for the "Pay Attention to Subject Matter Expertise" category, comparing ISO 31000:2018 and COSO ERM Framework across various criteria:

- Number of reported incidents related to lack of expertise within a given time period
- Percentage of team members with relevant expertise or qualifications
- Frequency of seeking advice or guidance from team members with relevant expertise
- Effectiveness of the solutions implemented based on advice or guidance from team members with relevant expertise

Both frameworks show similar ratings across these criteria, highlighting their consistent approach in recognizing the importance of subject matter expertise in risk management and decision-making processes (Fig. 3.6).

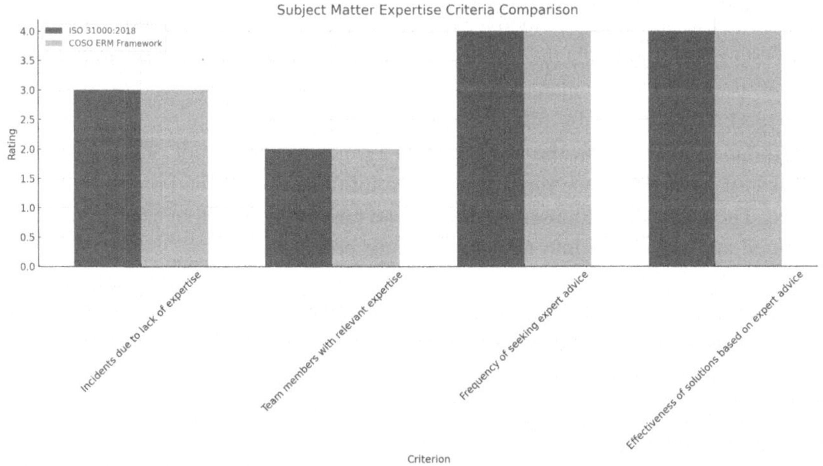

Fig. 3.6 Bar chart comparing the ISO 31000:2018 and COSO ERM Framework for Pay Attention to Subject Matter Expertise Criteria

3.3 The GEMS Model Criteria

3.3.1 Skill-based Errors (Slips and Oversights)

Table 3.23 Frequency of certain errors compared to the expected number of errors given the task complexity and individual skill level: ISO 31000:2018 and COSO ERM Framework

Criterion (TC 3.1.1)	ISO 31000:2018	COSO ERM Framework
Frequency of certain errors compared to the expected number of errors given the task complexity and individual skill level.	2	2

ISO 31000:2018 (2—Does not apply in part):

ISO 31000 offers a general risk management framework that encourages organizations to assess risks and take appropriate actions, including those related to operational risks and errors. However, ISO 31000 does not provide specific guidance or metrics for measuring the frequency of errors in relation to task complexity and individual skill level. The framework's primary focus is on risk assessment, treatment, and continuous improvement, rather than prescribing specific measures for monitoring error rates. ISO 31000 can inform an organization's risk management practices, which could indirectly influence error reduction efforts. Still, the actual measurement and management of errors in relation to task complexity and skill level typically fall under quality management and process improvement practices, which are managed separately from ISO 31000. As such, ISO 31000 is in a similar position as COSO and does not directly address this specific criterion.

COSO ERM Framework (2—Does not apply in part)

The COSO ERM framework does emphasize the importance of considering the human element and potential errors in internal control processes. Chapter 5, "Control Environment," addresses the need to attract, develop, and retain competent individuals, which indirectly relates to managing the risk of errors based on skill levels. The provided text highlights that the control environment includes standards, processes, and structures to support internal control, with a focus on competence and human resources management. Specific Texts are as follows:

"The control environment is the set of standards, processes, and structures that provide the basis for carrying out internal control across the organization. The board of directors and senior management establish the tone at the top regarding the importance of internal control including expected standards of conduct. Management reinforces expectations at the various levels of the organization" (COSO ERM 2012 Chapter 5, Page 31).

"The commitment to competence is supported by and embedded in the human resource management processes for attracting, developing, evaluating, and retaining the right fit of management, other personnel, and outsourced service providers. The adequate number of resources is determined and periodically readjusted considering the relative importance of risks to be mitigated to support the achievement of the entity's objectives" (COSO ERM 2012 Chapter 5, Page 51).

While COSO ERM underscores the significance of internal controls and the control environment, which includes managing human factors and competence, it does not provide specific metrics or detailed methodologies for measuring error frequencies in relation to task complexity and skill level. Therefore, the application remains partial and does not fully meet the specific criterion.

In summary, both the COSO ERM Framework and ISO 31000:2018 do not fully apply in part (2) to the criterion of measuring the frequency of certain errors compared to the expected number of errors given the task complexity and individual skill level. While they emphasize the importance of effective risk management and controls, they do not provide specific guidance or metrics for quantifying error rates. The measurement and management of errors typically fall under quality management and operational improvement practices, which are managed separately from these risk management frameworks (Table 3.23).

Table 3.24 Time taken to complete a task compared to the expected time given the task complexity and individual skill level: ISO 31000:2018 and COSO ERM Framework

Criterion (TC 3.1.2)	ISO 31000:2018	COSO ERM Framework
Time taken to complete a task compared to the expected time given the task complexity and individual skill level.	2	2

COSO ERM Framework (2—Does not apply in part):

The COSO framework primarily focuses on risk management, internal controls, and governance practices. It doesn't provide specific guidance or metrics for measuring task completion time in relation to task complexity and individual skill level. COSO promotes a risk-aware culture and effective internal reporting mechanisms, but it doesn't directly address the measurement of task completion time. COSO does indirectly support the idea of optimizing operational processes, which could include improving task efficiency. However, it doesn't offer explicit recommendations for assessing this specific aspect. The measurement of task completion time compared to expectations typically falls under operational performance and process improvement practices, areas that are managed separately from COSO's governance-oriented framework. While COSO can provide a context for understanding and managing operational risks, it does not provide tools or metrics for directly evaluating task completion times.

ISO 31000:2018 (2—Does not apply in part):

ISO 31000 offers a general risk management framework that encourages organizations to assess risks and take appropriate actions, including those related to operational performance. However, ISO 31000 does not provide specific guidance or metrics for measuring task completion time in relation to task complexity and individual skill level. The framework's primary focus is on risk assessment, treatment, and continuous improvement, rather than prescribing specific measures for monitoring task completion times. ISO 31000 can inform an organization's risk management practices, which could indirectly influence efforts to optimize task completion times. Still, the actual measurement and management of task efficiency typically fall under operational and process improvement practices, which are managed separately from ISO 31000. As such, ISO 31000 is in a similar position as COSO and does not directly address this specific criterion.

In summary, both the COSO ERM Framework and ISO 31000:2018 do not fully apply in part (2) to the criterion of measuring the time taken to complete a task compared to the expected time given the task complexity and individual skill level. While they emphasize the importance of effective risk management and controls, they do not provide specific guidance or metrics for quantifying task completion times. The measurement and management of task efficiency typically fall under operational performance and process improvement practices, which are managed separately from these risk management frameworks (Table 3.24).

Table 3.25 Consistency in performing the task correctly over multiple attempts: ISO 31000:2018 and COSO ERM Framework

Criterion (TC 3.1.3)	ISO 31000:2018	COSO ERM Framework
Consistency in performing the task correctly over multiple attempts.	2	2

COSO ERM Framework (2—Does not apply in part):

The COSO framework primarily focuses on risk management, internal controls, and governance practices. It doesn't provide specific guidance or metrics for measuring the consistency in performing tasks over multiple attempts.

COSO promotes a risk-aware culture and effective internal controls, which can indirectly support the idea of consistency in task performance. However, it doesn't offer explicit recommendations for assessing this specific aspect.

COSO emphasizes the importance of reliable processes and internal controls, which are relevant to achieving consistency in task execution. However, the framework itself doesn't directly address this criterion.

The measurement of consistency in task performance is typically associated with quality management and operational performance practices, areas that are managed separately from COSO's governance-oriented framework.

While COSO can provide a context for understanding and managing operational risks, it does not provide tools or metrics for directly evaluating task consistency.

ISO 31000:2018 (2—Does not apply in part):

ISO 31000 offers a general risk management framework that encourages organizations to assess risks and take appropriate actions, including those related to operational performance.

However, ISO 31000 does not provide specific guidance or metrics for measuring the consistency in performing tasks correctly over multiple attempts.

The framework's primary focus is on risk assessment, treatment, and continuous improvement, rather than prescribing specific measures for monitoring task consistency.

ISO 31000 can inform an organization's risk management practices, which could indirectly influence efforts to achieve consistency in task performance. Still, the actual measurement and management of task consistency typically fall under quality management and process improvement practices, which are managed separately from ISO 31000.

As such, ISO 31000 is in a similar position as COSO and does not directly address this specific criterion.

In summary, both the COSO ERM Framework and ISO 31000:2018 do not fully apply in part (2) to the criterion of measuring the consistency in performing a task correctly over multiple attempts. While they emphasize the importance of effective risk management and controls, they do not provide specific guidance or metrics for quantifying task consistency. The measurement and management of task consistency are typically associated with quality management and operational performance practices, which are managed separately from these risk management frameworks (Table 3.25).

Table 3.26 Reaction time to unexpected events or changes in the task: ISO 31000:2018 and COSO ERM Framework

Criterion (TC 3.1.4)	ISO 31000:2018	COSO ERM Framework
Reaction time to unexpected events or changes in the task.	2	2

COSO ERM Framework (2—Does not apply in part):

The COSO framework primarily focuses on risk management, internal controls, and governance practices. It doesn't provide specific guidance or metrics for measuring reaction time to unexpected events or changes in a task.

COSO promotes a risk-aware culture and effective internal controls, which can indirectly support the need for a prompt reaction to unexpected events. However, it doesn't offer explicit recommendations for assessing this specific aspect.

While COSO emphasizes the importance of monitoring and responding to risks, it doesn't provide detailed instructions on measuring reaction times.

The measurement of reaction time to unexpected events or changes in a task is typically associated with operational performance and incident response practices, areas that are managed separately from COSO's governance-oriented framework.

COSO can provide a context for understanding and managing operational risks, but it does not provide tools or metrics for directly evaluating reaction times.

ISO 31000:2018 (2—Does not apply in part):

ISO 31000 offers a general risk management framework that encourages organizations to assess risks and take appropriate actions, including those related to incident response.

However, ISO 31000 does not provide specific guidance or metrics for measuring reaction time to unexpected events or changes in a task.

The framework's primary focus is on risk assessment, treatment, and continuous improvement, rather than prescribing specific measures for monitoring reaction times.

ISO 31000 can inform an organization's risk management practices, which could indirectly influence efforts to improve reaction times to unexpected events.

Still, the actual measurement and management of reaction times typically fall under incident response and operational performance practices, which are managed separately from ISO 31000.

As with COSO, ISO 31000 is in a similar position and does not directly address this specific criterion.

In summary, both the COSO ERM Framework and ISO 31000:2018 do not fully apply in part (2) to the criterion of measuring reaction time to unexpected events or changes in a task. While they emphasize the importance of effective risk management and controls, they do not provide specific guidance or metrics for quantifying reaction times. The measurement and management of reaction times are typically associated with incident response and operational performance practices, which are managed separately from these risk management frameworks (Table 3.26) (Fig. 3.7).

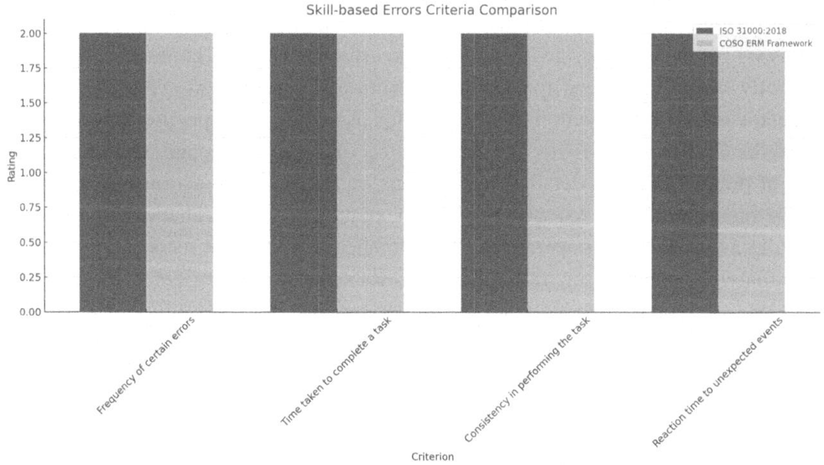

Fig. 3.7 Bar chart comparing the ISO 31000:2018 and COSO ERM Framework for Errors Criteria

3.3.2 Rule-based Errors (Errors of Confusion and Recognition)

Table 3.27 Number of times a rule was misinterpreted or not followed correctly: ISO 31000:2018 and COSO ERM Framework

Criterion (TC 3.2.1)	ISO 31000:2018	COSO ERM Framework
Number of times a rule was misinterpreted or not followed correctly.	2	2

COSO ERM Framework (2—Does not apply in part):

The COSO framework primarily focuses on risk management, internal controls, and governance practices. It doesn't provide specific guidance or metrics for measuring the number of times a rule was misinterpreted or not followed correctly. COSO promotes a risk-aware culture and effective internal controls, which can indirectly support the importance of following rules correctly. However, it doesn't offer explicit recommendations for assessing this specific aspect. While COSO emphasizes the need for strong internal controls and compliance, it doesn't provide detailed instructions on measuring rule misinterpretations or non-compliance incidents. The measurement of rule misinterpretations or non-compliance is typically associated with compliance management and quality control practices, areas that are managed separately from COSO's governance-oriented framework. COSO can provide a context for understanding and managing operational risks related to compliance, but it does not provide tools or metrics for directly evaluating the number of misinterpretations or rule violations.

ISO 31000:2018 (2—Does not apply in part):

ISO 31000 offers a general risk management framework that encourages organizations to assess risks and take appropriate actions, including those related to compliance and rule adherence. However, ISO 31000 does not provide specific guidance or metrics for measuring the number of times a rule was misinterpreted or not followed correctly. The framework's primary focus is on risk assessment, treatment, and continuous improvement, rather than prescribing specific measures for monitoring rule compliance. ISO 31000 can inform an organization's risk management practices, which could indirectly influence efforts to improve rule adherence. Still, the actual measurement and management of rule violations are typically addressed through compliance management and quality control practices, which are managed separately from ISO 31000. As with COSO, ISO 31000 is in a similar position and does not directly address this specific criterion.

In summary, both the COSO ERM Framework and ISO 31000:2018 do not fully apply in part (2) to the criterion of measuring the number of times a rule was misinterpreted or not followed correctly. While they emphasize the importance of compliance and internal controls, they do not provide specific guidance or metrics for quantifying rule violations or misinterpretations. The measurement and management of rule adherence typically fall under compliance management and quality control practices, which are managed separately from these risk management frameworks (Table 3.27).

Table 3.28 Frequency of incorrect responses to specific stimuli or cues: ISO 31000:2018 and COSO ERM Framework

Criterion (TC 3.2.2)	ISO 31000:2018	COSO ERM Framework
Frequency of incorrect responses to specific stimuli or cues.	2	2

COSO ERM Framework (2—Does not apply in part):

The COSO framework primarily focuses on risk management, internal controls, and governance practices. It doesn't provide specific guidance or metrics for measuring the frequency of incorrect responses to specific stimuli or cues. COSO promotes a risk-aware culture and effective internal controls, which can indirectly support the importance of making correct decisions in response to stimuli. However, it doesn't offer explicit recommendations for assessing this specific aspect. While COSO emphasizes the need for strong internal controls and decision-making processes, it doesn't provide detailed instructions on measuring the frequency of incorrect responses. The measurement of incorrect responses to stimuli or cues is typically associated with cognitive psychology, human factors engineering, and behavior analysis, areas that are managed separately from COSO's governance-oriented framework. COSO can provide a context for understanding and managing operational risks related to decision-making, but it does not provide tools or metrics for directly evaluating the frequency of incorrect responses.

ISO 31000:2018 (2—Does not apply in part):

ISO 31000 offers a general risk management framework that encourages organizations to assess risks and take appropriate actions, including those related to decision-making. However, ISO 31000 does not provide specific guidance or metrics for measuring the frequency of incorrect responses to stimuli or cues. The framework's primary focus is on risk assessment, treatment, and continuous improvement, rather than prescribing specific measures for monitoring decision-making accuracy. ISO 31000 can inform an organization's risk management practices, which could indirectly influence efforts to improve decision-making accuracy. Still, the actual measurement and management of cognitive errors are typically addressed through cognitive psychology and human factors engineering practices, which are managed separately from ISO 31000. As with COSO, ISO 31000 is in a similar position and does not directly address this specific criterion.

In summary, both the COSO ERM Framework and ISO 31000:2018 do not fully apply in part (2) to the criterion of measuring the frequency of incorrect responses to specific stimuli or cues. While they emphasize the importance of effective risk management, controls, and decision-making processes, they do not provide specific guidance or metrics for quantifying cognitive errors. The measurement and management of decision-making accuracy in response to stimuli typically fall under cognitive psychology, human factors engineering, and behavior analysis practices, which are managed separately from these risk management frameworks (Table 3.28).

Table 3.29 Percentage of correct responses to similar but distinct stimuli or cues: ISO 31000:2018 and COSO ERM Framework

Criterion (TC 3.2.3)	ISO 31000:2018	COSO ERM Framework
Percentage of correct responses to similar but distinct stimuli or cues.	2	2

COSO ERM Framework (2—Does not apply in part):

The COSO framework primarily focuses on risk management, internal controls, and governance practices. It doesn't provide specific guidance or metrics for measuring the percentage of correct responses to similar but distinct stimuli or cues. COSO promotes a risk-aware culture and effective internal controls, but it does not address the measurement of cognitive performance in response to such stimuli. While COSO emphasizes the importance of strong internal controls and decision-making processes, it doesn't provide detailed instructions on assessing the percentage of correct responses to nuanced stimuli. Measuring responses to distinct stimuli or cues is typically associated with cognitive psychology and human factors engineering, areas that are managed separately from COSO's governance-oriented framework. COSO can provide a context for understanding and managing operational risks related to decision-making but does not provide tools or metrics for directly evaluating the percentage of correct responses to distinct stimuli.

ISO 31000:2018 (2—Does not apply in part):

ISO 31000 offers a general risk management framework that encourages organizations to assess risks and take appropriate actions, including those related to decision-making. However, ISO 31000 does not provide specific guidance or metrics for measuring the percentage of correct responses to similar but distinct stimuli or cues. The framework's primary focus is on risk assessment, treatment, and continuous improvement, rather than prescribing specific measures for monitoring cognitive performance. ISO 31000 can inform an organization's risk management practices, which could indirectly influence efforts to improve cognitive performance. However, the actual measurement and management of such cognitive aspects are typically addressed through cognitive psychology and human factors engineering practices, which are managed separately from ISO 31000. As with COSO, ISO 31000 is in a similar position and does not directly address this specific criterion.

In summary, both the COSO ERM Framework and ISO 31000:2018 do not fully apply in part (2) to the criterion of measuring the percentage of correct responses to similar but distinct stimuli or cues. While they emphasize the importance of effective risk management, controls, and decision-making processes, they do not provide specific guidance or metrics for quantifying cognitive performance in response to nuanced stimuli. The measurement and management of cognitive responses to distinct stimuli typically fall under cognitive psychology, human factors engineering, and behavior analysis practices, which are managed separately from these risk management frameworks (Table 3.29).

Table 3.30 Time taken to recognize and correct an error: ISO 31000:2018 and COSO ERM Framework

Criterion (TC 3.2.4)	ISO 31000:2018	COSO Framework
Time taken to recognize and correct an error.	3	4

COSO ERM Framework (4 -Partly true):

The COSO ERM Framework is designed to provide comprehensive guidance on enterprise risk management, integrating various aspects such as governance, strategy, and performance. Similar to ISO 31000, it emphasizes the importance of effective risk management and internal controls but does not offer specific metrics for error correction times. However, it slightly surpasses ISO 31000 in terms of relevance due to its more detailed focus on internal controls and monitoring activities. COSO ERM covers a broader scope of enterprise risk management, which includes internal controls and continuous monitoring, potentially contributing to quicker error detection and correction. The framework's detailed attention to internal controls and monitoring activities indirectly supports the recognition and correction of errors, even though it does not prescribe specific metrics. Continuous monitoring and improvement processes embedded in the framework can enhance error correction capabilities. Overall, the COSO ERM Framework offers a more structured approach to internal controls and monitoring activities than ISO 31000, making it more relevant to the criterion, hence the higher score of 4.

ISO 31000:2018 (3—neither):

The framework's primary focus is on risk assessment, treatment, and continuous improvement, rather than prescribing specific measures for monitoring error correction times. ISO 31000 can inform an organization's risk management practices, which could indirectly influence efforts to reduce the time it takes to address errors. However, the actual measurement and management of error recognition and correction times are typically addressed through incident response and quality control practices, which are managed separately from ISO 31000. As with COSO, ISO 31000 is in a similar position and does not directly address this specific criterion.

In summary, the COSO ERM Framework does not provide specific guidelines for measuring error correction times, but its focus on internal controls and continuous monitoring helps to indirectly improve error correction. However, it does not offer concrete metrics for the time taken to recognize and correct an error. The ISO 31000:2018 framework promotes an overall risk management process but does not focus on measuring the time taken to recognize and correct errors. It provides a general approach to continuous improvement and incident management, which can indirectly assist in error correction (Table 3.30) (Fig. 3.8).

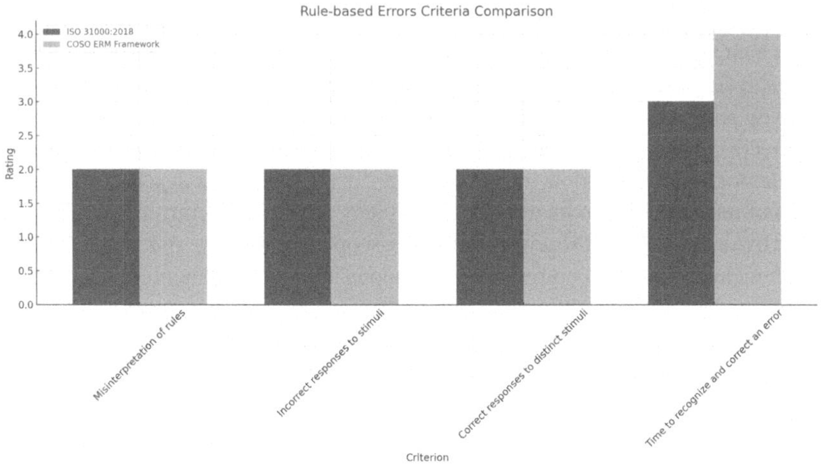

Fig. 3.8 Bar chart comparing the ISO 31000:2018 and COSO ERM Framework for Rule-based Errors Criteria

The bar chart above presents the comparison between ISO 31000:2018 and COSO ERM Framework for the "Rule-based errors" category, which includes:

- Number of times a rule was misinterpreted or not followed correctly
- Frequency of incorrect responses to specific stimuli or cues
- Percentage of correct responses to similar but distinct stimuli or cues
- Time taken to recognize and correct an error

Both frameworks generally show similar ratings across these criteria, except for the last criterion ("Time taken to recognize and correct an error"), where COSO ERM Framework has a slightly higher rating than ISO 31000:2018.

3.3.3 Knowledge-based Errors (Errors of Reasoning and Judgment)

Table 3.31 Number of logical fallacies committed during decision-making or problem-solving:: ISO 31000:2018 and COSO ERM Framework

Criterion (TC 3.3.1)	ISO 31000:2018	COSO ERM Framework
Number of logical fallacies committed during decision-making or problem-solving.	2	2

COSO ERM Framework (2—Does not apply in part):

The COSO framework primarily focuses on risk management, internal controls, and governance practices. It doesn't provide specific guidance or metrics for measuring the number of logical fallacies committed during decision-making or problem-solving. COSO promotes a risk-aware culture and effective internal controls, which can indirectly support the need for sound decision-making processes. However, it doesn't offer explicit recommendations for assessing this specific aspect related to logical fallacies. While COSO emphasizes the importance of robust internal controls and effective governance, it doesn't delve into the specifics of assessing logical reasoning errors during decision-making.

The identification and mitigation of logical fallacies in decision-making typically fall under critical thinking and logic training, areas that are managed separately from COSO's governance-oriented framework. COSO can provide a context for understanding and managing operational risks related to decision-making, but it does not provide tools or metrics for directly evaluating logical fallacies.

ISO 31000:2018 (2—Does not apply in part):

ISO 31000 offers a general risk management framework that encourages organizations to assess risks and take appropriate actions, including those related to decision-making. However, ISO 31000 does not provide specific guidance or metrics for measuring the number of logical fallacies committed during decision-making or problem-solving. The framework's primary focus is on risk assessment, treatment, and continuous improvement, rather than prescribing specific measures for monitoring logical reasoning errors. ISO 31000 can inform an organization's risk management practices, which could indirectly influence efforts to improve decision-making quality. However, the actual measurement and management of logical fallacies in decision-making are typically addressed through critical thinking training and logic assessment, areas that are managed separately from ISO 31000. As with COSO, ISO 31000 is in a similar position and does not directly address this specific criterion.

In summary, both the COSO ERM Framework and ISO 31000:2018 do not fully apply in part (2) to the criterion of measuring the number of logical fallacies committed during decision-making or problem-solving. While they emphasize the importance of effective risk management, controls, and decision-making processes, they do not provide specific guidance or metrics for quantifying logical fallacies. The identification and mitigation of logical reasoning errors in decision-making typically fall under critical thinking and logic assessment practices, which are managed separately from these risk management frameworks (Table 3.31).

Table 3.32 Consistency of decision-making with established principles or guidelines: ISO 31000:2018 and COSO ERM Framework

Criterion (TC 3.3.2)	ISO 31000:2018	COSO ERM Framework
Consistency of decision-making with established principles or guidelines.	4	4

COSO ERM Framework (4—Partly true):

The COSO framework places a strong emphasis on establishing and maintaining internal controls, governance structures, and risk management principles within an organization. COSO's principles and guidelines are aimed at ensuring that decisions are aligned with the organization's risk appetite and strategic objectives. While COSO encourages consistency in decision-making, it does not provide explicit guidance or metrics for measuring this consistency. The framework lacks specific tools for assessing the degree to which decisions align with established principles. Organizations implementing COSO may establish their own processes for monitoring and ensuring decision consistency, but this is not a direct focus of the framework. Overall, while COSO promotes the importance of consistency in decision-making, it does not fully provide a comprehensive methodology for evaluating it, making it partly true in this context.

ISO 31000:2018 (4—Partly true):

ISO 31000 offers a general risk management framework that encourages organizations to assess risks, establish risk criteria, and make informed decisions. The framework emphasizes aligning decisions with established risk criteria and principles, which contributes to decision-making consistency. However, ISO 31000 does not provide explicit tools or metrics for directly measuring the consistency of decision-making with established principles or guidelines. The framework sets the foundation for organizations to develop their own risk management processes, which may include mechanisms for ensuring decision consistency, but it does not prescribe a specific methodology. While ISO 31000 encourages the alignment of decisions with established principles, it does not fully address the detailed measurement of consistency, making it partly true in this context.

In summary, both the COSO ERM Framework and ISO 31000:2018 partially address the criterion of the consistency of decision-making with established principles or guidelines. While they emphasize the importance of aligning decisions with principles and risk criteria, neither framework provides specific tools or metrics for directly measuring the consistency of decision-making. Organizations implementing these frameworks typically need to develop their own processes or use additional tools to assess and ensure decision consistency effectively (Table 3.32).

Table 3.33 Time taken to reach a decision compared to the expected time given the complexity of the problem and available information: ISO 31000:2018 and COSO ERM Framework

Criterion (TC 3.3.3)	ISO 31000:2018	COSO ERM Framework
Time taken to reach a decision compared to the expected time given the complexity of the problem and available information.	2	2

COSO ERM Framework (2—Does not apply in part):

The COSO framework primarily focuses on risk management, internal controls, and governance practices. It does not directly address the measurement of the time taken to reach decisions. While COSO encourages sound decision-making as part of effective risk management, it does not provide specific guidance or metrics for assessing the timeliness of decisions. COSO emphasizes the importance of thorough risk assessments and data-driven decision-making, but it does not prescribe how to measure decision-making time against the complexity of the problem. The measurement of decision-making time is generally considered an operational or process-related metric and is not a primary focus of COSO. Organizations implementing COSO may incorporate time-related metrics into their risk management and decision-making processes, but this is not a direct aspect of the framework.

ISO 31000:2018 (2—Does not apply in part):

ISO 31000 offers a general risk management framework that encourages organizations to assess risks, make informed decisions, and continuously improve their risk management processes. However, ISO 31000 does not provide specific guidance or metrics for measuring the time taken to reach a decision compared to the expected time based on problem complexity. ISO 31000 emphasizes the importance of timely risk responses and decision-making but does not offer a structured approach for assessing this aspect. The framework sets the foundation for organizations to develop their risk management processes, and they may choose to include time-related metrics if they find it valuable for their specific context. Similar to COSO measuring decision-making time against problem complexity and available information is typically considered an operational or process-related metric and is not a primary focus of ISO 31000.

In summary, both the COSO ERM Framework and ISO 31000:2018 do not fully apply (2) to the criterion of measuring the time taken to reach a decision compared to the expected time given the complexity of the problem and available information. While they emphasize the importance of risk management and timely decision-making, neither framework provides specific guidance or metrics for directly evaluating decision-making time against problem complexity. Organizations may choose to incorporate such metrics into their processes, but it is not a central aspect of these risk management frameworks (Table 3.33).

Table 3.34 The degree of deviation from optimal outcomes or solutions: ISO 31000:2018 and COSO ERM Framework

Criterion (TC 3.3.4)	ISO 31000:2018	COSO ERM Framework
The degree of deviation from optimal outcomes or solutions.	4	4

COSO ERM Framework (4—Partly true):

The COSO framework primarily focuses on risk management, internal controls, and governance practices. It doesn't directly address the measurement of the degree of deviation from optimal outcomes. COSO emphasizes the importance of effective risk management processes and internal controls to mitigate risks. While not explicitly stated, one of the implicit goals is to reduce deviations from optimal outcomes. COSO encourages organizations to identify, assess, and manage risks that could affect the achievement of objectives. By doing so, organizations aim to minimize deviations from their intended outcomes. While COSO doesn't provide specific tools for measuring the degree of deviation, it provides a framework that can contribute to reducing such deviations through risk mitigation and control measures. Measuring the degree of deviation from optimal outcomes typically requires the use of performance metrics, which organizations may incorporate into their COSO-based risk management practices.

ISO 31000:2018 (4—Partly true):

ISO 31000 offers a general risk management framework that encourages organizations to assess risks, make informed decisions, and continuously improve risk management processes. While ISO 31000 does not directly address the measurement of the degree of deviation from optimal outcomes, its focus on risk assessment and treatment aligns with the objective of minimizing deviations. ISO 31000 emphasizes the importance of monitoring and reviewing risk treatment measures, which indirectly contributes to reducing deviations from optimal outcomes. The framework sets the foundation for organizations to develop their risk management processes, which may include performance metrics to measure and minimize deviations. ISO 31000 provides a risk-aware context that aligns with the goal of reducing deviations, but it does not offer specific tools or metrics for quantifying the degree of deviation.

In summary, both the COSO ERM Framework and ISO 31000:2018 partially address the criterion of measuring the degree of deviation from optimal outcomes or solutions. While they emphasize the importance of risk management, internal controls, and risk assessment, neither framework provides explicit tools or metrics for directly quantifying the degree of deviation. However, organizations implementing these frameworks often use performance metrics and monitoring processes as part of their risk management practices to reduce deviations from optimal outcomes (Table 3.34) (Fig. 3.9).

Here is the bar chart for the "Knowledge-based errors" category, comparing ISO 31000:2018 and COSO ERM Framework across various criteria:

- Number of logical fallacies committed during decision-making or problem-solving
- Consistency of decision-making with established principles or guidelines
- Time taken to reach a decision compared to the expected time
- The degree of deviation from optimal outcomes or solutions

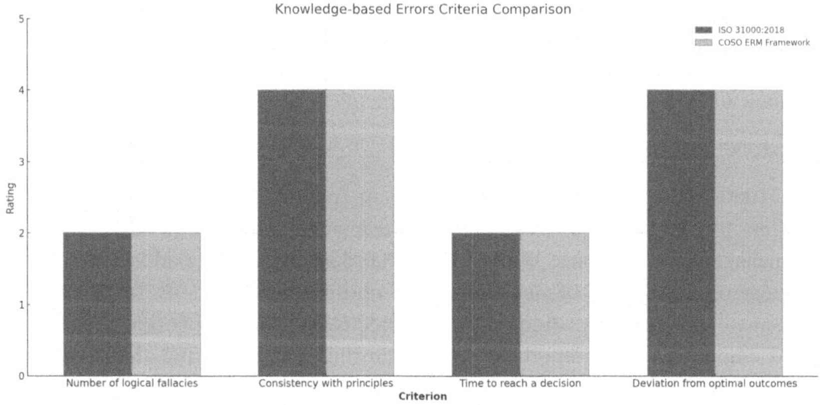

Fig. 3.9 Bar chart comparing the ISO 31000:2018 and COSO ERM Framework for Knowledge-based Error Criteria

Both frameworks show same ratings for the four criteria. They have a higher rating (4—Partly true) for the second ("Consistency of decision-making with established principles or guidelines" and fourth criterion ("Deviation from optimal outcomes") indicating a stronger alignment with these aspects.

3.4 SHELL-criteria

3.4.1 Software

Table 3.35 Robust incident response plan in place: ISO 31000:2018 and COSO ERM Framework

Criterion (TC 4.1.1)	ISO 31000:2018	COSO ERM Framework
Robust incident response plan in place.	4	4

COSO ERM Framework (4—Partly true):

The COSO framework primarily focuses on risk management, internal controls, and governance practices, and it indirectly supports having an incident response plan. While COSO emphasizes the importance of identifying, assessing, and managing risks, including those related to incidents, it doesn't provide specific guidance or templates for creating incident response plans. COSO's framework promotes a risk-aware culture and effective internal controls, which can contribute to the development of robust incident response capabilities. Organizations implementing COSO often integrate incident response planning into their broader risk management and internal control frameworks, making it partly true. However, the detailed development and maintenance of an incident response plan typically require specific expertise and guidance beyond what COSO provides.

ISO 31000:2018 (4—Partly true):

ISO 31000 offers a general risk management framework that encourages organizations to assess risks, make informed decisions, and establish risk treatment measures, including incident response plans. While ISO 31000 provides a foundational framework for risk management, it does not offer a detailed incident response plan template or step-by-step guidance. The framework promotes the need for a structured and well-documented approach to risk management, which includes incident response planning. ISO 31000's emphasis on monitoring and reviewing risk treatment measures indirectly supports the development of robust incident response capabilities. Organizations using ISO 31000 typically complement it with specialized guidance and standards for incident response planning to fully meet the requirement of having a robust incident response plan.

In summary, both the COSO ERM Framework and ISO 31000:2018 partly address the criterion of having a robust incident response plan in place. While they provide a foundation for risk management and indirectly support the development of incident response plans, they do not offer detailed templates or specific guidance for creating such plans. Organizations typically need to supplement these frameworks with specialized incident response standards and expertise to ensure they have a robust incident response plan in place (Table 3.35).

Table 3.36 Regularly updating software and ensuring it is secure and up-to-date: ISO 31000:2018 and COSO ERM Framework

Criterion (TC 4.1.2)	ISO 31000:2018	COSO ERM Framework
Regularly updating software and ensuring it is secure and up-to-date.	2	2

ISO 31000:2018 (2—Does not apply in part):

General Risk Management Framework: ISO 31000:2018 provides a broad framework for risk management that does not specifically address the technical aspects of software updates or cyber security (International Organization for Standardization (ISO), 2018a). The standard emphasizes assessing and managing risks related to organizational objectives, which may include IT-related risks, but lacks specifics on software maintenance (Purdy, 2010). While ISO 31000 encourages consideration of various risks, it does not provide detailed guidance on software maintenance (Hubbard, 2020). Organizations typically follow IT-specific standards like ISO 27001 for information security management to ensure software is regularly updated and secure (Calder and Watkins, 2019).

COSO ERM Framework (2—Does not apply in part):

The COSO framework centers on risk management, internal controls, and governance, without directly addressing software updates (Committee of Sponsoring Organizations of the Treadway Commission (COSO), 2017). While emphasizing risk management, including IT risks, COSO does not provide specific guidelines for software updates and cybersecurity (Beasley et al., 2005). The framework promotes a risk-aware culture, which may indirectly involve considerations for software security, but lacks specifics in software maintenance. IT Operational Practice Outside COSO Scope: Regular software updates and security are typically IT operational practices, addressed by IT governance and cybersecurity frameworks.

Summary: Both the COSO ERM Framework and ISO 31000:2018 partially apply to the criterion of regularly updating software and ensuring it is secure and up-to-date. These frameworks focus on broader risk management and governance principles and do not provide specific guidance on the technical aspects of software maintenance and cybersecurity. For specific practices in software updates and security, organizations often refer to IT governance and security standards and practices (Table 3.36).

Table 3.37 Conducting software testing to identify any potential vulnerabilities or weaknesses: ISO 31000:2018 and COSO ERM Framework

Criterion (TC 4.1.3)	ISO 31000:2018	COSO ERM Framework
Conducting software testing to identify any potential vulnerabilities or weaknesses.	2	2

ISO 31000:2018 (2—Does not apply in part):

General Risk Management Framework: ISO 31000:2018 provides a broad framework for risk management that does not specifically address software testing for vulnerabilities (International Organization for Standardization (ISO), 2018a).

Focus on Organizational Risks: The standard emphasizes assessing and managing risks related to organizational objectives, which may include IT-related risks, but lacks specifics on software testing (Purdy, 2010).

Consideration of a Wide Range of Risks: While ISO 31000 encourages consideration of various risks, it does not provide detailed guidance on the technical aspects of software testing (Hubbard, 2020).

Organizations typically follow cybersecurity standards like ISO 27001 or Open Worldwide Application Security Project (OWASP) guidelines for software testing (Calder and Watkins, 2019).

COSO ERM Framework (2—Does not apply in part):

The COSO framework centers on risk management, internal controls, and governance, without directly addressing software testing for vulnerabilities (Committee of Sponsoring Organizations of the Treadway Commission (COSO), 2017).

While emphasizing risk management, including IT risks, COSO does not provide specific guidelines for software testing (Beasley et al., 2005).

The framework promotes a risk-aware culture, which may indirectly involve considerations for secure software, but lacks specifics in software testing (Committee of Sponsoring Organizations of the Treadway Commission (COSO), 2017).

Regular software testing is typically an IT operational practice, addressed by IT governance and cybersecurity frameworks (Arena et al., 2010).

Summary: Both the COSO ERM Framework and ISO 31000:2018 partially apply to the criterion of conducting software testing to identify potential vulnerabilities or weaknesses. These frameworks focus on broader risk management and governance principles and do not provide specific guidance on the technical process of software testing for vulnerabilities. For specific practices in software testing, organizations often refer to IT governance and cybersecurity standards and practices (Table 3.37).

Table 3.38 Training to employees on how to use software and technology tools properly: ISO 31000:2018 and COSO Framework

Criterion (TC 4.1.4)	ISO 31000:2018	COSO ERM Framework
Training to employees on how to use software and technology tools properly.	2	2

ISO 31000:2018 (2—Does not apply in part):

ISO 31000:2018 provides a broad framework for risk management that does not specifically address employee training for software and technology tools (International Organization for Standardization (ISO), 2018a). The standard emphasizes assessing and managing risks related to organizational objectives, which may include technology use risks, but lacks specifics on training (Purdy, 2010). While ISO 31000 encourages consideration of a wide range of risks, including human factors, it does not provide detailed guidance on employee training (Hubbard, 2020). Specific training practices are typically covered under separate training and HR-related standards (International Organization for Standardization (ISO), 2018a).

COSO ERM Framework (2—Does not apply in part):

The COSO framework centers on risk management, internal controls, and governance, without directly addressing software and technology training (Committee of Sponsoring Organizations of the Treadway Commission (COSO), 2017). While emphasizing risk management, including IT risks, COSO does not provide specific guidelines for employee training in technology (Beasley et al., 2005). The framework promotes a risk-aware culture, which may indirectly involve training, but lacks specifics in technology training (Committee of Sponsoring Organizations of the Treadway Commission (COSO), 2017). COSO supports the importance of employee competence yet does not delve into technical training processes (Arena et al., 2010).

In summary, both ISO 31000:2018 and the COSO ERM Framework provide overarching guidelines on risk management and governance, with an indirect or minimal focus on specific employee training practices for software and technology tools (Table 3.38).

Here is the bar chart comparing the ISO 31000:2018 and COSO ERM Framework for various Software criteria. Each criterion is rated on a scale, with ratings reflecting the degree to which each framework addresses the criterion:

- Robust incident response plan
- Regularly updating software
- Conducting software testing
- Training on software use

Both frameworks received equal ratings for each criterion, as reflected in the chart (Fig. 3.10).

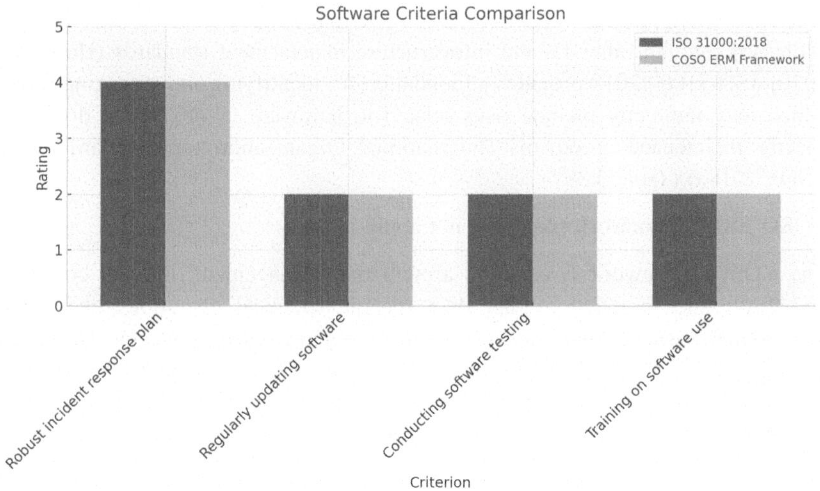

Fig. 3.10 Bar chart comparing the ISO 31000:2018 and COSO ERM Framework for various Software criteria

3.4.2 Hardware

Table 3.39 Conducting regular inspections and maintenance of hardware to ensure it is in good working condition: ISO 31000:2018 and COSO ERM Framework

Criterion (4.2.1)	ISO 31000:2018	COSO ERM Framework
Conducting regular inspections and maintenance of hardware to ensure it is in good working condition.	2	2

ISO 31000:2018 (2—Does not apply in part):

ISO 31000:2018 provides a generic framework for risk management, applicable across various types of risks and industries. It does not delve into specific operational practices like hardware maintenance (ISO, 2018). While the standard encourages organizations to consider a wide range of risks, including those associated with technology infrastructure, it does not offer detailed guidance on hardware maintenance (Purdy, 2010). Operational Practices Outside Scope: Specific operational practices like hardware inspections and maintenance are typically addressed through other IT and infrastructure management standards (Hubbard, 2020). ISO 31000:2018 provides a foundation for identifying and managing risks, which may indirectly include risks related to hardware failure, but it does not specify maintenance protocols (International Organization for Standardization (ISO), 2018a) (Table 3.39)

COSO ERM Framework (2—Does not apply in part):

The COSO framework is centered around risk management, internal controls, and governance practices, rather than specific technical operations like hardware maintenance (Committee of Sponsoring Organizations of the Treadway Commission (COSO), 2017). While COSO emphasizes risk management, including IT risks, it does not provide specific guidelines for conducting hardware inspections and maintenance (Beasley et al., 2005). The framework promotes a risk-aware culture and effective internal controls, which may indirectly involve proper hardware maintenance, but without specific technical guidance (Committee of Sponsoring Organizations of the Treadway Commission (COSO), 2017). COSO supports the importance of infrastructure reliability, yet it does not delve into the technical processes of maintaining hardware (Arena et al., 2010).

Both the COSO ERM Framework and ISO 31000:2018 partially apply to the criterion of conducting regular inspections and maintenance of hardware. These frameworks focus on broader risk management and governance principles and do not provide specific guidance on the technical aspects of hardware maintenance. For specific operational practices like hardware maintenance, organizations often refer to IT-specific standards and best practices. They do not provide specific guidelines for operational tasks like hardware maintenance, highlighting a need for supplementary standards to cover these aspects.

Table 3.40 Using high-quality hardware that meets safety standards: ISO 31000:2018 and COSO ERM Framework

Criterion (TC 4.2.2)	ISO 31000:2018	COSO ERM Framework
Using high-quality hardware that meets safety standards.	3	3

COSO ERM Framework (3—Neither):

The COSO ERM Framework, detailed in "Enterprise Risk Management — Integrating with Strategy and Performance" (Committee of Sponsoring Organizations of the Treadway Commission (COSO), 2017), focuses on broad risk management, internal controls, and governance practices. It does not delve into operational specifics like hardware quality and safety standards, indicating a more strategic than operational focus. In "Internal Control—Integrated Framework" (2013), COSO emphasizes the importance of identifying and managing risks, including those related to technology and infrastructure (The Committee of Sponsoring Organizations (COSO), 2013). However, it does not provide specific guidelines for hardware selection or safety standards, suggesting a gap in operational detail in this area. While COSO promotes a risk-aware culture and effective internal controls that may indirectly involve technology risk mitigation, it does not specifically address hardware quality or safety standards (Beasley et al., 2005).

ISO 31000:2018 (3—Neither):

ISO 31000:2018 offers a comprehensive risk management framework but does not specifically focus on hardware procurement, quality, or safety standards (International Organization for Standardization (ISO), 2018a). This highlights a gap in addressing specific operational standards related to hardware.

ISO 31000:2018 is primarily focusing on assessing and managing risks related to organizational objectives, including technology hardware (International Organization for Standardization (ISO), 2018a). However, it lacks specific guidance on hardware quality or safety standards.

ISO 31000 encourages considering a wide range of risks but does not provide detailed guidance on hardware quality and safety standards (Hubbard, 2020).

Both the COSO ERM Framework and ISO 31000:2018 recognize the importance of risk management and governance, including aspects related to technology. However, neither framework provides specific guidance on the operational aspects of hardware procurement, quality evaluation, or safety standards compliance. Therefore, organizations should integrate these frameworks with specialized standards and practices relevant to IT, engineering, and procurement for effective hardware quality and safety management (Table 3.40).

Table 3.41 Providing training to employees on how to use hardware safely and effectively: ISO 31000:2018 and COSO ERM Framework

Criterion (4.2.3)	ISO 31000:2018	COSO ERM Framework
Providing training to employees on how to use hardware safely and effectively.	2	2

COSO ERM Framework (2—Does not apply in part):

The COSO framework primarily addresses risk management, internal controls, and governance practices, without specifically focusing on technical training for hardware usage (Committee of Sponsoring Organizations of the Treadway Commission (COSO), 2017). While COSO emphasizes the importance of identifying and managing risks, including those related to technology, it does not provide specific guidelines for employee training on hardware usage (The Committee of Sponsoring Organizations (COSO), 2013). COSO promotes a risk-aware culture and effective internal controls, which may indirectly involve aspects of training, but the framework does not delve into the specifics of hardware training (Beasley et al., 2005).

ISO 31000:2018 (2—Does not apply in part):

ISO 31000 provides a comprehensive framework for risk management but does not specifically address employee training for hardware usage (International Organization for Standardization (ISO), 2018a). The framework's primary focus is on assessing and managing risks related to organizational objectives, which may include technology hardware, but lacks specific guidance on training for hardware usage (Purdy, 2010). ISO 31000 encourages consideration of a broad spectrum of risks, including human factors, but does not offer detailed guidance on the specifics of hardware training (Hubbard, 2020).

In summary, both the COSO ERM Framework and ISO 31000:2018 partially address the criterion of providing training to employees on hardware usage, focusing on broader risk management and governance principles. They do not provide specific guidance on the technical training process for hardware usage. Typically, organizations rely on separate training standards, HR-related practices, and best practices specific to their industry and technological needs to fulfill these training requirements (Table 3.41).

The bar chart below illustrates the comparison between ISO 31000:2018 and COSO ERM Framework for various Hardware criteria:

- Regular inspections and maintenance
- Using high-quality hardware
- Training on hardware use

Both frameworks show similar ratings across these criteria, indicating a consistent approach in addressing hardware-related aspects (Fig. 3.11).

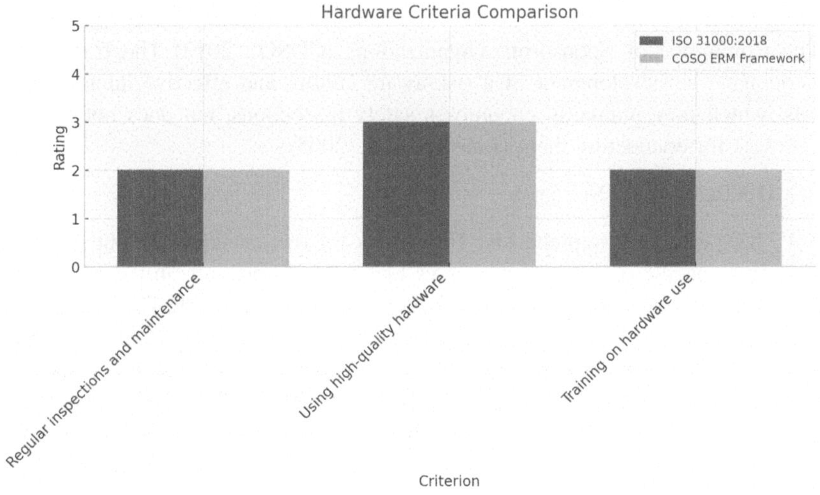

Fig. 3.11 Bar chart comparing the ISO 31000:2018 and COSO ERM Framework for various Hardware criteria

3.4.3 Environment

Table 3.42 Conducting regular safety inspections to identify potential hazards in the workplace: ISO 31000:2018 and COSO ERM Framework

Criterion (TC 4.3.1)	ISO 31000:2018	COSO ERM Framework
Conducting regular safety inspections to identify potential hazards in the workplace.	3	3

COSO ERM Framework (3—Neither):

The COSO ERM Framework focuses on broader aspects of risk management, internal controls, and governance practices, without specifically addressing operational practices like safety inspections (Committee of Sponsoring Organizations of the Treadway Commission (COSO), 2017). COSO emphasizes the importance of identifying and managing various risks, including those related to workplace safety, but it does not provide detailed guidance on conducting safety inspections (The Committee of Sponsoring Organizations (COSO), 2013) The framework encourages the development of a risk-aware culture and effective internal controls, which may indirectly encompass safety inspections, but does not specify processes for conducting them (Beasley et al., 2005).

ISO 31000:2018 (3—Neither):

ISO 31000 offers a comprehensive framework for risk management but does not delve into specific operational processes like safety inspections in the workplace (International Organization for Standardization (ISO), 2018a). The framework focuses on assessing and managing a wide range of risks associated with organizational objectives, which may include workplace safety, but lacks specific guidance on safety inspection procedures (Purdy, 2010). ISO 31000 encourages organizations to consider various risks, including safety risks, within its risk management processes, but it does not offer detailed guidance on conducting safety inspections (Hubbard, 2020).

In summary, both the COSO ERM Framework and ISO 31000:2018 do not fully address the specific criterion of conducting regular safety inspections to identify potential hazards in the workplace. They focus on broader principles of risk management and governance and lack specific guidance on the operational aspects of safety inspections. Organizations typically rely on industry-specific safety standards and regulations, such as those from OSHA in the United States, for detailed requirements regarding safety inspections (Table 3.42).

Table 3.43 Providing adequate lighting, ventilation, and other environmental controls to ensure a safe working environment: ISO 31000:2018 and COSO ERM Framework

Criterion (TC 4.3.2)	ISO 31000:2018	COSO ERM Framework
Providing adequate lighting, ventilation, and other environmental controls to ensure a safe working environment.	3	3

COSO ERM Framework (3—Neither):

The COSO ERM Framework primarily addresses broader aspects of risk management, internal controls, and governance practices, rather than delving into specific operational issues like environmental controls in the workplace (Reference: COSO, "Enterprise Risk Management — Integrating with Strategy and Performance," 2017).

While COSO emphasizes risk identification and management, including aspects related to workplace safety, it does not provide specific guidelines on environmental controls such as lighting and ventilation (The Committee of Sponsoring Organizations (COSO), 2013). COSO promotes a risk-aware culture which may indirectly encompass the maintenance of a safe working environment, but specifics on environmental control measures are not detailed within the framework (Beasley et al., 2005).

ISO 31000:2018 (3—Neither):

ISO 31000 provides a comprehensive framework for risk management but does not specifically address the technical details of environmental controls in the workplace (International Organization for Standardization (ISO), 2018a). The framework focuses on assessing and managing risks related to organizational objectives, including those associated with workplace safety and environment, but lacks detailed guidance on specific environmental (Purdy, 2010). ISO 31000 encourages organizations to consider a wide spectrum of risks, including environmental factors affecting the workplace, but does not delve into the specifics of implementing control measures like lighting and ventilation (Hubbard, 2020).

In summary, both the COSO ERM Framework and ISO 31000:2018 partially address the criterion of providing adequate environmental controls for a safe working environment, focusing on broader risk management and governance principles. They do not provide specific guidance on the technical aspects of implementing such environmental controls. Organizations typically need to refer to industry-specific safety and environmental standards and regulations, such as those from OSHA, for detailed requirements in these areas (Table 3.43).

Table 3.44 Providing training to employees on how to recognize and avoid environmental hazards: ISO 31000:2018 and COSO ERM Framework

Criterion (TC 4.3.3)	ISO 31000:2018	COSO ERM Framework
Providing training to employees on how to recognize and avoid environmental hazards.	2	2

COSO ERM Framework (2—Does not apply in part):

The COSO framework is primarily concerned with risk management, internal controls, and governance practices, and does not specifically focus on the technical aspects of environmental hazard recognition and avoidance training (Committee of Sponsoring Organizations of the Treadway Commission (COSO), 2017). While COSO emphasizes the importance of identifying and managing risks, including those related to environmental hazards, it does not provide detailed guidelines or requirements for specific employee training in this area (The Committee of Sponsoring Organizations (COSO), 2013) COSO promotes a risk-aware culture and effective internal control structures, which may indirectly involve training aspects, but it does not delve into the specifics of environmental hazard training (Beasley et al., 2005).

ISO 31000:2018 (2—Does not apply in part):

ISO 31000 provides a broad framework for risk management but does not offer specific guidance on the technical aspects of environmental hazard recognition and avoidance (International Organization for Standardization (ISO), 2018a). The framework's primary focus is on assessing and managing risks related to organizational objectives, which may include environmental hazards, but it does not offer detailed guidance on specific hazard recognition training (Purdy, 2010). ISO 31000 encourages organizations to consider a broad spectrum of risks, including environmental risks, but it does not delve into the specifics of hazard recognition training (Hubbard, 2020).

In summary, both the COSO ERM Framework and ISO 31000:2018 do not fully address the specific criterion of providing training to employees on recognizing and avoiding environmental hazards. These frameworks focus on broader risk management and governance principles and do not delve into the technical details of environmental hazard training. Organizations typically look to industry-specific safety and environmental standards and regulations to address these specific training requirements (Table 3.44).

Table 3.45 Encouraging a safety culture within the organization through regular communication, training, and feedback: ISO 31000:2018 and COSO ERM Framework

Criterion TC 4.3.4	ISO 31000:2018	COSO ERM Framework
Encouraging a safety culture within the organization through regular communication, training, and feedback.	4	4

COSO ERM Framework (4—Partly true):

The COSO framework, with its focus on risk management, internal controls, and governance practices, indirectly supports the development of a safety culture by emphasizing risk awareness and effective control structures (Committee of Sponsoring Organizations of the Treadway Commission (COSO), 2017).While not specifically geared towards safety culture, COSO encourages the establishment of a risk-aware culture that includes elements such as regular communication, training, and feedback, which are integral to safety culture (The Committee of Sponsoring Organizations (COSO), 2013). COSO recognizes the critical role of leadership in promoting a culture of risk management, which inherently includes considerations for safety (Beasley et al., 2005).

ISO 31000:2018 (4—Partly true):

ISO 31000 acknowledges the significance of organizational culture in effective risk management. This includes aspects that contribute to a safety culture, such as communication, training, and feedback (International Organization for Standardization (ISO), 2018a). The framework encourages organizations to develop a culture that is aware of risks, including safety risks, through effective communication and training strategies (Purdy, 2010). ISO 31000 emphasizes the importance of involving all levels of the organization in risk management processes, which is a key element in fostering a comprehensive safety culture (Hubbard, 2020).

In summary, both the COSO ERM Framework and ISO 31000:2018 partially address the criterion of encouraging a safety culture within the organization. They focus primarily on risk management and governance but indirectly support the development of a safety culture by promoting risk awareness, communication, and feedback mechanisms. However, organizations may need to complement these frameworks with specialized safety management standards and practices for a more comprehensive approach to developing a safety culture (Table 3.45).

Table 3.46 Holding employees accountable for following security policies and procedures. ISO 31000:2018 and COSO ERM Framework

Criterion (TC 4.3.5)	ISO 31000:2018	COSO ERM Framework
Holding employees accountable for following security policies and procedures.	4	4

COSO ERM Framework (4—Partly true):

The COSO ERM Framework's primary focus is on establishing and maintaining effective risk management, internal controls, and governance practices, which indirectly relate to the enforcement of security policies and procedures (Committee of Sponsoring Organizations of the Treadway Commission (COSO), 2017).

COSO emphasizes the significance of establishing robust internal controls and governance structures to manage various risks, including those related to security(The Committee of Sponsoring Organizations (COSO), 2013)

The framework recognizes the need for accountability in risk management, including adherence to security policies, but does not provide specific mechanisms or tools for enforcement (Beasley et al., 2005).

ISO 31000:2018 (4—Partly true):

ISO 31000 provides a general framework for risk management, which encompasses the management of security risks and compliance with security policies and procedures (International Organization for Standardization (ISO), 2018a). The standard encourages organizations to assess various risks, including security risks, and to take appropriate actions to manage these risks effectively (Purdy, 2010). ISO 31000 emphasizes the importance of accountability in the risk management process, supporting the idea that employees should adhere to security policies and procedures. However, it does not offer specific enforcement mechanisms (Hubbard, 2020).

In summary, both the COSO ERM Framework and ISO 31000:2018 partially address the criterion of ensuring employee accountability for following security policies and procedures. While they focus primarily on risk management and governance, they indirectly support the concept of accountability in security. However, they do not provide specific enforcement mechanisms or tools, leaving it to organizations to develop and implement these measures within their internal control and risk management frameworks (Table 3.46).

Table 3.47 Encouraging employees to report safety concerns or incidents: ISO 31000:2018 and COSO ERM Framework

Criterion (TC 4.3.6)	ISO 31000:2018	COSO Framework
Encouraging employees to report safety concerns or incidents.	4	4

COSO Framework (4—Partly true):

The COSO Framework encourages the identification of a wide range of risks, including safety-related risks. It emphasizes the importance of creating a culture where employees are encouraged to report any concerns (Committee of Sponsoring Organizations of the Treadway Commission (COSO), 2017). Organizations using COSO principles are advised to cultivate an environment where employees feel safe and comfortable reporting safety concerns, although this may require the implementation of specific measures beyond what COSO directly provides (The Committee of Sponsoring Organizations (COSO), 2013).

ISO 31000:2018 (4—Partly true):

ISO 31000 provides a general risk management framework that encompasses a variety of risks, including safety risks. It highlights the significance of risk reporting and communication within the organization (International Organization for Standardization (ISO), 2018a). The framework encourages the development of a culture that prioritizes risk awareness and open communication, which includes the reporting of safety concerns or incidents (Purdy, 2010). While ISO 31000 underscores the need for open communication channels, it does not provide detailed guidance on specific mechanisms for facilitating the reporting of safety concerns (Hubbard, 2020).

In summary, both the COSO ERM Framework and ISO 31000:2018 partially address the criterion of encouraging employees to report safety concerns or incidents. These frameworks highlight the importance of a risk-aware culture and open communication, but they do not offer detailed practices or mechanisms for safety reporting. Therefore, organizations may need to develop and implement specific strategies to encourage and facilitate the reporting of safety issues effectively (Table 3.47).

Table 3.48 Monitoring the level of cognitive, physical, and emotional demands placed on individuals or teams, as well as the distribution of workload among team members: ISO 31000:2018 and COSO ERM Framework

Criterion (TC 4.3.7)	ISO 31000:2018	COSO ERM Framework
Monitoring the level of cognitive, physical, and emotional demands placed on individuals or teams, as well as the distribution of workload among team members.	2	2

COSO ERM Framework (2—Does not apply in part):

The COSO ERM Framework is centered on risk management, internal controls, and governance practices, without directly addressing the monitoring of cognitive, physical, or emotional demands or workload distribution among employees (Committee of Sponsoring Organizations of the Treadway Commission (COSO), 2017). While COSO emphasizes effective risk management and control structures, it does not provide specific guidance on the assessment or monitoring of cognitive, physical, and emotional demands or workload distribution (The Committee of Sponsoring Organizations (COSO), 2013). COSO indirectly supports the concept of ensuring that employees are not overburdened with work as part of effective risk management but lacks specific tools or methodologies for this purpose (Beasley et al., 2005).

ISO 31000:2018 (2—Does not apply in part):

ISO 31000 provides a general framework for risk management but does not specifically address the monitoring of cognitive, physical, or emotional demands or workload distribution (International Organization for Standardization (ISO), 2018a). The framework focuses on identifying and managing risks related to organizational objectives, which may indirectly involve considerations related to workload and demands but does not provide specific tools for monitoring these aspects (Purdy, 2010). Organizations using ISO 31000 may need to integrate it with other relevant standards or frameworks that address workload management and employee well-being, such as occupational health and safety standards and human resources management practices (Hubbard, 2020).

In summary, both the COSO ERM Framework and ISO 31000:2018 partially address the criterion of monitoring cognitive, physical, and emotional demands and workload distribution among team members. They focus on risk management and governance but do not provide specific guidance or tools for managing workload-related aspects. Organizations should look to specialized frameworks and practices, like occupational health and safety standards and human resources management practices, to address these specific considerations comprehensively (Table 3.48).

Table 3.49 Stress and Fatigue: ISO 31000:2018 and COSO ERM Framework

Criterion (TC 4.3.8)	ISO 31000:2018	COSO ERM Framework
Stress and Fatigue: This includes the impact of stress, fatigue, and other psychological factors on individual and team performance, as well as strategies for managing and mitigating these factors; e.g. stress and fatigue management: Implementing programs to manage stress and fatigue, such as providing opportunities for rest and recovery, offering stress reduction techniques, and promoting healthy lifestyle habits.	2	2

COSO ERM Framework (2—Does not apply in part):

The COSO ERM Framework is centered on risk management, internal controls, and governance practices, and does not explicitly address the management of stress and fatigue (Committee of Sponsoring Organizations of the Treadway Commission (COSO), 2017). While COSO recognizes the importance of human factors in risk management, it does not provide specific guidance or tools for assessing or managing stress, fatigue, or other psychological factors (The Committee of Sponsoring Organizations (COSO), 2013). COSO may indirectly support stress and fatigue management by encouraging organizations to consider human factors in risk assessments, but it does not offer detailed strategies for managing these aspects (Beasley et al., 2005).

ISO 31000:2018 (2—Does not apply in part):

ISO 31000 provides a general framework for risk management, which includes the identification and management of a wide range of risks that could affect individual and team performance, potentially encompassing stress and fatigue (International Organization for Standardization (ISO), 2018a). However, ISO 31000 does not offer specific guidance or programs for managing stress and fatigue, focusing more broadly on risk management (Purdy, 2010). The framework emphasizes a holistic approach to risk management, considering various internal and external factors that could impact organizational objectives, including stress and fatigue indirectly (Hubbard, 2020).

In summary, both the COSO ERM Framework and ISO 31000:2018 partially address the criterion of stress and fatigue management. They focus primarily on risk management and governance and do not provide detailed guidance or tools for managing stress, fatigue, or psychological factors. Organizations should look to specialized standards, guidelines, and best practices in occupational health and safety and human resources management to effectively address stress and fatigue management (Table 3.49) (Fig. 3.12).

The bar chart below shows the comparison between ISO 31000:2018 and COSO ERM Framework for various Environment criteria:

- Conducting regular safety inspections
- Providing adequate environmental controls
- Training on recognizing and avoiding environmental hazards
- Providing training to employees on how to recognize and avoid environmental hazards.
- Encouraging a safety culture
- Encouraging employees to report safety concerns
- Monitoring cognitive, physical, and emotional demands and workload
- Managing stress and fatigue

Both frameworks demonstrate equal ratings across these environmental criteria, indicating a consistent approach in addressing environmental aspects within organizations.

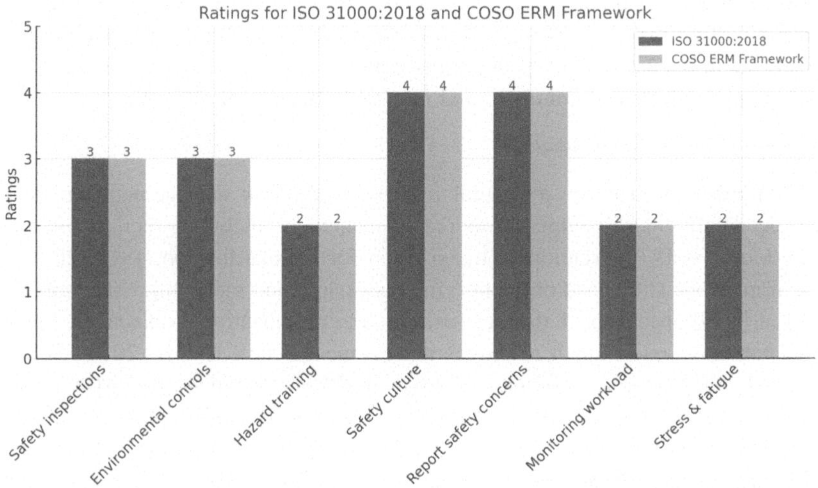

Fig. 3.12 Bar chart comparing the ISO 31000:2018 and COSO ERM Framework for various Environment criteria

3.4.4 Liveware

Table 3.50 Recruiting and Retention of qualified and experience staff: ISO 31000:2018 and COSO ERM Framework

Criterion (TC 4.4.1)	ISO 31000:2018	COSO ERM Framework
Recruiting and Retention of qualified and experience staff	3	3

COSO ERM Framework (3—Neither):

The COSO ERM Framework's primary focus is on risk management, internal controls, and governance practices. It does not delve into the specifics of human resources management, including aspects of recruiting and retention (Committee of Sponsoring Organizations of the Treadway Commission (COSO), 2017).

While COSO recognizes the significance of having skilled and experienced personnel for effective risk management, it does not provide explicit strategies or tools for their recruitment and retention (The Committee of Sponsoring Organizations (COSO), 2013). COSO underscores the value of qualified personnel in risk management but stops short of providing detailed guidance on how organizations should approach their recruitment and retention (Beasley et al., 2005).

ISO 31000:2018 (3—Neither):

ISO 31000:2018 provides a general framework for risk management but does not specifically address human resources management, including recruitment and retention of staff (International Organization for Standardization (ISO), 2018a). The framework is focused on identifying, assessing, and managing risks, considering a broad spectrum of risk factors affecting organizational objectives, but it does not delve into human resources management details (Purdy, 2010). While acknowledging the role of human resources in risk management, ISO 31000 does not offer specific guidance on recruitment or retention strategies (Hubbard, 2020).

In summary, both the COSO ERM Framework and ISO 31000:2018 do not fully address the criterion of recruiting and retaining qualified and experienced staff, as they primarily focus on risk management and governance. They lack specific guidance or tools for human resources management, necessitating that organizations refer to dedicated human resources practices and standards to effectively manage recruitment and retention (Table 3.50).

Table 3.51 Conducting background checks on all employees who have access to sensitive information: ISO 31000:2018 and COSO ERM Framework

Criterion (TC 4.4.2)	ISO 31000:2018	COSO ERM Framework
Conducting background checks on all employees who have access to sensitive information.	4	4

COSO ERM Framework (4—Partly true):

The COSO ERM Framework places a strong emphasis on establishing robust internal controls and effectively managing risks, including those related to information security, which is an integral component of an organization's risk management process (Committee of Sponsoring Organizations of the Treadway Commission (COSO), 2017). COSO's framework, while not explicitly addressing background checks, stresses the importance of assessing and managing risks associated with handling sensitive information, thereby implying the need for thorough vetting procedures such as background checks (The Committee of Sponsoring Organizations (COSO), 2013).

The framework advocates for the implementation of appropriate controls and safeguards to protect sensitive information, underlining the role of comprehensive security measures including background checks (Beasley et al., 2005).

ISO 31000:2018 (4—Partly true):

ISO 31000 provides a broad framework for risk management, encouraging organizations to address all relevant risks, including those related to information security, which can encompass strategies such as conducting background (International Organization for Standardization (ISO), 2018a). The standard emphasizes the importance of identifying and assessing risks associated with sensitive information, suggesting the implementation of controls and mitigation strategies that could include background checks (Purdy, 2010). ISO 31000 encourages the implementation of effective controls and mitigation strategies to manage risks, inclusive of those related to information security, where background checks could be a key component (Hubbard, 2020).

In summary, both the COSO ERM Framework and ISO 31000:2018 partially address the criterion of conducting background checks, focusing on managing information security risks, which indirectly supports the practice. However, they do not provide explicit instructions for conducting background checks, suggesting that organizations should integrate these frameworks with specific information security standards and best practices (Table 3.51).

Table 3.52 Training and Experience: ISO 31000:2018 and COSO ERM Framework

Criterion (TC 4.4.3)	ISO 31000:2018	COSO ERM Framework
Training and Experience: This includes the knowledge, skills, and experience of individuals or teams, as well as the training and development opportunities provided to support their performance.	4	4

COSO ERM Framework (4—Partly true):

The COSO ERM Framework recognizes the need for qualified and competent personnel in managing risks and implementing internal controls effectively. This requirement is critical for identifying, assessing, and mitigating risks (Committee of Sponsoring Organizations of the Treadway Commission (COSO), 2017).

COSO underscores the importance of having personnel with the right knowledge and skills in risk management. However, it does not provide detailed guidelines on specific training and development programs (The Committee of Sponsoring Organizations (COSO), 2013). While emphasizing the importance of personnel competence, COSO leaves the responsibility of implementing appropriate training and development initiatives to individual organizations (Beasley et al., 2005).

ISO 31000:2018 (4—Partly true):

ISO 31000:2018 encourages organizations to consider the competency and expertise of individuals or teams involved in risk management. It highlights the role of personnel competence in the effectiveness of risk management processes(International Organization for Standardization (ISO), 2018a). Although the framework acknowledges the necessity of knowledgeable and skilled personnel in risk management, it does not delve into specifics regarding training and development programs (Purdy, 2010). ISO 31000 places the onus on organizations to establish their own training and development initiatives, ensuring personnel possess the necessary expertise for effective risk management (Hubbard, 2020).

In summary, both the COSO ERM Framework and ISO 31000:2018 partially address the criterion of "Training and Experience." They emphasize the importance of competent individuals or teams in effective risk management but stop short of providing specific guidance on training and development programs. Consequently, organizations employing these frameworks are advised to complement them with their own human resources and training standards to ensure their personnel are adequately equipped with the required knowledge and skills (Table 3.52).

Table 3.53 Providing training to employees on how to work safely and effectively: ISO 31000:2018 and COSO ERM Framework

Criterion (TC 4.4.4)	ISO 31000:2018	COSO ERM Framework
Providing training to employees on how to work safely and effectively.	3	3

COSO ERM Framework (3—Neither):

The COSO framework primarily focuses on risk management, internal controls, and governance practices but does not explicitly address workplace safety. Safety is a critical aspect of overall risk management. However, the COSO framework's broader focus on risk management does not extend into detailed instructions on safety training (Fraser et al., 2021). While COSO emphasizes the importance of managing risks and internal controls, it does not explicitly delve into the specifics of workplace safety or safety training (Beasley et al., 2005),(Fraser et al., 2021). Organizations using COSO may need to complement it with workplace safety standards and regulations to ensure that employees receive proper training in safety practices. COSO indirectly supports the criterion by emphasizing the importance of competent personnel, which includes being trained to work safely, but it does not provide specific safety training guidelines.

ISO 31000:2018 (3—Neither):

While ISO 31000 underscores the importance of competent personnel in effective risk management, it stops short of addressing specific areas such as workplace safety training (International Organization for Standardization (ISO), 2018a). ISO 31000 provides a high-level approach to risk management, focusing more on the overarching strategy and process rather than delving into the detailed operational aspects like safety training (Purdy, 2010). Organizations adopting ISO 31000 are encouraged to integrate specific operational practices, such as safety training, into their overall risk management framework, even though the standard itself does not explicitly cover these aspects (Hubbard, 2020). ISO 31000 indirectly supports the criterion of having competent individuals by emphasizing their role in risk management. However, the framework does not provide specific guidelines or methodologies for safety training, suggesting the need for additional standards or practices focused on this area (Talbot and Jakeman, 2011). Similar to COSO, ISO 31000 indirectly supports the criterion by emphasizing the importance of competent individuals, who should be trained to work safely, but it does not offer specific safety training guidance.

In summary, both the COSO ERM Framework and ISO 31000:2018 neither fully apply (3—Neither) to the criterion of providing training to employees on how to work safely and effectively. These frameworks primarily focus on risk management, internal controls, and governance, and they do not provide specific guidance on workplace safety training. Organizations should refer to dedicated safety standards and regulations to establish proper safety training programs for their employees (Table 3.53) (Fig. 3.13).

The bar chart below presents the comparison between ISO 31000:2018 and COSO ERM Framework for the Liveware criteria:

- Recruiting and retention of qualified and experienced staff
- Conducting background checks on employees with access to sensitive information

- Training and experience
- Providing training to employees on how to work safely and effectively

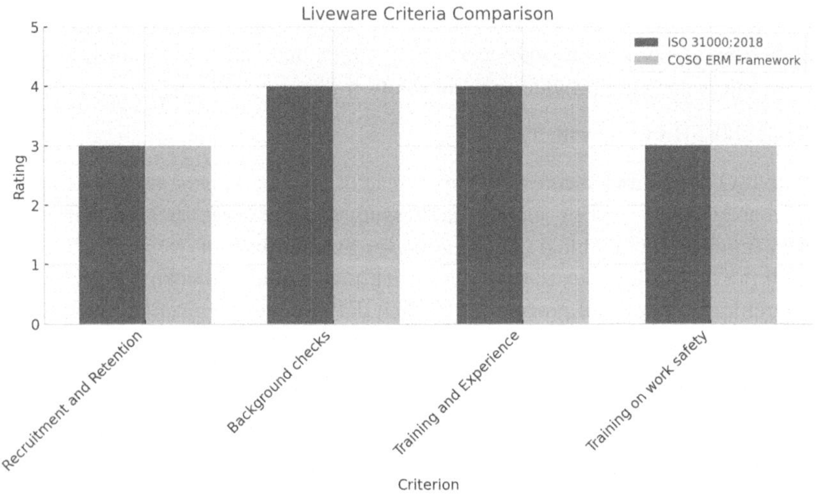

Fig. 3.13 Bar chart comparing the ISO 31000:2018 and COSO ERM Framework for various Liveware criteria

Both frameworks have received similar ratings for each of these criteria, highlighting their consistent approach in addressing aspects related to Liveware.

3.4.5 Liveware-Liveware Interface

Table 3.54 Communication: ISO 31000:2018 and COSO ERM Framework

Criterion (TC 4.5.1)	ISO 31000:2018	COSO ERM Framework
Communication: This includes the methods and channels of communication between individuals or teams, including verbal, written, and electronic communication.	4	5

COSO ERM Framework (5—Fully applicable):

The COSO ERM Framework places significant emphasis on communication as a key component of effective risk management and internal control. It underscores the need for effective and efficient communication channels within an organization (Committee of Sponsoring Organizations of the Treadway Commission (COSO), 2017). COSO highlights the importance of clear, transparent, and ongoing communication to foster a risk-aware culture within organizations, emphasizing both formal and informal communication channels (The Committee of Sponsoring Organizations (COSO), 2013). The framework offers specific guidance on how to establish effective communication processes, ensuring that risk information is adequately disseminated and understood throughout the organization (Beasley et al., 2014).

ISO 31000:2018 (4—Partly true):

ISO 31000 recognizes the importance of communication in the context of risk management, although it provides a more high-level approach compared to the COSO framework (International Organization for Standardization (ISO), 2018a). While ISO 31000 underscores the significance of communication, it offers high-level guidance as part of its broader risk management principles, rather than detailed methodologies (Purdy, 2010).

The standard encourages organizations to establish a communication framework as part of their risk management strategy, facilitating the sharing and understanding of risk-related information (Hubbard, 2020).

In summary, the COSO ERM Framework is fully applicable (5—Fully applicable) to the criterion of communication, providing comprehensive guidance on establishing effective communication processes within organizations. On the other hand, ISO 31000:2018 is partly true (4—Partly true) for this criterion as it recognizes the importance of communication but provides less detailed guidance compared to COSO. Organizations looking for more specific direction on communication methods may find COSO more beneficial, while ISO 31000 offers a broader perspective on risk management principles (Table 3.54).

Table 3.55 Teamwork: ISO 31000:2018 and COSO ERM Framework

Criterion (4.5.2)	ISO 31000:2018	COSO ERM Framework
Teamwork: This includes the collaboration and coordination of work between individuals or teams, as well as the development of shared goals and objectives.	4	4

COSO ERM Framework (4—Partly true):

The COSO ERM Framework highlights the importance of collaboration and coordination in achieving risk management objectives. It advocates for integrated risk management processes that require teamwork across different organizational levels (Committee of Sponsoring Organizations of the Treadway Commission (COSO), 2017).

COSO emphasizes the role of teamwork in effective internal control systems, suggesting that collaboration among various departments is crucial for identifying and managing risks effectively (The Committee of Sponsoring Organizations (COSO), 2013).

ISO 31000:2018 (4—Partly true):

ISO 31000:2018 promotes the development of shared risk management objectives, emphasizing the role of teamwork in achieving these goals. However, it offers a high-level approach rather than specific methods for fostering teamwork (International Organization for Standardization (ISO), 2018a). While ISO 31000 recognizes the importance of teamwork in risk management, it does not provide extensive guidance on specific practices to enhance collaboration or coordination among (Purdy, 2010). Organizations implementing ISO 31000 may need to develop additional strategies for promoting effective teamwork and achieving shared risk management goals, as the standard provides guiding principles rather than detailed instructions (Hubbard, 2020).

In summary, both the COSO ERM Framework and ISO 31000:2018 recognize the significance of teamwork in risk management, focusing on collaboration, coordination, and shared objectives. However, they provide less detailed guidance on how to foster these aspects. As a result, organizations using these frameworks should develop their strategies for promoting effective teamwork within their specific contexts (Table 3.55).

Table 3.56 Leadership style and conflict resolution: ISO 31000:2018 and COSO ERM Framework

Criterion (TC 4.5.3)	ISO 31000:2018	COSO ERM Framework
Leadership style and conflict resolution: Developing effective leadership practices that support communication, collaboration, and teamwork, such as setting clear expectations, providing feedback and coaching in conflict situations.	3	3

COSO ERM Framework (3—Neither):

The COSO ERM Framework primarily concentrates on risk management, internal controls, and governance, without delving deeply into leadership styles or conflict resolution. Its core focus is the strategic integration of risk management with overall organizational governance (Committee of Sponsoring Organizations of the Treadway Commission (COSO), 2017). While COSO recognizes the importance of leadership and the tone at the top in fostering a risk-aware culture, it does not offer detailed guidance on specific leadership practices or conflict resolution strategies (The Committee of Sponsoring Organizations (COSO), 2013). COSO implies that it is the responsibility of individual organizations to define their own leadership practices and conflict resolution strategies within the broader context of their risk management framework (Beasley et al., 2014).

ISO 31000:2018 (3—Neither):

ISO 31000:2018 is mainly oriented towards providing guidelines for risk management principles and processes and does not specifically address leadership styles or conflict resolution (International Organization for Standardization (ISO), 2018a). The standard acknowledges the crucial role of leadership in risk management but stops short of providing explicit guidance on how to develop leadership practices or conflict resolution strategies (Purdy, 2010). ISO 31000 encourages organizations to integrate risk management into their overall governance structures, implying the importance of leadership, but does not prescribe specific approaches to leadership style or conflict resolution (Hubbard, 2020).

In conclusion, both the COSO ERM Framework and ISO 31000:2018 provide a foundational understanding of the role of leadership in risk management. However, neither framework fully addresses the specific aspects of leadership style and conflict resolution, leaving the responsibility to the organizations to develop and implement these practices within the context of their risk management strategies.

Here is the bar chart for the "Liveware-Liveware Interface" category, comparing ISO 31000:2018 and COSO ERM Framework:

- Communication
- Teamwork
- Leadership style and conflict resolution

The COSO ERM Framework shows a slightly higher rating for the criterion "Communication" compared to ISO 31000:2018. For the other two criteria, both frameworks have similar ratings, indicating a consistent approach in addressing teamwork and leadership style and conflict resolution (Table 3.56) (Fig. 3.14).

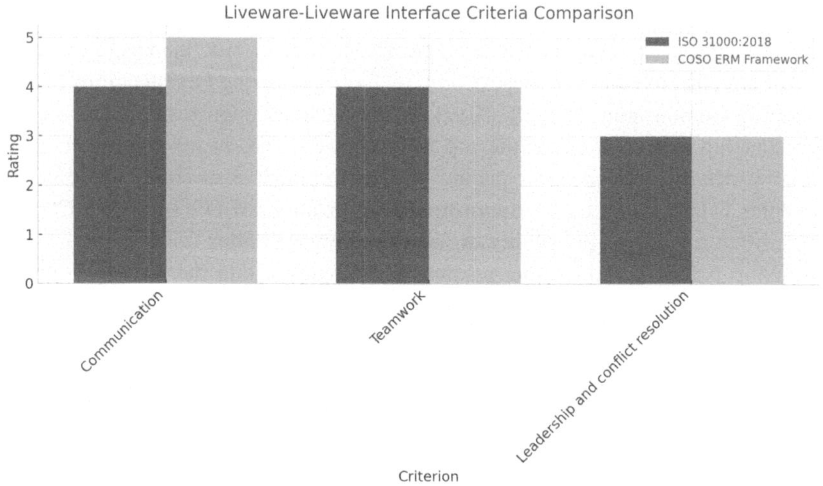

Fig. 3.14 Bar chart comparing the ISO 31000:2018 and COSO ERM Framework for various Liveware-Liveware criteria

The table of overall results can be found on the following page (Table 3.57).

Table 3.57 Overall findings

Spalte1	Spalte2	Spalte3	Spalte4
Test criteria (TC)	Sub criteria	ISO 3100:2018	COSO ERM Framework
TC 1.1: Competition versus partnership orientation dilemma	–	5	4
TC 1.2: Stable continuity versus dynamic change		5	1
TC 2.1: Deal with failure	Number of reported failures within a given period (TC 2.1.1)	3	4
	Percentage of reported failures that were analyzed and addressed (TC 2.1.2)	3	4
	Time taken to analyze and address failures (TC 2.1.3)	3	4
	Effectiveness of the solutions implemented to address failures (TC 2.1.4)	4	4
TC 2.2: Questioning simplistic interpretations	Frequency of questioning by team members during meetings or discussions (TC 2.2.1)	4	4
	Number of different perspectives considered when making decisions (TC 2.2.2)	4	4
	Percentage of decisions made after considering multiple perspectives (TC 2.2.3)	4	4
	Effectiveness of decisions made after considering multiple perspectives (TC 2.2.4)	4	4
TC 2.3: Sensitivity to operational processes	Number of reported process deviations within a given period (TC 2.3.1)	3	4
	Percentage of process deviations that were analyzed and addressed (TC 2.3.2)	3	4

(continued)

Table 3.57 (continued)

Spalte1	Spalte2	Spalte3	Spalte4
	Time taken to analyse and address process deviations (TC 2.3.3)	3	4
	Effectiveness of the solutions implemented to address process deviations (TC 2.3.4)	4	4
TC 2.4: Striving for resilience	Frequency of proactive measures taken to prevent failures or process deviations (TC 2.4.1)	4	4
	Number of backup or redundancy systems in place (TC 2.4.2)	3	3
	Time taken to recover from failures or process deviations (TC 2.4.3)	3	3
	Effectiveness of the solutions implemented to recover from failures or process deviations (TC 2.4.4)	3	3
TC 2.5: Pay attention to subject matter expertise	Number of reported incidents related to lack of expertise within a given time period (TC 2.5.1)	3	3
	Percentage of team members with relevant expertise or qualifications (TC 2.5.2)	2	2
	Frequency of seeking advice or guidance from team members with relevant expertise (TC 2.5.3)	4	4
	Effectiveness of the solutions implemented based on advice or guidance from team members with relevant expertise (TC 2.5.4)	4	4
TC 3.1: Skill-based errors (slips and oversights)	Frequency of certain errors compared to the expected number of errors given the task complexity and individual skill level (TC 3.1.1)	2	2

(continued)

Table 3.57 (continued)

Spalte1	Spalte2	Spalte3	Spalte4
	Time taken to complete a task compared to the expected time given the task complexity and individual skill level (TC 3.1.2)	2	2
	Consistency in performing the task correctly over multiple attempts (TC 3.1.3)	2	2
	Reaction time to unexpected events or changes in the task (TC 3.1.4)	2	2
TC 3.2: Rule-based errors (errors of confusion and recognition)	Number of times a rule was misinterpreted or not followed correctly (TC 3.2.1)	2	2
	Frequency of incorrect responses to specific stimuli or cues (TC 3.2.2)	2	2
	Percentage of correct responses to similar but distinct stimuli or cues (TC 3.2.3)	2	2
	Time taken to recognize and correct an error (TC 3.2.4)	3	4
TC 3.3: Knowledge-based errors (errors of reasoning and judgment)	Number of logical fallacies committed during decision-making or problem-solving (TC 3.3.1)	2	2
	Consistency of decision-making with established principles or guidelines (TC 3.3.2)	4	4
	Time taken to reach a decision compared to the expected time given the complexity of the problem and available information (TC 3.3.3)	2	2
	The degree of deviation from optimal outcomes or solutions (TC 3.3.4)	4	4

(continued)

Table 3.57 (continued)

Spalte1	Spalte2	Spalte3	Spalte4
TC 4.1: Software	Having a robust incident response plan in place (TC 4.1.1)	4	4
	Regularly updating software and ensuring it is secure and up-to-date (TC 4.1.2)	2	2
	Conducting software testing to identify any potential vulnerabilities or weaknesses (TC 4.1.3)	2	2
	Training to employees on how to use software and technology tools properly (TC 4.1.4)	2	2
TC 4.2: Hardware	Conducting regular inspections and maintenance of hardware to ensure it is in good working condition (TC 4.2.1)	2	2
	Using high-quality hardware that meets safety standards (TC 4.2.2)	3	3
	Providing training to employees on how to use hardware safely and effectively (TC 4.2.3)	2	2
TC 4.3: Environment	Conducting regular safety inspections to identify potential hazards in the workplace (TC 4.3.1)	3	3
	Providing adequate lighting, ventilation, and other environmental controls to ensure a safe working environment (TC 4.3.2)	3	3
	Providing training to employees on how to recognize and avoid environmental hazards (TC 4.3.3)	2	2
	Encouraging a safety culture within the organization through regular communication, training, and feedback (TC 4.3.4)	4	4

(continued)

Table 3.57 (continued)

Spalte1	Spalte2	Spalte3	Spalte4
	Holding employees accountable for following security policies and procedures (TC 4.3.5)	4	4
	Encouraging employees to report safety concerns or incidents (TC 4.3.6)	4	4
	Monitoring the level of cognitive, physical, and emotional demands placed on individuals or teams, as well as the distribution of workload among team members (TC 4.3.7)	2	2
	Stress and Fatigue includes the impact of stress, fatigue, and other psychological factors on individual and team performance, as well as strategies for managing and mitigating these factors; e.g. stress and fatigue management: Implementing programs to manage stress and fatigue, such as providing opportunities for rest and recovery, offering stress reduction techniques, and promoting healthy lifestyle habits (TC 4.3.8)	2	2
TC 4.4: Liveware	Recruiting and Retention of qualified and experienced staff (TC 4.4.1)	3	3
	Conducting background checks on all employees who have access to sensitive information (TC 4.4.2)	4	4
	Training and Experience: This includes the knowledge, skills, and experience of individuals or teams, as well as the training and development opportunities provided to support their performance (TC 4.4.3)	4	4

(continued)

Table 3.57 (continued)

Spalte1	Spalte2	Spalte3	Spalte4
	Providing training to employees on how to work safely and effectively (TC 4.4.4)	3	3
TC 4.5: Liveware-Liveware Interface	Communication includes the methods and channels of communication between individuals or teams, including verbal, written, and electronic communication (TC 4.5.1)	4	5
	Teamwork includes the collaboration and coordination of work between individuals or teams, as well as the development of shared goals and objectives (TC 4.5.2)	4	4
	Leadership style and conflict resolution: Developing effective leadership practices that support communication, collaboration, and teamwork, such as setting clear expectations, providing feedback and coaching in conflict situations (TC 4.5.3)	3	3

Interpretation of Results: Evaluating ISO 31000:2018 and COSO ERM Frameworks in Capturing Error Culture and Potential Improvement through AI Solutions using a Holistic Approach with MOS

4

4.1 Adaptability and Response to Failures

ISO 31000:2018 demonstrates a higher degree of adaptability in managing dynamic changes and addressing failures, indicating a more flexible and adaptive risk management approach. This framework's ability to better accommodate unpredictability and learn from failures is pivotal in operational environments where change is constant. Scientifically, this suggests an emphasis on holistic and principle-based risk management that prioritizes flexibility and continuous learning.

COSO ERM Framework, scoring lower in these aspects, potentially exhibits structural limitations or a philosophical orientation towards more static risk management models. These limitations may hinder its capacity to effectively respond to and mitigate rapidly evolving risks, particularly those involving complex human behaviours.

4.2 Handling of Operational Sensitivities

Both frameworks show moderate capabilities in recognizing and managing operational sensitivities like process deviations. This outcome indicates a foundational but not exceptional approach, pointing towards the potential benefit of integrating more advanced real-time data analytics and decision-making tools to enhance operational responsiveness.

H. Becker, *Using Artificial Intelligence (AI) to Minimize Errors in Business Enterprise Management*, https://doi.org/10.1007/978-3-658-47243-6_4

4.3 Management of Human Error

The handling of skill-based, rule-based, and knowledge-based errors by both frameworks is adequate but not comprehensive. Integrating cognitive and behavioural science principles could significantly bolster their approaches, providing a deeper understanding of human error mechanisms and more effective strategies for mitigation.

4.4 Technological Aspects of Risk Management

Adequate management of software and hardware risks is observed in both frameworks, but the absence of high scores suggests a need for innovation, possibly through the use of artificial intelligence and machine learning, to optimize risk responses and predict potential failures more accurately; particularly in areas like real-time monitoring and predictive analytics.

4.5 Leadership and Communication in Risk Management

ISO 31000:2018 slightly outperforms the COSO ERM in promoting effective leadership and communication strategies, which are essential in managing 'liveware' components of organizations. Exploring how different leadership styles and communication methods impact organizational risk could further clarify this difference, particularly in contexts such as change management.

Conclusion and Recommendations 5

The dissertation confirms the validity of the working hypothesis that artificial intelligence has the potential to minimize errors in business enterprise management. The supporting four sub-hypotheses are subsequently confirmed by the research results of this dissertation:

Sub-Hypothesis 1 (Error management approaches developed for High Reliability Organizations (HRO) can be largely transferred to all other business enterprises and organizations subject to risk management systems) is a reasonable hypothesis, as HROs are known for their rigorous error management practices and focus on maintaining safety and reliability. However, the extent to which these approaches can be directly transferred may vary depending on the specific context and industry. While HRO principles can provide valuable insights and guidance, adaptation to different organizational cultures and operational environments may be necessary.

Given the capabilities of AI in processing large datasets, identifying patterns, and suggesting solutions, it's plausible that MOS principles could be incorporated into AI-driven systems to improve error management practices. This supports the Sub-**Hypothesis 2** (MOS has the potential to be transferred into an AI solution in order to sustainably promote error culture and error management in the organization). However, the feasibility and effectiveness of such integration would depend on factors such as the sophistication of the AI system, the quality of data inputs, and the alignment with organizational goals and processes.

The implications of Sub-**Hypotheses 1 und 2** extend beyond theoretical discourse, suggesting practical applications that could reshape organizational approaches to error management. The adoption of HRO strategies in varied business contexts could lead to enhanced safety, efficiency, and operational integrity.

H. Becker, *Using Artificial Intelligence (AI) to Minimize Errors in Business Enterprise Management*, https://doi.org/10.1007/978-3-658-47243-6_5

Moreover, the AI-driven evolution in error management promises a future of more proactive and intelligent organizational practices.

Future research should focus on empirical evaluations of these hypotheses across diverse organizational settings. This involves exploring the practicality and impact of implementing HRO strategies in non-HRO contexts. Such empirical investigations would not only substantiate the theoretical propositions but also offer actionable insights for organizations seeking to innovate their error management practices.

Sub-Hypothesis 3 (The error culture can be measured and operationalized by an AI system) suggests that error culture can indeed be effectively measured and operationalized by an AI system. Through the discussion of various measurement methods, including questionnaires and surveys tailored to assess safety culture, as well as the development of objective test criteria derived from the MOS questionnaire, the text underscores the feasibility of utilizing AI systems in this context. Moreover, the incorporation of factors such as professional experience into the assessment process further strengthens the case for employing AI in measuring error culture. The correlations between employee experience levels and aspects of safety culture highlight the potential for AI systems to provide valuable insights independent of human bias or interpretation. Overall, the evidence presented suggests that AI systems can play a crucial role in enhancing error management and promoting safety within organizations by providing objective and reliable assessments of error culture. This underscores the significance of continued research and development in leveraging AI technology to improve organizational safety practices.

Sub-Hypothesis 4 (The risk management systems ISO 31000:2018 and COSO ERM Integrated Framework show significant weaknesses on the field of human factors that can be mitigated by MOS criteria, operationalized by an AI system). While ISO 31000:2018 and COSO ERM Framework provide a foundation for risk management, they fall short in addressing the nuanced aspects of human factors and error culture. The integration of AI systems shows promise in mitigating these identified weaknesses. AI tools offer predictive models for process deviation analysis, automate incident detection and response, and tailor risk mitigation strategies using real-time data. Additionally, AI-driven tools can assess decision inclusivity, monitor operational processes, and track Key Performance Indicators (KPIs) for evaluating recovery solutions. The integration of AI and MOS into these frameworks could significantly enhance their effectiveness, particularly in predictive risk management and error culture assessment, aligning with the evolving needs of modern, complex business environments. While AI can certainly assist in analyzing large amounts of data and identifying patterns related to error occurrence and management, measuring and operationalizing something as complex as organizational culture may require more than just data analysis. Cultural aspects often involve qualitative elements such as norms, beliefs, and behaviors, which may be challenging for an AI system to fully capture and interpret. However, AI could potentially complement other methods of assessing organizational culture, such as measuring the MOS criteria. They are a significant sign for the grade of mindful organizing which is a visible sign of an error management culture. Even if the organizational culture cannot be completely analyzed with AI, risk management systems can be strengthened through the selective and specialized use of AI to measure mindful organizing by the MOS criteria. For the first time, MOS criteria were transformed into objective measurement variables and thus made operable for AI use.

Furthermore, the emphasis on training, communication, and error reporting within the frameworks highlights an acknowledgment of the importance of an error culture. However, the absence of detailed methodologies underscores the need for more focused strategies in fostering a robust error culture for organizational resilience.

Integrating the Mindful Organizing Scale (MOS) into an AI framework could address the frameworks' lack of specific tools for quantitatively assessing organizational behavior and error culture. This integration would enable a more nuanced analysis, converting subjective cultural elements into quantifiable data points for precise risk assessments.

Moreover, the application of High Reliability Organization (HRO) principles in broader business contexts is supported by the general applicability of these frameworks across various sectors. This suggests that principles effective in HROs could enhance error management practices across diverse organizational types.

The limited focus of the frameworks on proactive risk mitigation strategies can be addressed by AI's predictive capabilities. AI's ability to identify potential errors based on data trends aligns with proactive risk management principles, offering a more advanced approach to risk identification and mitigation.

Future research is tasked to find out the efficacy of AI-integrated MOS in real-world scenarios.

Future research should also address the question of whether the MOS criteria should be supplemented with the qualifications and professional experience of the actors involved. There appears to be a significant positive correlation here. The more qualified and experienced employees are, the stronger the reliability and resistance of the organization appears to be.

ISO 31000:2018 and the COSO ERM Framework serve as foundational frameworks for risk management and governance. However, they may need to be complemented with specialized standards, practices, and strategies to address specific aspects related to error culture, the Liveware-Liveware Interface, and other criteria effectively.

This assessment aids in recognizing the importance of adaptability, comprehensive risk assessment, and the integration of diverse perspectives in effective risk management. The analysis also highlights areas for future research and development, particularly in closing the gap between theoretical frameworks and practical applications in various organizational contexts.

Organizations should tailor their risk management approaches to their unique needs and contexts.

Bibliography

AKTIONSBÜNDNIS PATIENTENSICHERHEIT (APS) (2016) *Empfehlungen zur Einführung von Critical Incident Reporting Systemen CIRS), Praxistipps für Krankenhäuser*, [cited: February 23, 2024]. Available from https://www.aps-ev.de/wp-content/uploads/2016/08/07-07-25-CIRS-Handlungsempfehlung.pdf.

AKTIONSBÜNDNIS PATIENTENSICHERHEIT (APS) (2016) *Glossar.* Aktionsbündnis Patientensicherheit (APS), [cited: February 16, 2023]. Available from https://www.aps-ev.de/patientensicherheit/glossar/.

AMERICAN SOCIETY FOR INDUSTRIAL SECURITY (ASIS) (2015) *Risk Assessment.* [cited: January 27, 2024]. Available from https://www.asisonline.org/publications--resources/standards--guidelines/ra/scope/.

AO, S.-I., et al. (2010) *Machine learning and systems engineering.* Vol. 68. Springer Science & Business Media.

ARENA, M., et al. (2010) The organizational dynamics of enterprise risk management. *Accounting, Organizations and Society,* **35** (7), pp. 659–675.

AUSSERHOFER, D., et al. (2012) Die Bestimmung der Inhaltsvalidität anhand des Content Validity Index am Beispiel eines Instrumentes zur Erfassung des Sicherheitsklimas im Krankenhaus. *Pflegewissenschaft,* **14** (3), pp. 151–158.

AUSSERHOFER, D., et al. (2013a) Validity and reliability on three European language versions of the Safety Organizing Scale. *Int J Qual Health Care,* **25** (2), pp. 157–166.

AUTHORITY FINANCIAL CONDUCT (FCA) (2018) *Transforming culture in financial services.*Updated 12/03/2018. [cited: January 7, 2024]. Available from https://www.fca.org.uk/publications/discussion-papers/dp18-2-transforming-culture-financial-services.

AVEN, T. (2008) *Risk Analysis: Assessing Uncertainties beyond Expected Values and Probabilities.* Hoboken, NJ, United States: John Wiley & Sons, Inc.

BADAR, M. E. (2013) The Concept of Mens Rea in International Criminal Law-The Case for a Unified Approach. 1 ed. London, Bloomsbury Publishing.

BAKER, B. (1995) The role of feedback in assessing information systems planning effectiveness. *The Journal of Strategic Information Systems,* **4** (1), pp. 61–80.

BATES, D. W. and GAWANDE, A. A. (2000) Error in medicine: What have we learned? *Ann Intern Med,* **132** (9), 763–7.

H. Becker, *Using Artificial Intelligence (AI) to Minimize Errors in Business Enterprise Management*, https://doi.org/10.1007/978-3-658-47243-6

BAUER, J., et al. (2004) Fehlerorientierung im betrieblichen Arbeitsalltag. Ein Vergleich zwischen Führungskräften und Beschäftigten ohne Führungsfunktion. *Zeitschrift für Berufs und Wirtschaftspädagogik,* **100**, pp. 65–82.

BEASLEY, M. S., et al. (2014) *Report on the Current State of Enterprise Risk Oversight: Opportunities to Strengthen Integration with Strategy.* Raleigh: The ERM Initiative in the Poole College of Management at North Carolina State University.

BEASLEY, M. S., et al. (2005) Enterprise risk management: An empirical analysis of factors associated with the extent of implementation. *Journal of accounting and public policy,* **24** (6), pp. 521–531.

BECKER, H. (2016) Fehlerkultur und Fehlermanagement in der Krankenhauspflege—eine Analyse am Beispiel der Frankfurter Rotkreuz Kliniken e.V., unpublished, Technical University of Munich (TUM).

BEHÖRDE FüR SOZIALES, FAMILIE, GESUNDHEIT UND VERBRAUCHERSCHUTZ DER FREIEN UND HANSESTADT HAMBURG (2010) *Aus Fehlern lernen, Curriculumbausteine Patientensicherheit,* [cited: February 16, 2023]. Available from https://www.hamburg.de/contentblob/2670294/a6aedde5c37a3ad309f11ce85519a7da/data/aus-fehlern-lernen.pdf.

BHALLA, A. (1995) Collapse of Barings Bank: Case of market failure. *Economic and Political Weekly*, pp. 658–662.

BHAVNANI, S. P., et al. (2017) Roadmap for Innovation-ACC Health Policy Statement on Healthcare Transformation in the Era of Digital Health, Big Data, and Precision Health: A Report of the American College of Cardiology Task Force on Health Policy Statements and Systems of Care. *J Am Coll Cardiol,* **70** (21), pp. 2696–2718.

BIESINGER, F., et al. (2019) A digital twin for production planning based on cyber-physical systems: A Case Study for a Cyber-Physical System-Based Creation of a Digital Twin. *Procedia CIRP,* **79**, pp. 355–360.

BIRD, F. E. (1974) *Management guide to loss control.* Atlanta, Georgia, USA,: Institute Press.

BLEGEN, M. A., et al. (2009) AHRQ's hospital survey on patient safety culture: psychometric analyses. *J Patient Saf,* **5** (3), pp. 139–144

BOOTH, R. (1993) Safety culture: concept, measurement, and training implications. In: *Proceedings of British Health and Safety Society Spring Conference, 19-20. April, 1993 : Safety Culture and the Management of Risk.* British Health and Safety Society, p.5

BOSTROM, N. (2014b) *Superintelligence : Paths, Dangers, Strategies.* Oxford University Press, Oxford, United Kingdom.

BOSTROM, N. and YUDKOWSKY, E. (2014) The ethics of artificial intelligence. In: FRANKISH, K. and RAMSEY, W. M. (Eds.) *The Cambridge Handbook of Artificial Intelligence.* Cambridge: Cambridge University Press, pp. 316–334.

BRÜGGE, M. (2007) Fehlerkultur im Krankenhaus–Ein Status quo des Umgangs mit Fehlern und mögliche Einflussfaktoren auf die Fehlerkultur am Beispiel einer Klinikabteilung. In: VON EIFF, W. (Ed.) *Risikomanagement – Kosten-/Nutzen-basierte Entscheidungen im Krankenhaus,.* (Schriftenreihe Gesundheitswirtschaft) Vol. 2. Wegscheid: WIKOM Verlag, pp. 271–307.

BURANAPIN, S., et al. (2023) Enhancing Organizational Resilience through Mindful Organizing. *Sustainability,* **15**, 2681. https://doi.org/10.3390/su15032681.

CALDER, A. and WATKINS, S. (2019) IT Governance: An international guide to data security and ISO27001/ISO27002.) 7 ed. London, Philadelphia, New Delhi, Kogan Page Publishers.

CAMERON, K. (2009) *An introduction to the competing values framework.* [Organizational culture white paper.] Haworth, [cited: January 20, 2024]. Available from https://media.haworth.com/asset/28512/An_Introduction_to_the_Competing_Values_Framework_White_Paper.pdf.

CAMERON, K. and QUINN, R. E. (1999) *Diagnosing and Changing Organizational Culture: Based on the Competing Values Framework.* Addison-Wesley.

CAMERON, K. S., et al. (2006) *Competing Values Leadership.* Cheltenham, UK: Edward Elgar Publishing.

CAMPBELL, J. P. (1977) On the nature of organizational effectiveness. In: GOODMAN, P. S., PENNINGS, JOHANNES M., AND ASSOCIATES (Ed.) *New perspectives on organizational effectiveness.* Vol. 13. San Francisco; London: Jossey-Bass, pp. 13–55.

CAMPBELL, R. D. and BAGSHAW, M. (2002) *Human performance and limitations in aviation.* Hoboken, New Jersey, USA: John Wiley & Sons.

CANTAMESSA, M., et al. (2018) Startups' Roads to Failure. *Sustainability,* **10** (7), 2346. https://doi.org/10.3390/su10072346.

CARROLL, J. S. and RUDOLPH, J. W. (2006) Design of high reliability organizations in health care. *Qual Saf Health Care,* **15** (Suppl 1), pp. i4–9.

COLLINS, C., et al. (2021) Artificial intelligence in information systems research: A systematic literature review and research agenda. *International Journal of Information Management,* **60**, 102383.

COMMISSION ON THE BP DEEPWATER HORIZON OIL SPILL (2011) *Deep Water: The Gulf Oil Disaster And The Future Of Offshore Drilling—Report to the President (BP Oil Spill Commission Report).* Updated 2011, January 11. Available from https://www.govinfo.gov/app/details/GPO-OILCOMMISSION.

COMMITTEE OF SPONSORING ORGANIZATIONS OF THE TREADWAY COMMISSION (COSO) (2017) *Enterprise Risk Management Integrating with Strategy and Performance-Executive Summary.* Committee of Sponsoring Organizations of the Treadway Commission, [cited: January 7, 2024]. Available from https://www.coso.org/_files/ugd/3059fc_61ea5985b03c4293960642fdce408eaa.pdf.

COMMITTEE ON ENERGY AND COMMERCE (2018) Facebook : Transparency and use of consumer data- Hearing before the committee on energy and commerce—House of Representatives. Washington D.C., U.S. Government Publishing Office.

COMMITTEE ON SCIENCE AND TECHNOLOGY—HOUSE OF REPRESENTATIVES (1986) *INVESTIGATION OF THE CHALLENGER ACCIDENT.* U.S.GOVERNMENT PRINTING OFFICE, [cited: January 27, 2024]. Available from https://www.govinfo.gov/content/pkg/GPO-CRPT-99hrpt1016/pdf/GPO-CRPT-99hrpt1016.pdf.

COOPER, M. D. (2000) Towards a model of safety culture. *Safety Science,* **36**, pp. 111–136.

COUNCIL OF THE EUROPEAN UNION (COUNCIL) (2024) Proposal for a Regulation of the European Parliament and of the Council laying down harmonised rules on artificial intelligence (Artificial Intelligence Act) and amending certain Union legislative acts—Analysis of the final compromise text with a view to agreement.) Brussels, Council of the European Union.

DAVENPORT, T. H. and RONANKI, R. (2018) Artificial intelligence for the real world. *Harvard business review,* **96** (1), 108–116.

DiCUCCIO, M. H. (2015) The Relationship Between Patient Safety Culture and Patient Outcomes: A Systematic Review. *J Patient Saf,* **11** (3), pp. 135–142.DOI: https://doi.org/10.1097/PTS.0000000000000058.

DUPONT, G. (1997) The dirty dozen errors in maintenance.) *The 11th FAA/AAM Meeting on Human Factors in Aviation Maintenance and Inspection "Human Error in Maintenance".* San Diego, California, USA, FAA Office of Aviation Medicine.

EDMONDSON, A. C. (2004) Learning from failure in health care: Frequent opportunities, pervasive barriers. *Qual Saf Health Care,* (13), pp. ii3–9.

EDWARDS, E. (1972) Man and machine: Systems for Safety. Proceedings of the British Airline Pilots Association (BALPA). *Technical symposium, London, pp. 21-36*

EIFF, W. V. (2007) *Risikomanagement: Kosten-/Nutzen-basierte Entscheidungen im Krankenhaus.* (Risk management: Decisions based on cost-benefit analysis in hospitals) Wegscheid: WIKOM-Verl.

EISENBERG, N., et al. (1985) Children's justifications for their adult and peer-directed compliant (prosocial and nonprosocial) behaviors. *Developmental Psychology,* **21** (2), 325.

EISENBERG, N. and SPINRAD, T. L. (2014) Multidimensionality of Prosocial Behavior: Rethinking the Conceptualization and Development of Prosocial Behavior. In: PADILLA-WALKER, L. M. and CARLO, G. (Eds.) , Prosocial development: A multidimensional approach,Oxford University Press. pp. 17–39. https://doi.org/10.1093/acprof:oso/9780199964772.003.0002.

EUROCONTROL (2005) *Guidelines on the Systemic Occurrence Analysis Methodology (SOAM).* EuroControl Brussels, Belgium, [cited: January 20,2024]. Available from https://www.eurocontrol.int/sites/default/files/2019-06/eam2-gui8-e1.0.pdf.

EUROPEAN COMMISSION (2020) *On Artificial Intelligence—A European approach to excellence and trust.* [White Paper] Updated 19.02.2020. [cited: January 27, 2024]. Available from https://eur-lex.europa.eu/legal-content/EN/TXT/PDF/?uri=CELEX:52020DC0065.

EUROPEAN COMMISSION (2024) *Shaping Europe's digital future: AI Act.* [cited: February 24, 2024]. Available from https://digital-strategy.ec.europa.eu/en/policies/regulatory-framework-ai.

EUROPEAN PARLIAMENT (2024) Artificial Intelligence Act: MEPs adopt landmark law, Press Release March 13, 2024. Press Service, Directorate General for Communication European Parliament.

FARRELL, M. and GALLAGHER, R. (2015) The valuation implications of enterprise risk management maturity. *Journal of Risk and Insurance,* **82** (3), 625–657.

FLORIDI, L. (2016) *The 4th revolution : How the infosphere is reshaping human reality.* Oxford: Oxford University Press.

FORMAN, R., et al. (2021) COVID-19 vaccine challenges: What have we learned so far and what remains to be done? *Health Policy,* **125** (5), pp. 553–567.

FRASER, J. R., et al. (2021) *Enterprise risk management: Today's leading research and best practices for tomorrow's executives.* Hoboken, New Jersey, USA: John Wiley & Sons.

GEMEINSAMER BUNDESAUSSCHUSS (G-BA) (2016) Bestimmung des Gemeinsamen Bundesausschusses von Anforderungen an einrichtungsübergreifende Fehlermeldesysteme (üFMS-B) in der Fassung vom 17. März 2016. Bundesanzeiger (BAnz AT vom 4. Juli 2016 B3).

GLANS, T. B., GRAD, B., HOLSTEIN, D., MEYERS, W. E., & SCHMIDT, R. N. (1968) *Management systems.* Holt Reinhardt and Winston, New York

GLENDON, A. I. and STANTON, N. A. (2000) Perspectives on safety culture. *Safety science,* **34** (1–3), pp. 193–214.

GLOBAL AVIATION INFORMATION NETWORK (GAIN) WORKING GROUP E (2004) *Roadmap to a just culture: Enhancing the safety environment.* Global Aviation Information Network (GAIN), Updated September 2004. [cited: January 14, 2024]. Available from https://flightsafety.org/files/just_culture.pdf.

GOERZEN, A., et al. (2023) *Research Handbook on International Corporate Social Responsibility.* (Chapter 12: Governance failure and firm-level crises: The case of the Volkswagen emissions scandal. Edward Elgar Publishing.

GRANT, A. M. (2008) Does intrinsic motivation fuel the prosocial fire? Motivational synergy in predicting persistence, performance, and productivity. *Journal of applied psychology,* **93** (1), 48.

GULDENMUND, F. W. (2000) The nature of safety culture: A review of theory and research. *Safety Science,* **34**, pp. 215–257.

GUSTON, D. H. (2008) Presenting Futures. In: FISHER E, SELIN C., WETMORE JM (Ed.) *The Yearbook of Nanotechnology in Society: Presenting Futures.* Vol. 1. New York: Springer, pp. v–viii.

GUSTON, D. H. (2014) Understanding 'anticipatory governance'. *Social Studies of Science,* **44** (2), pp. 218–242.

HAENLEIN, M. and KAPLAN, A. (2019) A Brief History of Artificial Intelligence: On the Past, Present, and Future of Artificial Intelligence. *California Management Review,* **61** (4), pp. 5–14.

HANSSON, S. O. and HELGESSON, G. (2003) What is stability? *Synthese,* **136**, pp. 219–235.

HÄRTER, M. and KOCH-GROMUS, U. (2022) Qualitätsentwicklung im Gesundheitswesen: Sind wir schon so weit, wie wir wollten? *Bundesgesundheitsblatt—Gesundheitsforschung—Gesundheitsschutz,* **65** (3), pp. 267–269.

HAWKINS, F. H. and ORLADY, H. W. (1993) *Human Factors in Flight.* Farnham, United Kingdom: Ashgate.

HAWKINS, F. H. and ORLADY, H. W. (2017) *Human Factors in Flight.* London (UK): Routledge.

HEALTH SAFETY EXECUTIVE (HSE) (1999) *Reducing error and influencing behaviour.* Health Safety Executive, [cited: January 20, 2024]. Available from https://thecpi.org.uk/library/PDF/Public/health-safety/General/Human%20Factors/General%20Guidance/01%20HSG%2048%20-%20Reducing%20Error%20and%20Influencing%20Behaviour.pdf.

HEALY, P. M. and PALEPU, K. G. (2003) The fall of Enron. *Journal of economic perspectives,* **17** (2), pp. 3–26.

HEINRICH, H. W. (Ed.) (1941) *Industrial Accident Prevention. A Scientific Approach.* New York, London: McGraw-Hill Book Company, Inc.

HELFRICH, C. D., et al. (2007) Assessing an organizational culture instrument based on the Competing Values Framework: Exploratory and confirmatory factor analyses. *Implementation science,* **2** (1), pp. 1–14.

HELMREICH, R. L. (2000) On error management: Lessons from aviation. *British Medical Journal (BMJ),* **320**, pp. 781-785.

HELMREICH, R. L., et al. (1999a) Models of threat, error, and CRM in flight operations. In: *Proceedings of the tenth international symposium on aviation psychology.* pp. 677–682.

HELMREICH, R. L., et al. (1999b) The evolution of Crew Resource Management training in commercial aviation. *Int J Aviat Psychol,* **9** (1), pp. 19–32.

HELMREICH, R. L. and MUSSON, D. M. (2000) Surgery as team endeavour. *Canadian Journal of Anaesthesia,* **47** (5), pp. 391–392.

HENRI, J.-F. (2006) Management control systems and strategy: A resource-based perspective. *Accounting, Organizations and Society,* **31** (6), pp. 529–558.

HOFFMANN, B. and ROHE, J. (2010) Übersichtsarbeit Patientensicherheit und Ursachen unerwünschter Ereignisse und Maßnahmen zu ihrer Vermeidung. *Deutsches Arzteblatt-Arztliche Mitteilungen-Ausgabe B,* **107** (6), 92.

HOLZHAUER, H. M. (2015) The Future of Risk Management. *Investment Risk Management,* pp. 580-598.

HU, B. and MENG, L. (2022) Understanding awe elicitors in the workplace: A qualitative inquiry. *Journal of Managerial Psychology,* **37**, pp. 697–715.

HUBBARD, D. W. (2020) *The failure of risk management: Why it's broken and how to fix it.* Hoboken, New Jersey, USA: John Wiley & Sons, Inc.

HUDSON, P. (2001) Safety management and safety culture: The long, hard and winding road. *Occupational health and safety management systems,* **2001**, pp. 3–32.

INSTITUTE OF MEDICINE (US) COMMITTEE ON QUALITY OF HEALTH CARE IN AMERICA (2000) *To Err is Human: Building a Safer Health System.* Washington (DC): National Academy of Sciences.

INTERNATIONAL ATOMIC ENERGY AGENCY (IAEA) (2015) *The Fukushima Daiichi Accident—Report by the Director General.* Vienna (Austria): International Atomic Energy Agency.

INTERNATIONAL ELECTROTECHNICAL COMMISSION (IEC) (2024) *What we do: What we do for safety, sustainability and global trad.* International Electrotechnical Commission (IEC),[cited: February 24, 2024]. Available from https://www.iec.ch/what-we-do.

INTERNATIONAL ORGANIZATION FOR STANDARDIZATION (ISO) (2018a) *ISO 31000: 2018 (en) Risk management — Guidelines.* International Organization for Standardization (ISO), [cited: January 20, 2024]. Available from https://www.iso.org/obp/ui/# iso:std:iso:31000:en.

INTERNATIONAL ORGANIZATION FOR STANDARDIZATION (ISO) (2018b) *ISO 45001:2018(E) : Occupational Health and Safety Management Systems: Requirements with Guidance for Use.* International Organization for Standardization (ISO), Updated 2018–03.

INTERNATIONAL ORGANIZATION FOR STANDARDIZATION (ISO) (2024a) *About us.* International Organization for Standardization (ISO),[cited: February 24, 2024]. Available from https://www.iso.org/about-us.html.

INTERNATIONAL ORGANIZATION FOR STANDARDIZATION (ISO) (2024b) *What is a management system?* International Organization for Standardization (ISO),[cited: February 24, 2024]. Available from https://www.iso.org/management-system-standards.html.

INTERNATIONAL TELECOMMUNICATION UNION (ITU) (2024) *About International Telecommunication Union (ITU).* [cited: February 24, 2024]. Available from https://www.itu.int/en/about/Pages/default.aspx.

JOHNSTON, N. and MCDONALD, N. (2017) *Aviation psychology in practice.* London: Routledge.

KAHLA-WITZSCH, H. A. (2005) *Praxis des klinischen Risikomanagement.* Landsberg/Lech: ecomed Medizin.

KAPLAN, R. S. and MIKES, A. (2012) Managing risks: A new framework. *Harvard Business Review,* **90** (6), pp. 48–60.

KIESER, A. and WALGENBACH, P. (2003) Organisation. 4., überarb. und erw. *Aufl. Stuttgart: Schäffer-Poeschel.*

KIZZA, J. M., et al. (2013) *Guide to computer network security.* Springer.

KOCH, P. J. (1987) Emotional Ambivalence. *Philosophy and Phenomenological Research,* **48** (2), pp. 257–279.

KRITZINGER, W., et al. (2018) Digital Twin in manufacturing: A categorical literature review and classification. *IFAC-PapersOnLine,* **51** (11), pp. 1016–1022.

KUSUMANINGTYAS, A., et al. (2021) Why Start-ups Fail: Cases, Challenges, and Solutions. In: *Conference Towards ASEAN Chairmanship 2023 (T-A-C 23 2021).* Atlantis Press, Amsterdam, Holland, pp. 155–159.

LAM, J. (2014) *Enterprise risk management: From incentives to controls.* Hoboken, New Jersey, United States: John Wiley & Sons, Inc.

LAZARI, A. and MIKAC, R. (2022) *The external dimension of the European Union's Critical Infrastructure Protection Programme: From neighbouring frameworks to transatlantic cooperation.* Boca Raton, Florida,USA: CRC Press.

LEAPE, L. (1994) Error in medicine. *The Journal of the American Medical Association (JAMA),* **272** (23), pp. 1851–1857.

LEVESON, N. G. and TURNER, C. S. (1993) An investigation of the Therac-25 accidents. *Computer,* **26** (7), pp. 18–41.

LÖBER, N. (2012) *Fehler und Fehlerkultur im Krankenhaus: Eine theoretisch-konzeptionelle Betrachtung.* Wiesbaden: Gabler Verlag.

LYKE, B. and JICKLING, M. (2002) WorldCom: The accounting scandal. In: *Congressional Research Service Report for Congress, August.* Vol. 29, pp. 1–6.

MACEY, J. R. (2008) *Corporate governance: Promises kept, promises broken.* New York: Princeton University Press.

MAGNANO, P., et al. (2017) Validation of the italian version of the mindfulness organizing scale (MOS) in organizational contexts. *TPM: Testing, Psychometrics, Methodology in Applied Psychology,* **24** (1).

MARX, D. (1997) Discipline:The role of rule violations. *Ground Effects,* **2** (4), pp. 1–4.

MCCARTNEY, F. (2006) *National Security Space Launch Report.* RAND CORP., [cited: February 3, 2024]. Available from https://www.rand.org/content/dam/rand/pubs/monographs/2006/RAND_MG503.pdf.

MENG, L. and WANG, X. (2023) Awe in the workplace promotes prosocial behavior. *PsyCh Journal.* Vol.12, pp. 44-53.

MILDENBERGER, D. and ULSENHEIMER, K. (2003) Incident Reporting für ein produktives Riskmanagement. *Das Krankenhaus,* **7**, pp. 539–543.

MITTELSTADT, B. D., et al. (2016) The ethics of algorithms: Mapping the debate. *Big Data & Society,* **3** (2), DOI: 10.1177/2053951716679679

MOELLER, R. R. (2007) *COSO enterprise risk management: Understanding the new integrated ERM framework.* Hoboken, New Jersey, USA: John Wiley & Sons,Inc.

MOLLOY, G. J. and O'BOYLE, C. A. (2005) The SHEL model: A useful tool for analyzing and teaching the contribution of Human Factors to medical error. *Academic Medicine,* **80** (2), pp. 152–155.

MOOR, J. (2006) The Nature, Importance, and Difficulty of Machine Ethics. *IEEE Intelligent Systems,* **21**, pp. 18–21.

MORAY, N. (2018) Error reduction as a systems problem. In: *Human error in medicine.* Boca Raton, Florida,USA: CRC Press, pp. 67–91.

MORGESON, F. P. and HOFMANN, D. A. (1999) The structure and function of collective constructs: Implications for multilevel research and theory development. *Academy of management review,* **24** (2), 249–265.

NASA AREOSPACE SAFETY ADVISORY PANEL (2021) *Third Quarterly Meeting Report.* Washington, DC 20546: National Aeronautics and Space Administration.

NATIONAL INSTITUTE OF STANDARDS AND TECHNOLOGY (NIST) (2018) *Framework for improving critical infrastructure cybersecurity.* Updated April 16, 2018. [cited: January 7, 2024]. Available from https://nvlpubs.nist.gov/nistpubs/cswp/nist.cswp.04162018.pdf.

NATIONAL INSTITUTE OF STANDARDS AND TECHNOLOGY (NIST) (2023) Artificial Intelligence Risk Management Framework (AI RMF 1.0).

NATIONAL TRANSPORTATION SAFETY BOARD (NTSB) (2019) *Safety Recommendation Report:Assumptions Used in the Safety Assessment Process and the Effects of Multiple Alerts and Indications on Pilot Performance.* Washington, DC 20594: NTSB.

NERDINGER, F. W., et al. (2011) *Arbeits- und Organisationspsychologie.* Heidelberg: Springer.

O'NEILL, D., et al. (2021) Leadership and community healthcare reform: A study using the Competing Values Framework (CVF). *Leadership in Health Services,* **34** (4), pp. 485–498.

ÖNDAS, V. and AKPINAR, M. (2021) Applying the SHELL model to study the causes of high-tech start-up failures and finding ways to prevent them. *Finnish Business Review,* **8**, pp. 10–20.

POTTER, K. and DORIS, L. (2024) Ethical Considerations in the Development and Deployment of Artificial Intelligence Systems. *Artificial Intelligence.* (ePub ahead of print)

POWER, M. (2007) *Organized uncertainty: Designing a world of risk management.* Oxford: Oxford University Press.

PURDY, G. (2010) ISO 31000: 2009 - Setting a new standard for risk management. *Risk Analysis: An International Journal,* **30** (6), pp. 881-886.

REASON, J. (1990) *Human Error.* Cambridge: Cambridge University Press.

REASON, J. (1991) Identifying the latent causes of aircraft accidents before and after the event. In: *Proceedings of the 22nd ISASI Annual Air Safety Seminar.* Canberra, Australia: International Society of Air Safety Investigators (ISASI), Sterling, VA.

REASON, J. (1995) Understanding adverse events: Human factors. *BMJ Quality & Safety,* **4** (2), 80–89.
REASON, J. (1998) Achieving a safe culture: Theory and practice. *Work & Stress,* **12** (3), pp. 293–306.
REASON, J. (2000a) Human error: Models and management. *BMJ,* **320** (7237), pp. 768–770.
REASON, J. (2000b) Safety paradoxes and safety culture. *Injury Control and Safety Promotion,* **7**, pp. 3–14. doi: https://doi.org/10.1076/1566-0974(200003)7:1;1-V;FT003.
REASON, J. (2016) Managing the Risks of Organizational Accidents.) 1 ed. London, Routledge.
RENECLE, M., et al. (2020) Spanish validation of the mindful organizing scale: A questionnaire for the assessment of collective mindfulness. *Accident Analysis & Prevention,* **134**, 105351. DOI: https://doi.org/10.1016/j.aap.2019.105351.
RICE, J. B. and SHEFFI, Y. (2005) A supply chain view of the resilient enterprise. *MIT Sloan Management Review,* **47**, pp. 41–48.
ROGOVIN, M. and FRAMPTON GEORGE T. (1979) *Three Mile Island: A report to the commissioners and to the public.* Washington, DC (USA): Nuclear regulatory commission—special inquiry group. NUREG/CR–1250.
RUSSELL, S. J. and NORVIG, P. (2010) *Artificial intelligence : A modern approach.* Upper Saddle River, New Jersey, USA: Prentice Hall.
SACHVERSTÄNDIGENRAT FÜR DIE KONZERTIERTE AKTION IM GESUNDHEITSWESEN (2003) Gutachten. Baden-Baden, Nomos Verl.-Ges.
SANTOS, C., et al. (2015) Towards a classification of technology strategy frameworks. In Proceedings of the European Conference on IS Management and Evaluation (ECIME), Vol. 9, pp. 180-187.
SCHAEFER, H. G., et al. (1994) Human factors and safety in emergency medicine. *Resuscitation,* **28** (3), pp. 221–225.
SCHEIN, E. H. (1985) *Organizational culture and leadership.* San Francisco, CA: Jossey-Bass.
SCHEIN, E. H. (1992) *Organizational Culture and Leadership.* Bulletin of Science, Technology & Society, Vol. 14. San Francisco, CA: Jossey-Bass.
SCHEIN, E. H. (1995) *Unternehmenskultur: Ein Handbuch für Führungskräfte.* Frankfurt am Main: Campus-Verlag.
SCHEIN, E. H. (2004) *Organizational Culture and Leadership.* Hoboken, New Jersey, United States: John Wiley & Sons,Inc.
SEXTON, J. B., et al. (2006) The Safety Attitudes Questionnaire: Psychometric properties, benchmarking data, and emerging research. *BMC health services research,* **6** (1), pp. 1–10.
SIDNEY, W. and DEKKER, A. (2009) Just culture: Who gets to draw the line? *Cognition, Technology & Work,* **11** (3), 177.
SIEBERT, H. (2014) *Das APS – Aktionsbündnis Patientensicherheit.* Berufsverband der Deutschen Chirurgie e.V. (BDC), Updated 01.05.2014. [cited: January 20, 2024].
SIMKINS, B. J. and FRASER, J. (2010) *Enterprise risk management:Today's Leading Research and Best Practices for Tomorrow's Executives.* Hoboken, New Jersey, United States: John Wiley & Sons,Inc.

SORRA, J. S. and DYER, N. (2010) Multilevel psychometric properties of the AHRQ hospital survey on patient safety culture. *BMC health services research,* **10** (1), pp. 1–13.

TALBOT, J. and JAKEMAN, M. (2011) *Security risk management body of knowledge.* Vol. 69. Hoboken, New Jersey, USA: John Wiley & Sons.

TAO, F., et al. (2018) Digital twin-driven product design, manufacturing and service with big data. *The International Journal of Advanced Manufacturing Technology,* **94** (9), pp. 3563–3576.

TEICHMANN, F., et al. (2023) Wirecard scandal. A commentary on the biggest accounting fraud in Germany's post-war history. *Journal of Financial Crime,* **31** (1).DOI: 10.1108/JFC-12-2022-0301

COMMITTEE OF SPONSORING ORGANIZATIONS (COSO) (2013) *Internal Control - Intergrated Framework : Executive Summary.* [cited: December 20, 2023]. Available from https://www.coso.org/_files/ugd/3059fc_1df7d5dd38074006bce8fdf621a942cf.pdf.

THE EUROPEAN UNION INFORMATION AGENCY FOR OCCUPATIONAL SAFETY AND HEALTH (EU-OSA) (2022) Updated 03/06/2022. [cited: January 27, 2024]. Available from https://oshwiki.osha.europa.eu/en/themes/safety.

THE HEALTH FOUNDATION (2011) *Evidence Scan: Does improving safety culture affect patient outcomes ?* [cited: January 14, 2024]. Available from https://www.health.org.uk/publications/does-improving-safety-culture-affect-patient-outcomes.

THE INTERNATIONAL TELECOMMUNICATION UNION (ITU) (2024) *Definition of cybersecurity.* [cited: January 24. 2024]. Available from https://www.itu.int/en/ITU-T/studygroups/com17/Pages/cybersecurity.aspx.

THE WHITE HOUSE (2013) *Presidential Policy Directive/PPD-21: Critical infrastructure Security and Resilience.* [cited: January 20, 2024]. Available from https://obamawhitehouse.archives.gov/the-press-office/2013/02/12/presidential-policy-directive-critical-infrastructure-security-and-resil.

TOLK, J. N., et al. (2015) High reliability organization research:A literature review for health care. *Engineering Management Journal,* **27** (4), pp. 218–237.

TROMPENAARS, F., et al. (2004) *Managing change across corporate cultures.* Vol. 3. Chichester: Capstone.

TUCKER, A. L., et al. (2007) Implementing New Practices: An Empirical Study of Organizational Learning in Hospital Intensive Care Units. *Management Science,* **53** (6), pp. 894–907.

TURING, A. M. (1950) Computing Machinery and Intelligence. *Mind,* **59** (236), pp. 433–460.

TURNBULL, N. (1999) Internal control, guidance for directors on the combined code. London Institute of chartered accountants in England and Wales. *Accounting Horizons Supplement*, pp. 37–48.

U.S. DEPARTMENT OF TRANSPORTATION (DOT) (2012) *Semiannual report to congress (October 1, 2011 – March 31, 2012).* Office of Inspector General, [cited: February 3, 2024]. Available from https://www.oig.dot.gov/sites/default/files/DOT-OIG%20Semiannual%20Report%20to%20Congress%5EOctober%201%2C%202011%20-%20March%2031%2C%202012.pdf.

U.S. DEPARTMENT OF TRANSPORTATION (DOT) (2019) *U.S. Department Of Transportation Releases Results From NHTSA-NASA study of unintended acceleration in Toyota vehicles.* Updated August 1, 2019. [cited: February 2, 2024]. Available from https://www.transportation.gov/briefing-room/us-department-transportation-releases-results-nhtsa-nasa-study-unintended-acceleration.

VAN DYCK, C., et al. (2005) Organizational error management culture and its impact on performance: A two-study replication. *Journal of applied psychology,* **90** (6), 1228.

VOGUS, T. J., et al. (2014) The affective foundations of high-reliability organizing. *Journal of Organizational Behavior,* **35** (4), pp. 592–596.

VOGUS, T. J. and SUTCLIFFE, K. M. (2007) The Safety Organizing Scale: Development and Validation of a Behavioral Measure of Safety Culture in Hospital Nursing Units. *Medical Care,* **45** (1), pp. 46–54.

VOGUS, T. J. and SUTCLIFFE, K. M. (2012) Organizational mindfulness and mindful organizing: A reconciliation and path forward. *Academy of Management Learning & Education,* **11** (4), pp. 722–735.

WACHTER, R. M. (2010) *Fokus Patientensicherheit: Fehler vermeiden, Risiken managen.* Berlin: ABW Wissenschaftsverlagsgesellschaft.

WEBER, M. (1976) Wirtschaft und Gesellschaft–Grundriss der Verstehende Soziologie, JCB Mohr (Paul Siebeck), Tübingen, 5. *Auflage, Studienausgabe.*

WEICK, K. E. and SUTCLIFFE, K. M. (2001) *Managing the unexpected.* Vol. 9. San Francisco: Jossey-Bass.

WEICK, K. E. and SUTCLIFFE, K. M. (2007) *Managing the unexpected: Resilient performance in an age of uncertainty.* Hoboken, New Jersey, USA: John Wiley & Sons.

WEICK, K. E., et al. (1999) Organizing for high reliability: Processes of collective mindfulness. In: SUTTON, R. I. and STAW, B. M. (Eds.) *Research in Organizational Behaviour.* Greenwich, Connecticut: Elsevier Science/JAI Press, pp. 81–123.

WEIR, C., et al. (2005) Nurse's role in tracking adverse drug events: the impact of provider order entry. *Nursing administration quarterly,* **29** (1), pp. 39–44.

WEISS, H. M. and CROPANZANO, R. (1996) Affective events theory. *Research in organizational behavior,* **18** (1), pp. 1–74.

WIEGMANN, D. A. and SHAPPELL, S. A. (2017) A Human Error Approach to Aviation Accident Analysis: The Human Factors Analysis and Classification System.) 1 ed. London: Routledge.

WIENER, E. L. and NAGEL, D. C. (1988) *Human factors in aviation.* Houston, TX: Gulf Professional Publishing.

WIENER, N. (1960) Some Moral and Technical Consequences of Automation. *Science,* **131** (3410), pp. 1355-1358

WIGGINS, R. Z. and METRICK, A. (2015) The Lehman Brothers Bankruptcy H: The Global Contagion," Journal of Financial Crises: Vol. 1 : Iss. 1, pp. 172-199.

WILSON, K. A., et al. (2005) Promoting health care safety through training high reliability teams. *BMJ Quality & Safety,* **14** (4), pp. 303–309.

WOODS, A. and DOAN-JOHNSON, S. (2002) Toward a taxonomy of nursing practice errors. *Nursing Management,* **33** (10), pp. 45–48.

WORLD HEALTH ORGANIZATION (WHO) (2005) *World alliance for patient safety: WHO draft guidelines for adverse event reporting and learning systems: from information to action.* World Health Organization (WHO), Updated 2005. [cited: January 20, 2024]. Available from https://apps.who.int/iris/handle/10665/69797.

WORLD HEALTH ORGANIZATION (WHO) (2009) *Conceptual framework for the international classification for patient safety version 1.1: final technical report January 2009.*

World Health Organization, Updated 2009. [cited: January 13., 2024]. Available from https://apps.who.int/iris/handle/10665/70882.

WORLD HEALTH ORGANIZATION (WHO) (2020) *Development of a draft global patient safety action plan.* World Health Organization. Regional Office for the Eastern Mediterranean, Updated 2020–10. [cited: January 13, 2024]. Available from https://apps.who.int/iris/handle/10665/335958.

WORLD HEALTH ORGANIZATION (WHO) (2021) *Global patient safety action plan 2021–2030: towards eliminating avoidable harm in health care.* [cited: January 20, 2024]. Available from https://iris.who.int/bitstream/handle/10665/343477/9789240032705-eng.pdf?sequence=1.

ZIPPER, S. G. (2006) Medical-Risk-Management. *Med Klin,* **101** (10), pp. 796–803.

ZOHAR, D. (1980) Safety climate in industrial organizations: Theoretical and applied implications. *Journal of applied psychology,* **65** (1), 96.

The manufacturer's authorised representative in the EU is Springer Nature Customer Service Centre GmbH, Europaplatz 3, 69115 Heidelberg, Germany. If you have any concerns regarding our products, please contact ProductSafety@springernature.com

Printed and bound by CPI Group (UK) Ltd, Croydon, CR0 4YY
02/10/2026
02227132-0001